The Family of Semen Gurba
1772 - 1927

A New Land...A New Beginning

by Brian Broda

ISBN 978-0-557-01255-8

The Family of Semen Gurba

    1772 – 1927

A New Land....A New Beginning

by

Brian Broda

Cover photo: Exaltation of the Holy Cross Ukrainian Catholic Church (Skaro).....picture taken by Brian Broda summer of 2007

Contents

iv

This book is dedicated to my Grandmother, Frances
Bezborodka (nee Gurba). She was the ninth
child born to Anton and Tekla Gurba and was
the source of much of my information relating to
the history of the Gurba family. She is the one
who taught me the most valuable
lesson in family history and genealogy:
"Just ask!"
At the age of 102 years, she continues to be a proud member
of the Gurba family. I know that
she is delighted that information about our
family will be passed along to future generations.

ACKNOWLEDGEMENTS

I am so intensely grateful to so many people. Firstly to my great-grandparents, Anton and Tekla Gurba for making that decision over 110 years ago to leave everything that was familiar to them and embark on a life-altering journey to a new and wonderful part of the world. I never met them but I am convinced in my own mind that they were amongst the bravest people this world has seen. People are often asked, if they had the choice, who they would invite over for supper. The person could be living or non-living. One of my top choices would be Anton and Tekla. There is so much I would like to know about their lives and times.

I am also blessed to have had my Grandmother Frances in my life for so very long. Her wonderful memory, her stories and her intense Gurba pride has kept me hooked on family history for many years! Her unconditional love of the Gurba family is apparent in everything she has shared with me. She is so proud of her parents, brothers and sisters, nieces and nephews, and of course her own blood kin.

My parents, Bob and Joyce, and my sister, Penny, have always been a pillar of strength and support for everything I have strived for. Their love of family and their strong desire to nurture extended familial bonds is unparalleled. My father, in particular, has shared my love of genealogy and the both of us have been hunched over many a microfilm reader here in Edmonton and in Salt Lake City trying to find an undiscovered document relating to the Gurba family. Dad never once complained about the occasions that I had lost track of time whilst researching and phoning him near mid-night telling him, "Guess what I just found out?"

I would also like to thank Marilyn Waingarten (nee Mack) for her efforts in preserving the Mack family history. Her excellent book called *Small Farms, Big Family...A Collective Memoir* published in 2004 provided me with very valuable information about Anna Gurba-Budynski's family who married into the Mack family in 1910. The Mack, Gurba and Budynski families have had close familial ties for well over a century.

Thanks must also be extended to the entire Gurba clan, here in Canada and in the United States. Not only have they provided me with stories, photographs and memories, they have always provided constant encouragement in my endeavours to preserve and document our family history. Receiving e-mails from 3rd cousins twice removed from around the continent, was always exciting.

Genealogy has become more than just a hobby for me. It has become a passion. It has combined the elements of history, geography and social studies with the best elements of a mystery "who-dun-it", all of which I love. I take full responsibility for the stories, content and pictures found between these covers. Despite my best efforts, I am sure that mistakes may have crept in and seemingly erroneous perceptions or interpretations of material may have occurred. I am also sure that there are many more stories that could have been included. Possibly, some people may question why I have included certain events. I appeal to the readers for forgiveness and understanding.

Brian Broda
September 2008

PREFACE

On July 3, 4, and 5, 1992, the Gurba family held a 95ᵗʰ year anniversary commemorating their arrival in Canada from Galicia in the Austro-Hungarian Empire. The reunion was held in the town of Radway, Alberta and hundreds of family members attended. To commemorate that event, members of the family put together an excellent book called *The Gurbas Then and Now*. It provided us with a wonderful description of who we were nearly a century after the arrival of Anton and Tekla Gurba from the old country. At that time, very little was known about the family prior to 1897. We were not even sure which ship the Gurba's had arrived on or whether or not they left behind any family members. The book was heavily based on the descendents of Anton and Tekla and very little was mentioned about Anton's sister, Anna or their 3 half sisters, Katie, Rosalia and Sophia. Anton's father, Semen, was mentioned in one sentence. Yet these were members of the Gurba family who arrived in Canada at about the same time as Anton and Tekla. The genealogy bug had already infected me a few years earlier when my father, Robert, and I were visiting the "family" graveyard at the Exaltation of the Holy Cross Parish in Skaro. While walking amongst the crosses and gravestones, many written in Ukrainian, we came upon the simple marker for Semen Gurba. At the time, neither of us had any idea who this man was. We asked my grandmother, Frances, who proudly told us that it was her Grandfather, a man who had immigrated with her father and mother back in 1897. When asked why she never told us about him, she replied, "You never asked".

I had learned my lesson and have been asking questions ever since. Unfortunately, it was too late to learn much about the earliest years of the Gurba family as most of the family members who would know the answers to my questions had passed away. Stories about Gurba family life before their arrival in Canada have been almost non-existent. It appears that those stories were never passed on down. Perhaps no one in Semen's or his children's generations discussed such things. Possibly no one really cared. Maybe everyone was so busy living and surviving day by day that there was no time for yesterday. Never-the- less, I was still determined to learn as much as I could about the early years of the Gurba family and if possible, to go back into history as far as I could to trace the Gurba roots. I could only speculate at certain events hoping that I could reconstruct their lives as best as I could.

I decided to use Semen as the focal point of this book as he was the patriarch of the family here in North America. We've known for quite awhile who his children and grandchildren were, right down to his g-g-g-g-grandchildren. Recent research has now revealed his parents (Stefan and Maria) and grandparents (Daniel and Ewa). We are now able to trace back 9 generations of Gurbas. I also decided to focus the events of this book to the century and a half from the birth of Semen's grandfather in 1772 until the death of Semen's son, Anton, in 1927. That leaves the next 80 some years for another book! I also deliberately avoided telling stories already recorded in the first Gurba family book mentioned earlier. In that book, for example, there is an excellent description of the development of Lucas and Pearl's homestead at Hollow Lake. The tribute to Pearl in that same book refers to a "great lady, a pioneer feminist, good and kind mother, neighbour and friend." I encourage family members to re-read that book.

In preparing this book, I gathered bits from archives here in Alberta and back in Poland, the Family History Library in Salt Lake City, the internet, individual memories and snatches of remembered history, especially from my grandmother Frances, the longest living member of the Gurba family.

A mention must be made about the spelling of many names. This is a very common problem genealogists encounter when researching immigrant ancestors. I have uncovered many different spellings for my ancestors. The name GURBA has been recorded as Gurban, Gorba, Gourba and Coubar. There have also been multiple spellings for other surnames like Dombroski, Dembroski, Dombrowski and Dombrowsky. I have also encountered Budynski spelled as Bodinske, Budinski and Budenski. First names are just as problematic. Anton has been recorded as Antoni, Anthony, Antonian and Antonius. Joseph has been written as Jozef, Johannes, Josef and Joe. Sometimes, even the spelling of names provided by the family is incorrect. For example, in the cemetery records for Albion, New York dated September 27, 1936, it states that Anne Budynski was the "wife of Joseph, daughter of Samuel Jurnba and Polly Chomik" (instead of Semen Gurba and Pelagia Chomik). I have decided to use the different spelling interchangeably, depending on the document being discussed. More often than not, however, I have opted to use the names and spellings that would be most familiar to the family members of today.

There is no doubt that there are many more stories out there and I will probably never learn all that I want to about this incredible family. The evolution of this family from its humble peasant roots in Galicia continues down to this day.

On a personal note, please remember to share your valuable family stories with your children, grandchildren.....right on down the line. In many ways, the stories of our lives are a valuable gift to pass on to the next generations.

Brian Broda (a great-great-grandson of Semen and Pelagia and great-great-great-great- grandson of Daniel and Ewa)

September 2008 (111 years after the arrival of the Gurba's in Canada)

CHAPTER 1
THE FAMILY BEFORE CANADA

Until a few years ago, very little was known about the Gurba family prior to their immigration to Canada from Skoloszow, Galicia in March of 1897. We knew that Anton, his wife Tekla and 4 of their children (Tylda, Lucas, Dmytro and Ivan) arrived in Canada on April 8, 1897 accompanied by Anton's father Semen and Anton's unmarried sister Sofia. Seven months later, Anton's sister Anna and her husband Josef Budynski arrived with their 3 children (Wladek, Rose and Wawrzenic). In April 1898, the remaining 2 daughters of Semen, Katie and Rosalia, arrived with their families. Accompanying Katie was her son Michael and accompanying Rosalia were her husband Paul Czternastek and their children, Anna, Marie, and Katherine. For a brief while, Semen was reunited with all of his children and grandchildren at the family homestead near Skaro (aka Edna-Star), Alberta. Any family history prior to that time was unknown for nearly a century. A more detailed description of their departure from Galicia and their subsequent arrival in Canada will be told in future chapters.

For several years, research at the Family History Library in Salt Lake City, Utah was undertaken to try to trace the family prior to the birth of Anton and his sisters. Unfortunately, nothing could be found. The next step would have to be physically search the records back in the old country. To achieve that goal, in 2007, I hired Adam Jedryka, a researcher from

Krakow, Poland, to search the Przemysl civil archives and the Radymno registration office, where I knew the records for the village of Skoloszow were kept. He was able to document and trace the family ancestry back an additional 3 generations to the birth of Daniel Gurba in 1772. This was indeed exciting news as was the realization that the Gurba family had lived in the same house (ie: house #139) for well over a century. On the previous page is a map showing the Radymno/Skoloszow area in 1900. Each black dot represents a house. Unfortunately, it is not known which dot is house #139. We can not even speculate. When house numbering was introduced, the numbering began near the village church. The lowest number house would be near there. After the initial house was numbered, new numbers were assigned whenever a new house was built. That meant the house numbers did not progress down the street in an orderly fashion. For example, if a house was assigned #140 and the next house built in town was at the other end of town, it would still get the #141 designation What we can assume however, is that the Gurba house was probably not near the church as they had quite a high house number.

The history of house #139 is first mentioned in the marriage records of Daniel Gurba and Eudoxia Blonarowicz on November 10, 1799. (See below in the column labeled Nrus Domus)

1799		S P O N S U S						S P O N S A						T E S T E S	
Dies et Mensis	Nrus Domus	NOMEN	Religio Catholica	Ant alia	Aetas	Coelebs	Viduus	NOMEN	Religio Catholica	Ant alia	Aetas	Coelebs	Vidua	NOMINA	CONDI- TIO.
Eadem	139	Daniel Gurba	1	"	27	1	"	Eudoxia Blonarowicz	1	"	15	1	"	Gabriel Gur ba Grego. mus Skupit	etto.

From this record, we can determine Daniel's birth is circa 1772 (as he was 27 at the time of his marriage). Eudoxia is listed as being 15 years old at the time of her marriage so this puts her birthdate circa

1783. Both were Catholic and single at the time of their marriage (ie: coelebs).

Another marriage had occurred earlier in house #139 in the year 1796. Ignacy Gurba married Maria Wolos on October 29, 1796. We assume Ignacy was Daniel's younger brother. This is based on the evidence that Daniel eventually was the one to inherit the family house at #139. This honour was usually granted to the oldest son.

Daniel and Ewa would have 6 children born at house #139 but only 3 would survive to adulthood: Stefan (Jan 6, 1808-April 28, 1857), Pelagia (May 6, 1811 - ?) and Simeon (May 10, 1817 - ?). Daughter Tatiana died at age 23 days old (Jan 24, 1805), son Basilius would die at age 5 (July 27, 1813- Sept 6, 1818) and a second son also named Basilius would die at 2 months of age (May 9, 1822-July 10, 1822). Stefan's birth as shown in the parish registers is seen below.

Daniel and Ewa's oldest surviving child, Stefan would marry the 19 year old Maria Kosteczko (Feb 16, 1810-Jan 30, 1854) at house #139 in November of 1829. They would have 8 children (Pantelemon, Simeon, Grzegorz, Salomea. Ewa, Elias, Izydor, and Anastasia) at the same house during the next 17 years. Their oldest son Pantelemon was born on Aug 8, 1830 but died 25 years later unmarried and childless. Simeon's birth record is shown below.

1832.				Reli-gio.	Se-xus				PARENTES		PATRINI
Mensis *Julius*	Nu-merus Do-	NOMEN					Legitimi	Illegitimi			
Na-tus	Bapti-satus	mus		Catholica	Aut alia	Puer	Puella	Thori	PATER	MATER	CONDITIO
10. *Septemo.* *anno 183?*	11.	139	*Simeon*	1	„	1	„	1	„	*Stefan Gur-ba .c?*	*Maria nata .. vente Clud Hoi .kie ho*	*Dmitro Braila Anna Pat..zg. .tha .c?*

The ownership of house #139 then passed on to their second son, Simeon (Sept 10, 1832- Dec 1, 1901). This Simeon would be the "Semen" who immigrated with his children and their families to Canada in 1897. He will be referred to as Semen for the rest of this book to differentiate him from his Uncle Simeon.

Semen, born at house #139 on Sept. 10, 1832, would marry his first wife, Pelagia Chomiak (born April 17, 1835) at the same house on September 29, 1857. Pelagia's parents are listed as Mathias Chomiak and Tatiana Dutkowa. She lived in House #52. Semen was 24 years old and Pelagia was 21. Their marriage is recorded below.

1857		Sponsus						Sponsa						Testes	
Dies & Mensis	Nrus Do-mus	NOMEN	Religio					NOMEN	Religio					NOMINA	Con-ditio.
			Catholica	Aut alia	Ætas	Cælebs	Viduus		Catholica	Aut alia	Ætas	Cælebs	Vidua		
29 September 1857	139 52.	Simeon Gurba fil. Stefhan Gurba & Maria Pretey Rowa r.g cum licent. al office De	1	„	24	1	„	Pelagia Chomi Roba filia Mi Chomiak et Tatiana Dut Towej r.g trinis	1	„	21	1	„	Mathens Hlaza R Andreas Pawlik 1? October 1857 et ??	

They would have 3 children born at the same house that Semen was born in: Anton (Oct 17, 1858), Anna (Feb.7, 1861) and Jan (June 25, 1863). Both Anton's and Anna's birth records are shown below. It is interesting to note that the priest reported that Anton was a female (ie: puella). I guess even priests can make mistakes!

Tragedy would strike in 1863. Pelagia would give birth to a second son, Jan, on June 25, 1863 but he would die the next day of "natural" causes. Pelagia herself, would die 3 days later on June 29, 1863 of tuberculosis (phtisis). Their deaths are recorded below. Semen would become a widower with 2 young children at the age of 31 after a marriage of only 6 years.

Annus 18 /3. Mensis Dies Mortis | Sepultu-ræ	Nrus Domus	NOMEN MORTUI	Religio		Sexus		Dies Vitae	MORBUS & qualitas Mortis
			Catholica	Aut alia	Masculin.	Fœmina		
(handwritten) 26. 28.	139	Joannes Filius Semionis Gurbarii	1		1		2.	Naturali
(handwritten) 29. 1.	130	Pelagia uxor... ...Gurba...	1			1	28	Debilius

Semen would then marry Maria Dziedzic (Didicz), who was born on June 12, 1828. They would have 3 daughters (Katie, Sofia, and Rosalia) but no records of their birth could be found as there is a gap in the records beginning in 1865.

When the elderly Semen immigrated to Canada with his children in 1897, it is not certain whether he left any surviving immediate family at home. We know that his oldest brother, Pantelemon died in 1855, his sister Ewa died at the age of 1 in 1840, and another sister Anastasia died at the age of 3 on April 16, 1850. We also know that he had four more siblings: Grzegorz (born Jan 17, 1835), sister Salomea (born Sept. 7, 1835), and 2 other brothers, Elias (born Oct 3, 1841) and Izydor (born Feb 14, 1844). Unfortunately, we can not find any documents regarding their lives and possible families. Perhaps they moved out of the area.

We do know for a fact that Semen left behind at least 2 much younger cousins when he left for Canada. These were Michal (b. Oct 30, 1864) and Jan (b. Mar 4, 1874) who were the sons of Semen's Uncle Simeon. There is the possibility of 5 more cousins still living at the time Semen left for Canada: Lukasz (b. Oct 9, 1859), Katarzyna (b. July 18, 1867), Maria (b. May 8, 1870), Antoni (b. Sept 20, 1871) and Mikolaj (b. May 10, 1879). Cousin Michal's sons would later track down the Gurba family here in Canada and would immigrate themselves in the 1950's and 1960's and became much welcomed additions to the Gurba family here in Canada. Michal's son, John and his wife Hilda, now reside in Edmonton and have attended every Gurba event held in the Edmonton area since their arrival in Canada.

CHAPTER 2

FROM WHENCE THEY CAME

Tradition had long held that the Gurba family came from a small village called Skoloszow, in the Austro-Hungarian province of Galicia. This was to be proven once we had found copies of the ship records a few years ago. As shall soon be shown, the Gurba's indicated to customs officials in Hamburg, that they lived in the town of Radymno, which was only 1.8 km away from Skoloszow. In all likelihood, they probably lived on a piece of land somewhere between the two, in house #139, as indicated in the church birth/marriage/death records referred to in the previous chapter of this book. At the present time, the area of Skoloszow/Radymno lies within the border of Poland, a few kilometers from the Ukrainian border. The star on the map below indicates the location of this village. Zooming in on the map indicates the close proximity of these two locations, less than 2 kilometres. (See map on next page.)

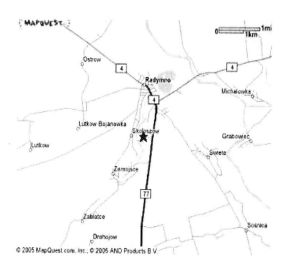

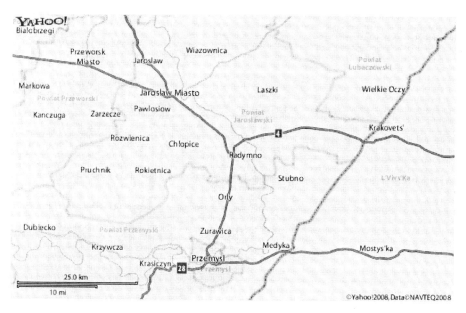

The dual towns of Skoloszow and Radymno   are located equidistant from the 2 larger cities of Jaroslaw and Przemysl. There is   a very interesting book called *"on long winter nights....Memoirs of a Jewish Family in a Galician Township (1870-1900)"*, written by Hinde Bergner. She was born on 11 October 1870 in Radymno and would therefore have been a contemporary of Tekla Gurba. Her father managed an estate in

Radymno for a Polish lord. She would live her entire life in Radymno. She would be arrested by Nazi forces when they occupied Radymno on 22 September 1939. She would perish in 1942 at the Belzec Concentration Camp. In her book, Hinde claimed that "at least once a week, half of Radymno would find itself either in Jaroslaw or in Przemysl—respectfully a quarter hour and half hour away by train." It would be interesting to discover how many times the Gurba's would have made that trip.

Skoloszow

Skoloszow derives from the word 'skole', the name of the river valley, and 'szow', hill on the other side of the river. People have lived in the area since the 2nd century as indicated by a major archeological find made in the area in 1958 that showed remnants of residential fireplaces, pottery, etc. By the year 1393, the land was given to the Bishop of the area for taking part in battles and demonstrating bravery during war. In March 1656, the Swedish king took control of the area for 3 days. In the next few years, the area was also attacked by the Cossacks and Hungarians. By 1772, the area settled back down to relative calm under the control of the Austro-Hungarian Emperor and the area around Skoloszow was once again controlled by the Bishop. Residents were required to work for the Bishop for 4 days a week.

Between the years of 1880-1902, the Austrian authorities published the _Slownik geograficzny Krolestwa Polskiego i innych krajow slowianskich_, which is a gazetteer of geographic points of interest in the lands that once belonged to the Kingdom of Poland. This period of time corresponds to when the Gurba's lived in the area. In 1880, it indicated that Skoloszow had 354 homes and 1983 residents (944 males and 1039 females). There were 650 Roman Catholics, 1249 Greek Catholics and 151 Jews. (It is interesting to note that these figures don't add up to the 1983 residents mentioned above.) In the year 1900, a census of the area was taken and then published in 1907 in a book entitled *Gemeindelixikon der im Reichsrate vertretenen Kongreiche und Lander*. Although the Gurba's were no longer in the area during the census, it is interesting to note that there was now a population of 2955 (1608 males and 1347 females plus 331 military personnel). Roman Catholics now numbered 1085, Greek Catholics 1585 and 27 Jews. When asked to identify their language/nationality, 105 replied German, 2619 Polish, 1 Ruthenian and 228 others. Total number of houses was 425. Also inhabiting Skoloszow were 630 horses, 743 cattle, 16 sheep and 371 pigs. The boundaries of Skoloszow included 1966 hectares of which 1630 ha were fields, 38 ha were meadows and 42 ha were gardens.

Covered market in Radymno, late 1890's. The Gurba's probably "shopped" here.

Early postcard of the town of Radymno

Radymno

The <u>Slownik geograficzny</u> classified Radymno as a "small town". Even though its population was apparently less than Skoloszow's when this gazetteer was published, Radymno was the economic and political centre of the area. It had the county court, the Roman Catholic church, the Greek Catholic church, the post office, the telegraph office, a notary, a physician, a pharmacy, a railroad station and 2 co-ed single class schools. The covered market, seen on the previous page, had "major" markets on the 20th day of May, August, September and December plus a weekly "trades" market. The town itself had 293 homes and 1919 residents (906 males and 1013 females) of which 850 were Roman Catholic, 171 Greek Catholic and 898 were Jewish. (As an aside, the *Encyclopaeida Judaica*, writes that even though the population of Radymno was 46.8% Jewish in 1880, there were none left in the town after the Holocaust, the entire population being exterminated at the Belzec concentration camp during World War II).

Market Square in Radymno 1880

Early photographs of the Radymno farmers market

Row of houses in the residential quarter of Radymno

World War II.) The area surrounding Radymno (including the villages of Skoloszow, Zagrody, Zasnie, Zagrodani and Michalowski) consisted of 4555 homes, and 25,990 residents (7830 Roman Catholics, 16,125 Greek Catholics, 8 Protestants and 2027 Jews.)

Marketplace in Radymno. The building in the forefront is the old town hall, built in 1800. The building with the tower is the new town hall, built in 1896, the year before the Gurba's left the area.

The Budynski (Anna Gurba's) family listed their residence on the ship's record as Surochow, which was NNW of Radymno. The village of Surochow had 42 homes with 522 residents. The "brick" parish church built in 1824 served the area and claimed 2825 "souls".

In the mid to late 1890's, the extended Gurba family made the decision to leave their homes in the Skoloszow/Radymno area and immigrate to the country of Canada. Their exact reasons for doing so may never be known. It may have been for economic reasons. As indicated in the census numbers referred to earlier, the population was increasing rapidly in the area. Land availability was obviously at a premium. My grandmother, Frances, recalls her father Anton telling her that there was never enough wood in the old country to keep the family warm. They just couldn't afford to buy it from the Polish overlords. Perhaps the Gurbas wanted to persue an adventurous dream. It may have been for political/racial reasons as well. In a book found at the Alberta Genealogical Society Library detailing the building of St. Mary's Greek Catholic Church in Rabbit Hill, Alberta, an interesting document is reproduced that contains a very revealing statement about the reasons for emigration of some of its parishioners. At a meeting held on March 26, 1900 to plan the building of a church in Rabbit Hill, a group of people, including Wasyl Kadryk from the village of Skoloszow signed a declaration which in part reads as follows:

We, the undersigned, Rusyny of the Greek Catholic rite from the land of Galicia in the state of Austria in Europe, emigrated from our land in the years 1896, 1897, 1898 partly because of poverty stricken conditions to which Ruthenians were subjected by Polish

(landlords) and Jewish (moneylenders) elements that drove us
Ruthenians from Galicia across the sea. It was on that account that
we sold our ancestral lands in our country and sought a happier
future for ourselves and our children in a far away land.

Did the Gurba family leave for the same reason as fellow villager Wasyl Kudryk? Did they attribute their peasant status to the landlord and moneylenders? The Gurba's did in fact have to sell their "ancestral land". House #139 in Skoloszow was in the Gurba family for at least 100 years prior to their immigration to Canada.

Whatever the ultimate reason, the patriarch of the family about to immigrate to Canada was the twice-widowed man, Semen Gurba. He was 65 years old at the time, which was considerable for that era. With his first wife, Pelagia Chomik, he had two children (Anton and Anna). With his second wife, Marina Didicz, he had 3 more daughters (Katie, Rose and Sofia).

His eldest child, son Anton, was already married to Tekla Albert, and at the time of leaving Skoloszow, they had four young children by the names of Tylda, Lukas, Dymetro and Ivan.

Semen's eldest daughter, Anna, was married to Josef Budenski and they had 3 children by the names of Wladek, Rosalie and Wawrzenic. They lived in the nearby settlement of Surochow.

Semen's first daughter with his second Marina, Katie, was married (possibly widowed) to Michal Danelko and had a son, Mihal (Mike). They lived in Skoloszow/Radymno.

Daughter Rosalie, married Paul Czternastek and had 3 children Anna, Marie and Katherine. They too listed their home on the ship records as Radymno.

Daughter Sofia was still unmarried and presumably living at home with her father, Semen.

Starting in March of 1897, Semen, his 5 children, 1 daughter-in-law, 2 sons-in-law and 11 grandchildren, made the arduous trip to Alberta Canada in a series of 3 journeys. A description of these 3 journeys follows in Chapter 4.

CHAPTER 3
MILITARY SERVICE

The extended Gurba family has a proud history of serving its adopted countries of Canada and the United States. We've had family members recently patrol in Afghanistan and in the former Yugoslavia. We've had family members serve in Viet Nam. World War II saw many members of the Gurba extended family serve overseas. Some were pilots. Some were medics, soldiers, nurses, even paratroopers. Some of them became Prisoners of War. Some were shot and/or wounded. Some have been decorated with medals, including the Bronze Star.

The history of the Gurba family in the military service goes back for many years even back to the "old country". In theory, all men living in the Austro-Hungarian Empire, of which Galicia was a province, were liable for conscription into the army. In fact, the highest numbers of men in the army were those conscripted by officials in several recruiting areas spread throughout the Austro-Hungarian Empire. Each of these areas had to supply a stated number of men each year. If the area fell short of their quota, it was added to the requisition for the following year. In practice however, rules were set so that only the lowest classes – peasants and urban working class- would bear the greatest burden. The Gurba family were by most accounts listed in birth, death and marriage records as "peasants" or "farmers". Conscription laws ordered all men who had reached the age of 19 be added to the Landstrum service list. It was not until the spring of his 21st birthday that a recruit was ordered to report to a selection centre. Once at the selection centre, the recruits were graded according to their fitness and then were required to take an Oath of Allegiance. In peace time, military service was for 3 years. Once that was completed, the soldier was required to begin a period of reserve service for 10 years. During this 10 year period, he was liable to be recalled for further training. He then spent a further 5 years as a First

Landsturm Reservist before passing into the Second Landsturm Reserve.

Standards of accommodation for the men were low and the infantry was often billeted in old, decrepit buildings or with an area family. Food and pay were also of low standard. For example, in 1874, a period close to the time that Anton Gurba would have served, soldiers received only one hot meal per day and this consisted of soup, 6 ounces of beef and a similar amount of vegetables and bread. They were allowed to ration the bread for consumption during the day, but 6 ounces of bread was all they received for the entire day. Low pay would not allow them to supplement their food situation as

Peter Budynski (Anna Gurba's brother-in-law) in his Austrian army uniform

they were required to pay for other things such as shoe polish and for the upkeep of their barracks. This Spartan lifestyle would certainly help Anton deal with what lay ahead for him on the work crews on the Crow's Nest Pass Railroad during his first year in Canada.

There is no doubt that many of the Gurba men would have been conscripted to fight for the Austro-Hungarian Army. From the early 1800's men living in the Przemysl region (which included Skoloszow) were conscripted into the 4th battalion of the 10th Regiment. It is probably this regiment that the Gurba's were involved with. It is also possible that they could have been conscripted into the 40th Regiment as these were made up of people from the settlements of Jaroslau and Rzeszow, both also in close proximity to Skoloszow.

Based on the conscription rules, Daniel Gurba would have had to begin his service in 1793. His son, Stefan, would have started in 1829. His son, Semen was born in 1832, which would coincide with the end of Stefan's 3 years of compulsory service. Semen's service began in 1854. His son, Anton would be born 4 years later. Again this timeline would fit with the end of the father's compulsory service. Anton began to serve in 1880. His first child, Tylda, would be born 6 years later, again following the pattern of starting a family after the completion of military service.

We do have documentary proof that Gurba family members served with the military in Galicia. We know for a fact that Daniel Gurba (1772-1827) was definitely a soldier. The birth certificate for Simeon Gurba (brother of Stefan and Semen Gurba's uncle) listed his father, Daniel Gurba, as a "reservist soldier" even at the age of 45. His death certificate dated Feb 11, 1827 also listed him as a "reservist soldier". On Izydor Gurba's (Semen's brother) birth certificate dated Feb 14, 1844, the father, Stefan, was listed as a "judge in Skoloszow". It is not hard to believe that someone appointed as a judge would have had the proper credentials and that probably would have included his compulsory military service. It is also very probable that Anton would have served in the military. As written above, Anton was 32 years old when his first child (Tylda) was born in 1890. It is highly probable that he was serving his compulsory military service until the age of 28 or 29. It was likely that he met and married his wife Tekla after he was discharged.

Anton's military experience is also confirmed by his daughter, Frances. She recalls that her father talked about his experience in the Austrian army but she can not recall any details. "We weren't too interested in knowing that stuff so we just forgot about those things." She does recall that Anton would always start his day by doing "exercises". She stated that he did them "almost to the day he died". Could these exercises that he religiously performed everyday be a holdover from his days in military training??

It is very interesting to speculate as to what would have happened if the Gurba family had chosen NOT to emigrate from Galicia in 1897. Anton's son, Lucas, would have begun his compulsory service in 1914-15, the onset of the First World War. This gives one pause to think of what might have been. The Austro-Hungarian Army was Canada's "enemy". Many hundreds of thousands of people were killed. Providence had led the Gurba's away from this area less than 2 decades earlier.

It is chilling to think that one of the most vicious battles on the Eastern Front during World War I, was fought on the Gurba's doorstep. The First Battle of Przemysl occurred shortly after the outbreak of the war. Przemysl was a ringed fortress city of the 1st class; the 3rd only to Verdun and Antwerp and was located only 16 km (9 miles) south of Skoloszow, the Gurba home base. It is quite likely that if the extended Gurba family hadn't emigrated some 20 years earlier, many of Semen's grandchildren would have been involved in this battle. At the very least, the Gurba's ancestral homeland was virtually on the front lines of the Eastern Front of World War I.

PRZEMYŚL. Totalansicht der Festung Przemyśl vor dem Kriege. Ogólny widok twierdzy przemyskiej przed wojną.

City of Przemysl before World War I

Due to its military importance, the Russians attacked the Przemysl area early. A contemporary description of the battle indicated that there were "2 ½ million troops whose fighting had no parallel in fierceness" and that the combatants were "most desperate and dreadful characters". Przemysl "crashed with explosions, great mushroom-shaped columns of smoke arose from the destroyed munitions stores". The city was besieged and cut off from all lines of communication and supplies from November 1914 until March of 1915. During this time, the garrison at Radymno was rescued by the Austro-Hungarian army as it too had be taken by the Russians, and they began a counter attack that ultimately was unsuccessful. The Russians completely cut off 131,000 people and 21,000 horses living in Przemysl from the outside world. Starvation hit the area and 13,000 horses eventually had to be slaughtered in Przemysl to feed the troops. In March of 1915, the Russians decided to "end" the siege and attacked the city. Almost 120,000 soldiers from the Przemysl area were taken prisoner. Czar Nicholas II of Russia visited the destroyed Fortress on April 25, 1915. Shortly afterwards, towards the end of May, troops from Germany helped the Austrian troops recapture the fort and returned it to the inhabitants. The Fortress, or what was left of it, once again played a role after the end of World War I, when the Polish and the Ukrainians became the principle combatants. The Ukrainians from the West Ukrainian Peoples Republic took control of the area for a short time until the Polish Army reclaimed the area and drove the Ukrainians out of the area.

Przemyśl. Das zerstörte Fort Prałkowce. — Przemyśl. Zburzony fort Prałkowce.

Fortress at Przeymsl after the siege.

*Street scene in Przemysyl during
the siege of 1914.*

CHAPTER 4

THE TRANS-ATLANTIC VOYAGES

Once the extended Gurba family made the decision to leave Galicia in the mid- 1890's, they would have triggered a series of events. Their first task would have to have been to raise enough capital to fund such a voyage. There were a variety of expenses that had to be covered: fees for passports (which apparently were not easy to obtain); travel expenses to get to a port, which in the Gurba's case was Hamburg; purchase of tickets for the trans-Atlantic voyage; costs to be incurred on route across Canada; payment of $10 for the homestead registration; money to buy supplies for the initial set up of the farm and enough cash to tide them over until they could make money on their homestead, which could be a couple of years. According to some sources, the total amount of money needed would be about $200 - $300. To raise this capital, the Gurba's would have to dispose of whatever they could have back in Skoloszow. It is not known what happened to "House #139". Whether Anton sold it to the local Lord or to members of his extended family is not known.

They would have sold whatever they deemed unnecessary and then packed whatever they could into wooden chests. These wooden chests were built to stand about knee high and usually had an undivided interior. It is not known exactly what the Gurba's would have packed with them for their long voyage to Canada. My grandmother, Frances, does not recall any specific item that was brought from the old country (aside from "Mom's Polish Bible"). Reading other accounts of the early settlers, it is not unreasonable to believe that the Gurba families would have packed similar items as fellow immigrants. In addition to pillows, linens and clothing, items such as household utensils, small tools, steel implements, packets of seed, felling axes, Austrian broad axes, saws, augers, sickle, scythes and whetstones commonly accompanied the new immigrants. They were limited to about 400 pounds of "baggage" per family. What the Gurba's obviously did take with them however, was courage, bravery and fortitude as they were now headed to a land of different language, culture, customs, law and agricultural practices.

Semen, his grown children and their spouses, and his young grandchildren embarked on 3 separate journeys to begin their new lives in Canada. During the course of a bit over one year, the Gurbas would make their way overland to Hamburg, Germany where they would undergo medical exams and then be permitted to board a ship that would, either directly or indirectly, take them to Canada. Even though there were 3 separate journeys, the Gurba families would have had some shared experiences. For example, we know that they all booked passages on the "Hamburg-America Linie", so they undoubtedly saw posters such as the one shown above, scattered throughout their villages.

Upon arriving at the port of Hamburg, they would have had to stay in quarantine, often in "hotels" converted to immigration stations

Port of Hamburg early 1890's

After passing all medical and legal checks, they would have walked up a rickety gangplank to board their respective ships to begin their journey to Canada.

Once aboard the ship, the Gurba's would begin their long, uncomfortable, and at times, harrowing, journey across the Atlantic Ocean.

Journey #1 (March 19 1897 – April 1897)

The first of the family to leave the "old country" was the aged Semen himself, his single daughter, Sofia and his son Anton and his family, (which consisted of his wife, Tekla and his 4 children Tylda, Lucas, Dymetro, and Ivan). They were the trailblazers and in some ways, had the most strenuous journey. They were the only family members to arrive in Canada through an "indirect" routing, thereby resulting in a 21 day voyage. (The other Gurba's voyages would last between 14-16 days.) They left Hamburg, Germany on March 19, 1897, along with 61 fellow "Galicians" aboard the nearly 50 year old ship called the Empress. They sailed to the city of West Hartlepool, England (located on the east coast of England) where they probably boarded a train to take them to Liverpool (which is on the Atlantic side of England).

In Liverpool, they boarded the ship the S.S. Lake Ontario, destined for Canada. They traveled in the ship's steerage compartment located below water level which was reached by descending a narrow, steep and slippery stairway. The ship was furnished with two- three- and four tiered wooden bunk beds. We know from discussions with Anton's daughter, Frances, that Anton and Tekla often spoke of the terrible inhumane conditions on the "cattle boat" and that everyone, excluding mother Tekla, was violently seasick for almost the entire voyage. It was a very rough passage. Tekla's daughter, Frances, recalls her mother explaining why Tekla's Polish Bible was is such a tattered state. Apparently, the Bible had many loose pages. Frances was curious as to why. When asked, Tekla related that while on route to Canada, a sudden lurch by the boat caused Tekla to drop her Bible whereupon it was tossed from side to side, causing many pages to rip out of the binding. Tekla managed to recover all the pages but the Bible was never rebound. The ship's quarters were hot, crowded, noisy, stuffy, ill smelling and dirty. The food was unpalatable and the drinking water was strictly rationed. In fact, Tekla often "blamed" the conditions of the voyage for the developmental difficulties experienced by her son, Dmetro.

S.S. LAKE ONTARIO, 1887 Beaver Line
Courtesy The Peabody Museum of Salem

The Gurbas arrived in St. John, New Brunswick at 6:00 P.M. on April 8, 1897 with 348 fellow passengers.

In both ships manifests, (i.e.: the Empress and Lake Ontario), Semen appears grouped with Anton and his family's name as an apparently non-related man named either as "Antonego

Senko" or "Antoni Senko". The ships manifest from the Empress (Hamburg to West Hartlepool) is shown below. There are no other Senkos listed on either passenger list. Nor does either list contain the name Semen Gurba or any name similar, yet it is clear that Semen did arrive with Anton and his family. That leads to the speculation that the name Antonego Senko on the passenger list in fact refers to Semen Gurba and probably the error occurred when the ship's officer preparing the list asked for the identity of Semen. He received a response from Semen that "Anton is my son"---in Ukrainian, "Anton me senko". The language difficulty resulted in the listing of Semen Gurba as Antonego (or Antoni) Senko.

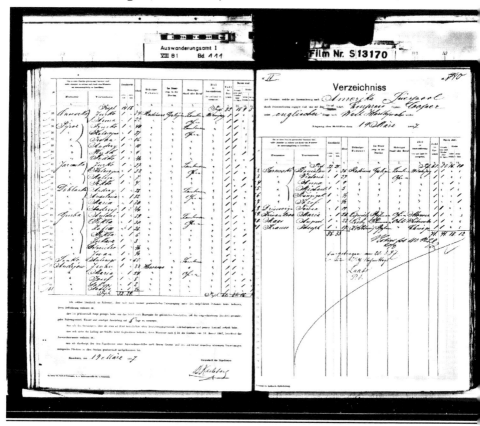

Ships manifest from Hamburg to West Hartlepool. The Gurba family is shown on lines 49-56. The ditto marks in column 5 indicated they all resided in "Radimno". Column 7 indicated that Antoni was a farmer. "Antengo Senko" is listed on line 56

Above is part of the ships log from the S.S. Lake Ontario recording the arrival of the Gurba clan in Canada on April 8, 1897 at 6:00 p.m. (from Antonio Gurba age 39, down to Dimeter. Above Ivan's name is Antony Senko age 65…believed to be Semen.)

Journey #2 (October 28, 1897 – November 13, 1897)

The second family group of Gurbas left for Canada 7 months later. Semen's daughter, Anna, her husband Josef Budenski and their 3 children, Wladek, Rose, and Wawrzenic, left Hamburg on Oct 28, 1897 and arrived in Quebec City on November 13, 1897 before heading to Montreal. The ship was called the Ambria. The ship was on its inaugural single round trip voyage between Hamburg and Quebec. This routing didn't last long. It soon became a Hamburg to Baltimore journey. It made 8 more such voyages until it switched to Far East routes. The ship was torpedoed and sunk in 1918.

The Budenski voyage was probably more comfortable and efficient than the Gurba's a few months earlier for two major reasons. The first reason is that there were not many passengers aboard the ship. Antoni's family arrived the previous year aboard a ship with 348 passengers and they would soon be followed by the Czternasteks the following year on a ship transporting 954 settlers. On the Budenski's ship however, there were only 154 passengers (87 adults, 54 children between the ages of 1-14 and 13 children under the age of 1). The other major reason for a more comfortable passing was that during 1897 – 1898, the Government of Canada ordered Canadian representatives to personally accompany 16 pre-determined voyages from Liverpool, England to Winnipeg, Manitoba. The immigrants aboard these ships would be known as "Personally Conducted Parties". The November 1897 sailing of the SS Ambria was one of those ships.

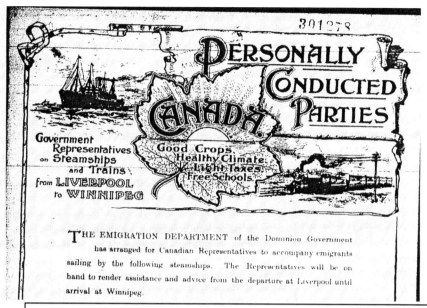

Part of a poster advertising Personally Conducted Parties. The SS Ambria carrying the Budenski family was one such voyage.

Documents pertaining to these Personally Conducted Parties have been microfilmed by the Canadian Archives (Record group 76, file 34186 film C-7300) but no records could be found specifically for the SS Ambria.

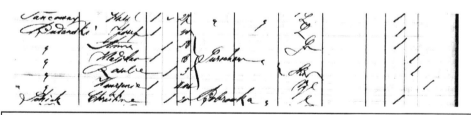

Ship's departing manifest from the Ambria. The Budynski listed their hometown as Surochow,

Journey #3 (April 10, 1898 – April 24, 1898)

The final group of Semen's children left Hamburg on April 10, 1898 aboard the Bulgaria. The Bulgaria was another one of the Personally Conducted Parties.

the Bulgaria

It was a brand new, massive ship and sailed direct from Hamburg to Halifax and then onto New York. (In fact, the Gurbas were on the Bulgaria's very first voyage!) This was a massive ship, capable of carrying over 2700 passengers in 2nd and 3rd class categories. (The ship would be scrapped in 1924.) On this, it's inaugural sailing, only 954 passengers would board in Hamburg. Aboard this ship were Semen's daughter, Katie and grandson Mihal and Semen's other daughter Rosalie, her husband Paul Czternastek and their children Anna, Marie and Katherine. There appears to be no record of Katie's husband accompanying them although it is interesting to note that another family of Danelko's from the same village as the Czternasteks and Katie, also traveled with them ... perhaps relatives?? It is also interesting to note, that travelling with the Gurba relatives was a family of Macks, also from Radymno. They are related to the same Mack family that Rose Budynski would marry into 12 years later.

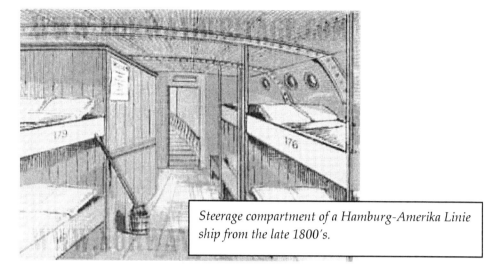

Steerage compartment of a Hamburg-Amerika Linie ship from the late 1800's.

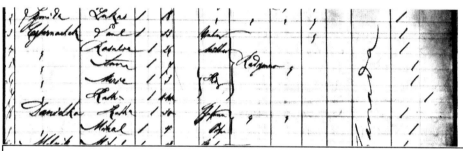

Ship's departing manifest from the Bulgaria. The Czternastek's and Katie Danelko & family are listed as residents of Radymno.

For her book, *Small Farms, Big Family,* Marilyn Waingarten interviewed Kathleen Rombalski Maxwell (aka Katherine Czternastek), who was 3 years old at the time of sailing on the Bulgaria,

> My mother said I was awful sick on the trip
> from Europe, with seasickness. They thought
> they were going to lose me.

As stated earlier, the Bulgaria was another one of the Personally Conducted Parties. Fortunately, a 3 page report from Alfred

Akerlindh, the Immigration Officer who met the Bulgaria passengers in Montreal, survives and it paints an interesting picture of the Czternastek's and Danelko's train trip across Canada.

Upon meeting the train, Mr. Akerlindh realized that there was a shortage of bread aboard the trains (there would be a convoy of two trains transporting the Bulgaria immigrants) and he quickly ordered that more be delivered. Once the bread was delivered, the trains commenced their trip to Winnipeg. Mr. Akerlindh then reported "that the cars I was supplied with at Montreal were large and comfortable and my passengers were not crowded but very comfortable and everything went smooth all along the North Shore." He then reports a sleet and snow storm at Rat Portage making it "a little uncomfortable at the depot", where he had to order "a large supply of bread". He then sadly reports that an 8 month old died of stomach problems near Birds Hill station. He arranged for burial in Winnipeg. Another "little boy" fell off the train a few days later but was ultimately OK. Shortly before arriving at Winnipeg, Mr. Akerlindh received a wire from Ottawa encouraging him to convince this trainload of immigrants to settle near Fish Creek, near Prince Albert. Stating that he got the wire too late to do much convincing, he regretfully reported that he was unsuccessful in this task. He wrote "a large number [of passengers] had friends and relations in the Edmonton district and were bound for there and would go nowhere else." I'm sure that Semen and his family already in Skaro would have been pleased that the Czternasteks and Danelkos stuck to their guns and refused to go to Fish Creek.

There is another statement written by Mr. Akerlindh that is quite interesting to ponder.

As to the quality of the people, should there be any difference to parties passing through my hands last year and the year before, I am pleased to be able to say that these were somewhat superior to former batches, and much cleaner in their habits, of course it must be understood that there is a great deal to be desired from them yet, but I had not quite as much trouble on this trip to keep the cars in somewhat decent state as on previous trips, and I must impress that the earlier I can meet these people should any further parties come out, the quicker I get them trained into more cleanliness, both to the comfort of themselves as well as those in charge.

I can't help but wonder would Paul, Anna and Katie would think knowing that they and their family were considered to be "somewhat superior to former batches" of immigrants from Galicia.

Once on Canadian Shores

Once their ships arrived in port, the next order of business for the Gurba family was to once again, undergo a medical examination and documentary control. Each family also had to declare how much money they had brought with them, $25 being the lowest amount acceptable. All the Gurba members passed these tests as none of them were required to stay behind.

The next ordeal would have been the crossing of the vast expanse of Canadian wilderness by train. This would be another long and tiresome journey aboard specially converted railcars provided by the Canadian Pacific Railway. Conditions aboard these trains varied greatly and we only have documentary evidence for the last two Gurba journeys as recorded above. The Gurba's would have been forced to get off the train in Winnipeg, where immigration officers would have met them and then determine where to send them to the next distribution centre. In the Gurba's situation, it was Edmonton (Strathcona).

Once in Edmonton, the family would have temporarily boarded at the Immigration Hall. The hall was small and very congested. The families were expected to sleep on wooden bunks and provide for their own food, often cooked communally with other immigrants. While at the Immigration Hall, the men would tour with an immigration agent looking at potential homestead sites. After paying the $10 registration fee, the family would pack up their meager belongings and head out

Glenbow Archives NC-6-560

Edmonton Immigration Hall 1900

to their chosen homestead.

Having ultimately chosen a homestead in the Edna-Star area, Semen, Anton and his family, would have had to travel along the South Victoria Trail between the North Saskatchewan River and the edge of Beaver Hills, a long established transportation route used by the Aboriginal people of the area. It is not known if they walked or "hitched" a communal ride with other settlers. There would be no train service to the area until 1905, when the Canadian National Railway arrived about 1 mile south of the Star post office.

By the middle of 1898, Semen and all of his children were reunited in their newly adopted home of Edna-Star, Alberta. Their new life was about to begin. It was inevitable that this group of 20 persons would eventually disburse and establish homes and families through Canada and the United States. Semen would pass away on December 1, 1901. His death certificate stated the cause of death as "old age not able to find any other cause of death". He was 69 years old.

Semen's grave at the Exaltation of the Holy Cross Ukrainian Catholic Church near the family homestead. The headstone incorrectly records his year of birth and death. On the back of the headstone is a marble plaque retelling the story of Semen's family's journey to Canada. The plaque was placed there in 2002. (See page 114)

The Anton Gurba family remained in Edna-Star until Anton's children reached adulthood and they moved to places in Alberta such as Edmonton, Hollow Lake, Danube, Radway and Eldorena. Two of Anton's daughters (Tylda and Anne) moved and settled in New York State. His son, Steve, was to stay on the homestead and raise his family, who still retained ownership into the new millennium.

Semen's daughter, Anna Budynski, and her family eventually settled in the Albion, New York area.

Semen's widowed second daughter, Katie Danelko, married Matjiv Stecyk and that family settled in the Eldorena, Alberta area.

Semen's third daughter, Rosalia Czternastek, and her family settled in the Round Hill area. Upon the sudden and tragic death of her husband, she married Anton Rombalski and moved to Glanford, Ontario. She remained there until Anton's death in 1920 where upon she moved to New York State.

Semen's fourth daughter, Sofia Gurba, stayed on the homestead for a while. She would soon marry a widowed neighbour, John Dombrosky and became an instant mother for his 5 children. They lived for a few years on John's homestead, which was near the Gurba's. A few years later, they moved to Edmonton to open a rooming house. Sofia and her 7 daughters would later take up a homestead near her nephew, Lucas' home near

Hollow Lake. She would later move to be near some of her married daughters in Canfield, Ontario.

CHAPTER 5

THE FIRST CANADIAN HOMESTEADS

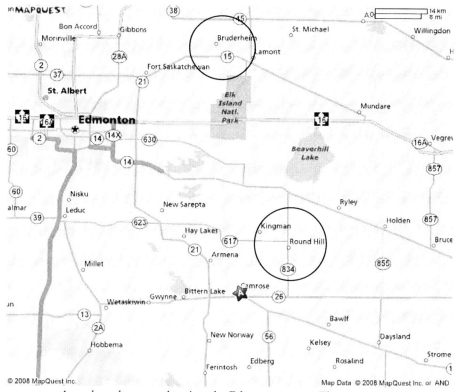

*A modern day map showing the Edmonton area. The community
of Edna Star is just north-east of the town of Bruderheim. The Budynski's
and Czternastek's settled near the community of Round Hill. See circles.*

One of the first orders of business for the Gurba families was to
establish a homestead. Back in Galicia, rumours were spreading
about the availability of land and freedom in a distant land called
Canada. One hundred and sixty acres of heavily wooded land would
be given to every family after they had paid a $10.00 registration fee,
cleared 30 acres of land and built a habitable dwelling within 3 years.
This seemed like an impossible dream but the stories continued and

the names of Ivan Pylypiw and Wasyl Eleniak and their experiences in Canada were gaining credibility. (These 2 men first came to Canada on September 7, 1891 to check out opportunities to start new lives in Canada. They liked what they saw and reported their findings to family back in the village of Nebyliw, Galicia. They are often called the trailblazers of Ukrainian emigration to Canada.) Although Anton was illiterate, his wife Tekla could read and write in Polish. It is not unreasonable to assume that she read reports from Dr. Jospeh Oleskiw, a highly regarded professor of Agriculture in Lviv, that confirmed what Pylypiw and Eleniak were saying. In discussions with my grandmother, Frances, there is no doubt that Anton was desirous of a better life for his family than what was potentially waiting for them if they stayed in the old country. Self sufficiency and education was very important to Anton and Tekla. The thought of nearly 160 free acres in a land known for its freedom from overlords had an attraction.   Anton and Tekla had made the decision. They began disposing of as many assets as possible in order to pay for the transportation to Canada and to raise as much capital as they could to get their 160 acres in Canada.

ANTON'S HOMESTEAD

Anton wasted little time in choosing his homestead. There are stories that Anton inspected possible sites in the Leduc-Calmar area but the abundance of trees and the quality of the soil convinced him that the area around Edna-Star was a much more desirable site. (A 1903 Dominion Land Survey of the area described the area as containing "dense growths of poplar and willow". By 1919, the same land was described as "fairly level country with light poplar and willow bluffs.") Anton acted quickly. On April 13, 1897 (a mere 5 days after arriving in Canada), he went to the Edmonton office of the Local Agent of Dominion Lands and applied for Homestead Entry on the NW ¼ of Section 30, Township 56, Range 19, West of the 4th Meridian. His dream of his own land suffered a severe setback when the Agents' records disclosed that 2 years earlier, on April 8, 1895, a man by the name of Joseph Ososke, had filed for homestead entry on the same property. Fortunately for Anton, he learned that if Mr. Ososke had not complied with the conditions of the homestead entry by clearing sufficient land and the construction of the required building, the entry would be cancelled and Anton's application would prevail. His examination of the property had shown no improvements to the land whatsoever so Anton apparently convinced the land agent to order an inspection. This was done and the Ososke entry was cancelled on July 14, 1897 and the Gurba application was duly filed.

A recent photo of the house at the homestead. The original log walls, plastered with mud, are seen under the more modern wooden planks.

The Gurba family immediately moved to their chosen quarter section. Several generations of Gurba's would work that quarter section of land for the next 100 years. On February 20, 1902, Anton Gurba applied for patent (or title) to the land and his application was supported by sworn declarations by Petro Skitsko and Stach Potiuk outlining in detail the improvements created on the property to date. From those statements, we learn that in 1897, Anton and his family had broken 3 acres of land and had cultivated the entire 3 acres. The following year, they broke an additional 2 acres and cultivated all 5 acres. In 1899 they broke another 3 acres and had crops on all 8 acres.

They didn't break any new land in 1900 but cultivated all previously broken land. In 1901, they had broken an additional 1 acre but still only had 8 acres cultivated. By 1902, the Gurbas had built a 15'X21' house, which was valued at $25.00. When asked, Anton's daughter Frances, is adamant that they family never built a temporary mud "burdei" as many immigrants had first constructed. Anton had insisted that his family would "never have mud for walls!" They had 10 acres fenced and had dug a water well, 3 stables and a granary, all valued at $110.00. The Application for Patent also indicated that in 1897, the Gurba family had 1 cow. In 1898, they had 3 cows and 2 pigs. The following year, 1899, they had 4 cows and 4 pigs. In 1900, the animal population doubled, as they reported having 6 cows, 6 pigs and 4 horses. In 1901, they had 6 cows, 8 pigs and 6 horses. The powers that be decided that Anton had met all the requirements to gain ownership of the homestead and the Patent was granted on December 1, 1902. The Gurba family was now firmly established in their new country of choice

ANNA GURBA AND JOZEF BUDYNSKI

Anna and her family were the second group of Gurbas to immigrate to Canada. Upon arriving in Canada in late 1897, they settled in the Clearwater School district area of Alberta on the NE ¼ of Section 10 Township 50 Range 23 W4., a few miles SE of Beaumont. Jozef made the application for the homestead on May 4, 1898. Jozef and his family would only stay on this section of land for about 1 year. During that year, he built a 14' X 20' house, a 16'X12' stable and had cleared 4 acres. On March 29, 1900, he made an application to abandon the land, claiming that it was "not fit for cultivation" and that it had "too much water and timber". He claimed total improvements in the value of $24.00 which he had to abandon to the government of Canada. The abandonment was registered on May 23, 1900.

One year later, Jozef applied for another homestead. (See the map on page 43 for the location of both the Budynski and Czternastek final homesteads.) On the exact day that Jozef and his family became naturalized citizens, (May 23, 1901), Jozef applied for a homestead on NE ¼ of Section 20 Township 48 Range 19 W4. In that first year, he cleared 3 acres and cropped all of it. He also claimed ownership of 2 cows. The following year, he cleared an additional 6 acres and cropped 9 acres. He doubled the cow population to 4 animals. By 1903, he claimed to have cleared an additional 6 acres and cropped 15. By then, he added to his animal population by acquiring 3 horses. By the time he filed for title to the land in 1904, he had cleared a total of 17 acres and farmed 15 of it. He also had built a 14'X26' log house valued at $150.00, a 20'X26' stable valued at $100.00, had 2 miles of fencing valued at $100.00 and had dug a well valued at $10.00. The Budynski's would not stay very long in this area however, and would soon begin their trek towards Albion, New York arriving in 1920.

Jozef Budynski had 4 brothers; Peter, John, Antoni and Mike. They would all follow Jozef to Canada but only Mike would settle near Jozef in the Round Hill area. Mike and his wife Anna Kontek would arrive in 1900. They had a son, Michael Junior. In 1912, Mike Junior would marry Tylda Gurba, the eldest daughter of Anton and Tekla Gurba.

KATIE GURBA-DANELKO AND MATVIJ STECYK

Katie arrived in Canada with the "third wave' of Gurba's in 1898 with her sister Rosalia's family. Accompanying her was her son, Mike Danelko. No record of her husband, Michal has been found. Shortly after her arrival, she married Matvij Stecyk. They homesteaded in the Skaro area.

Matvij had resided on the NE section of 20-56-19-W4 since December of 1894. The property was just south-east of the Gurba homestead. When he applied for patent in 1899, he stated that he was single when he started living on the land but was "now married with [a] mother, wife and 2 children". During the previous 5 years, he declared that he had broken 6 acres and cropped as much. He had 5 head of cattle. He had built a 12'X18' house that he valued at $75.00 and a 15'X21' stable valued at $400.00 On April 20, 1900 he abandoned the land claiming "my neighbours are making life unbearable for me." It is interesting to note that the stable was much bigger and more valuable than the house!

Matvij and Katie then took out another homestead at SW 22-57-20-W4. He built an 18'X18' house which he valued at only $3.00 and a 12'X12' stable valued at $2.00. The family only stayed at this homestead for less than a year, as Matvij abandoned this homestead on May 30, 1901 claiming it was "too low and rocky".

No other homestead records are found for the family for the next 8 years until September 3, 1909 when Katie's son Michael Danelko applied for homestead on NE 28-57-20-W4 across the North Saskatchewan River near Eldorena. The census record below indicates their presence.

1911 census image. Interesting to note that Katie Stecyk's son, Mike Danelko is listed as "head (age 20)". Below Katie's name is her daughter, Mary,. Matvij is not listed. Katie's other 2 children Ruska (Rose) age 5 and Fred age 7 are listed on the next page of the census.

A few months after the census, Katie herself applied for the homestead rights over that of her son. On that application, she indicated that she was a "widow", even though we know that Matvij didn't die until 1947. In her application for Patent, she declared that in 1913 she broke 5 acres and cropped 3 of it. By 1919, she had cleared a total of 19 acres and cropped 18 of it. She didn't have any animals until 1916 but by 1919, she had 7 cattle and 3 horses. She had also built a house valued at $250.00, a barn valued at $200.00, a granary valued at $200 and a well valued at $30.00. Katie would die of cancer 5 years later on May 18, 1924.

ROSALIA GURBA AND PAUL CZTERNASTEK

Czternastek and Budynski homesteads circled.

Rosalia and her family were also part of the third group of immigrants to arrive in Canada. Upon arriving in Alberta in 1898, they applied for a homestead on the SE ¼ of 10-50-23-W4, which was directly south of Jozef Budynski's first homestead. The application was made on May 4, 1898. Their land turned out to be less than ideal. On March 17, 1900, Paul filed the papers to abandon the homestead. On the application, he claimed that he had built a 10'X20' house valued at $10.00, a similar sized stable valued at $5.00 and had 4 acres cleared. He stated that the land was "not fit for cultivation". Less than a week letter, an agent of Dominion Lands in Edmonton wrote a letter to Ottawa asking for advice indicating that Paul Czternastek "informs me that he's unable to find a more suitable homestead than this one and therefore asked that his entry for [homestead] entry may stand". A reply from Ottawa was sent on March 30, indicating that since no action had yet been taken by land titles, they would ignore the abandonment request. However, by March 20, 1901, almost 3 years after first applying for the homestead, Paul had finally had enough and once again applied for abandonment. He claimed that during "the past 2 years, it has been almost completely under water and totally unfit for cultivation." (It is interesting to note that looking at a township map from the year 1926, there is a notation on Paul's section of land that reads "low land, liable to flooding".)

A month later, on April 16, 1901, the Czternastek's filed for a homestead on the NE ¼ of 18-48-19-W4 which was 10 ½ miles north and 2 miles east of Camrose in the Pretty Hill school district. This area would be later named Dinant where the hamlet was built along the railway ½ mile south and 2 miles west of the Czternastek farm. They would build a 20' X15' log house and a 20'X30' log stable on the land where 3 daughters were born. In his application for Patent, the Czternasteks claimed that he broke 2 acres in 1901 and cropped all of it. The next year he broke another 4 acres and cropped a total of 6 acres. In 1903, another 5 acres were broken and they farmed all 11 acres of land. Another 4 acres were broken in 1904 which now gave the family a total of 15 acres to crop, something that was accomplished. In 1901 Paul reported that they had 2 horses, 4 cows and 4 pigs. Not much changed in the next few years as they reported that in 1909, they still had 4 cows, 4 pigs but now had an additional horse for a grand total of 3.

In the book *Small Farms, Big Family,* Marilyn Waingarten interviewed Josephine R. Clark, who was Rosalia and Paul's daughter born in July 1903. She recalled:

> *we had a big coal mine next to our farm. About 80-90*
> *men worked there, a stones throw from our farm. It was*
> *the kind of mine all you had to do was dig a little ways,*
> *not very deep, and you'd get beautiful pieces of coal.*
> *They'd haul it to the train on a wagon. Nobody ever*
> *bought coal around there. You'd just pick it up on the*
> *roadside.*

Paul would die tragically in January of 1906, leaving Rosalia widowed. She would then meet Anton Rombalski from Independence, Wisconsin. They would soon sell the Czternastek farm and eventually move to Glanford, Ontario to farm in that area.

Enroute to Ontario, they spent some time in the United States because in the 1910 American census, Anton and Rosalia (along with 5 of their children) are listed as residents of Great Falls, Montana. Anton would die in Glandford, Ontario of "apoplexy" in 1921, leaving Rosalia once again widowed. She would then sell this farm and move with her family to Albion, New York.

SOFIA GURBA AND JOHN DOMBROSKY

Sofia arrived in Canada with her brother Anton and her father Semen. She would soon marry the widowed John Dombrowsky whose first wife Maria died in 1896, leaving him with several small children. He was one of the first immigrants to settle in the area as he arrived in 1895. On June 8, 1896 he applied for Homestead Entry for SW 6-57-19-W4, which was one section north of where the Gurba's would homestead. In that first year, he broke 14 acres but didn't farm any of it. In 1897, he broke 6 more acres and farmed 14 acres. In 1898, he broke another 10 acres and farmed 20 acres. By 1899, he had broken a total of 40 acres and farmed 30 of it. As efficient as he was in breaking the land, the same efforts didn't go into building his house. In 1899, he claimed that he had a 12'X12' log house valued at $30.00. Not a very large house for a family that he claimed had "a wife and 7 children". He also claimed that he built a 18'X24' stall, a 16'X24' granary, 2 wells and a milk house valued at $10.00.

1901 census showing the Dombrosky children. The names of Sophia and John appear on the previous page of the census but the quality is to poor to reproduce.

Those are the facts as reported on the Dombrosky patent application. There is a very interesting observation made by a Ukrainian Catholic priest by the name of Father Nestor Dmytriw who visited the Edna-Star area in April of 1897. In an article he published in 1897 called *Kanadiyska Rus: Podorozhni spomyny* (Canadian Ruthenia: Travel Remininscences), he writes quite extensively about John Dombrosky. His observations are below:

> Let us now take a settler who came two years ago from the
> village of Krasne, district of Zolochiw. As it happens, I know
> the conditions in the village very well. I know the quality of
> the soil, etc., and therefore it will be easy for me to evaluate
> whether Iwan Dombrowsky would have done better in two
> years of farming in Krasne than in Canada.
> Iwan Dombrowsky arrived in Winnipeg with $400 in cash.

During the first spring, he ploughed 4 acres of land and
sowed 8 bushels of wheat, harvesting 106 bs.; on the other
4 acres he sowed 8 bushels of wheat, 10 bs. of oats, 6 bs.
of barley, and also planted 12 bs. of potatoes. He added
another horse recently to his outfit and now has 4 horses,
2 cows, and a pair of pigs. He has a house, a modest house,
but clean and well kept. You can see that he is a "wheat-bread
country man," as people from Krasne are called. This man,
through his intelligence and perseverance, would have been
much better off than any of his neighbours if he had not been
hit by a misfortune—his wife died and he was left with 5 small
children. His two elder daughters (the oldest 10 years of age)
help him to run the household. This is his third farm. In
Krasne, Iwan probably would have owned a pair of horses
and a cow, which he would have had to pasture along the
road, leading it on a string.

Father Dmytriw obviously believed that John was much better off being in Canada than being back in the old country. Shortly after Father Dmytriw wrote that article, John would meet and then marry the daughter of Semen, Sofia. She was probably comfortable in the belief that she was marrying a very well off farmer, if we are to believe Father Dmytriw's assessment of John. Reality would not be so kind as will soon be shown in Chapter 9 of this book.

The land that the Dombrosky's homesteaded would eventually house the Svoboda School. My grandmother, Frances, recalls that Svoboda School was "on Auntie Sophie's land" until they sold it to the Pasemko family when the Dombrosky's sold the farm and moved to Edmonton. Upon John's passing in 1933, Sophia bought her own farm north of Waskatenau on the SW ¼ of 8-61-19-W4, next to her nephew, Lucas, farm.

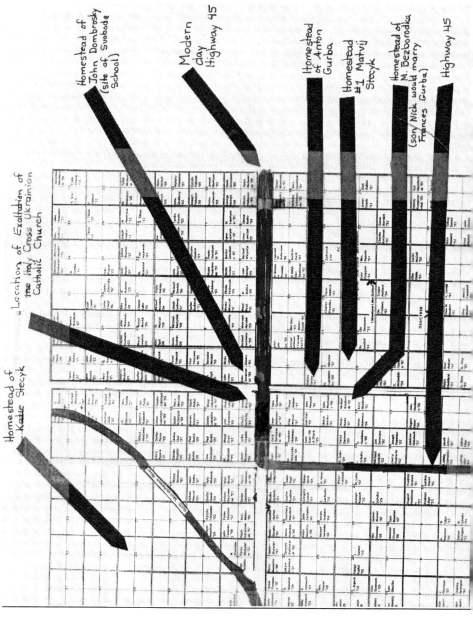

Map of the Edna-Star (Skaro) area showing places of interest to the Gurba family.

CHAPTER 6
ANTON'S FIRST YEAR IN CANADA

The first time the genealogy bug bit me was in early 1970 when I read a wonderful book called *Vilni Zemli* by John MacGregor. It was a book that described the early experiences of the Ukrainian settlers in the Edna-Star region of Alberta, a region that I knew the Gurba family had settled 80 years earlier. I distinctly recall my heart missing a beat when I first read the "Gurba" name in a history book. After reading the short paragraph, it left me wanting to learn more details. The chapter in the book described the experiences of Ivan Nimchuk, age 19, while working on the railroad. The Nimchuk's were the Gurba's neighbours to the south-east.

When Ivan got home [in the fall of 1898] , Mrs. Gurba came over to ask if they had any news of her husband. Like so many others, [Anton] could not read nor write and so could not let his wife know that he had decided to continue working. Rumour mills being seldom idle, someone started a story to the effect that all summer Gurba and a partner had worked together here and there. Then, the rumour said, at one camp the partner had turned up alone, presumably having killed Gurba and taken his money. The story might well have been fact. All winter Gurba's wife was left to tend the farm, haunted by the fear that it had been true.

Eventually, Anton did return home. He had walked injured all the way home from southern Alberta, with a few dollars in his pocket, some stories to tell, and a horse (whom Anton affectionately named Yoshka) that he claimed "an Indian" had given him.

Wanting to learn more, I had many conversations with my grandmother, Frances, Anton's daughter. Although the events in question occurred before Frances was born in 1906, she recalls her father relating to her certain details. For example, she recalls Anton telling her that during the first winter that the Gurba family spent in Canada, Anton went to work on the railway in southern Alberta while leaving his wife, Tekla, and their 4 young children, (Tylda, age 7, Lucas, age 5, Metro, age 3 , and John, age 2), in the care of his father Semen. They were to remain behind on the homestead to ready the farm for spring planting. Although Anton could not read or write, his wife Tekla, could read and write in Polish. (In a few short years, she would also learn how to read and write in Ukrainian as well.) The first few months that Anton was gone, Tekla would receive letters from Anton that he had dictated to fellow workers who were literate. Since not much of the homestead had been cleared that first summer in Canada, Anton and Tekla had arranged for neighbours to help Tekla plant their first crop in the spring of 1898. He had planned to be back that fall to help with the harvest. He had not returned and Tekla, her father in law Semen, and the neighbours had to harvest that first meager crop without Anton. The letters that Tekla had first received stopped coming for some reason and she had not known that Anton had decided to continue working on the rail lines during the winter of 1898-99, hence the rumours of his murder. Frances recalled that shortly after Tekla and the neighbours had planted the Gurba's second crop in Canada, Anton came hobbling up the road with Yoshka trailing behind. Anton related to Frances as she was growing up, how tough the work had been but that he was desperate for money so that they wouldn't have to "live like they did back in the old country". Frances also recalls her father telling her about labour strife on the worksite but no matter how bad it became, Anton always chose to work for the wages offered because the family was so desparate for money to ensure their future in this new country. "He even walked home from Southern Alberta to save train fare," recalled Frances.

I became curious to learn more about Anton's first year in Canada and undertook to do some research. I wanted to reconstruct, as best as I could, what life must have been like for Anton and his family during those pivotal first few months and years.

There is no doubt that Anton and his family were near destitute upon arriving in Canada. During the spring and early summer of 1897, several hundred families from Galicia arrived in the Edna-Star area. Immigration officials began to raise the alarm that the settlers were sold a bill of goods from the steamship companies leaving the settlers the impression that the Government of Canada would ensure their well being. Soon after their arrival in Edna-Star, most of the settlers meager means were quickly exhausted and authorities were becoming concerned . The Commissioner of the North West Mounted Police (the precursors to the RCMP), was the first to act and ordered Corporal G. G. Butler, stationed at Edna-Star, to "investigate the conditions of each family" in the area.

Corporal Butler enumerated 35 families who in his opinion required immediate relief. One of the 35 families he enumerated was Anton Gurba (whom he listed as Antonian Coubar). He wrote that the Gurba's had "2 children, 1 cow. Nothing else." This was obviously inaccurate as we know there were 4 children accompanying Anton, in addition to his wife Tekla and his father, Semen. None the less, it does appear that the Gurba's did not have a great deal of essentials.

The Commissioner of Immigration was annoyed that the NWMP appeared to be interfering into what should be the jurisdiction of his department and he ordered his agent, C. W. Sutter, to go to Edna-Star "to investigate the alleged destitution". In his report, Sutter confirmed that many of the settlers "would like [it] if the government would advance them some grain and flour." He further indicated in his report that he "gave them to understand that they must not expect any help from the government and that they must go out and work to earn their grain and flour and that there was plenty of work all over the country this year." Perhaps it was Agent Sutter's advice that convinced Anton that he would have to leave his family to go work on the railroad.

Inspector P.C.H. Primrose of the NWMP was then ordered by his superiors to confirm the reports of both Corporal Butler and Mr. Sutter. He submitted his report in January 1898. Inspector Primrose also visited the Gurba homestead (whom he reported as Antonie Gourba). He reported that that there was a "total family of 6. Stock 1 cow, 1 calf. 2lbs Potatoes, 15 lbs flour, 2 bags bran, 1 bag wheat". (The family of "6" probably referred to Semen, Tekla and the 4 children.) In his summary statement of all the homesteads he visited, he wrote that only "3 have teams at all, and only 3 have a horse....and only one has more than a cow and a calf...only one farm had any meat of any sort....many are deriving most of their sustenance from bread made of shorts, which diet is hardly suitable for humans here in mid-winter, and as the visit was made, the preparations were in progress for the celebration of their New Years Festival, it is to be presumed that they were as well provisioned as they could be". He also noted that "the children were also well kept. In no place did we see any want or suffering". The situation did not seem as bad as first reported by Corporal Butler, but it was obvious that the settlement of Edna-Star was struggling to keep it's people fed.

Shortly after the report of Inspector Primrose, Thomas Bennett, an Immigration Agent in Edmonton, visited the area and was authorized to give relief to 45 families in the area whom he deemed most needy. The relief given was to be secured by a lien on the settlers homesteads. In his report on the Anton Gurba family, he recorded that there was "a wife and 4 children. Has 5 acres broken. Log house, cook stove, 1 cow and calf. Would be short of provisions before he could do anything. Granted relief to the amount of $10.00". (It should be noted that Anton soon paid back the relief amount and the lien on the homestead was soon lifted.) Mr. Bennett also included a general statement about the physical appearances of the homes that he visited. He stated that "on the whole [the houses] are warm, the majority being heated with the Russian stove. Very few have cook stoves".. (the Gurba's being a rare exception, it appears). "The beds are broad and generally reach from the side of the stove to the end of the room and are generally large enough for the whole family to sleep on-the smallest children sleeping over the stove. The beds consist of straw or hay with a coarse linen cover but no blankets or eider down quilts were visible....but they are quite content to sleep in their sheep skin coats".

These reports paint a somewhat bleak picture of what life was like for Anton and his family immediately upon arrival in Canada. There is no doubting the reason why Anton felt he had to leave his family for the short term. He needed to raise more capital to ensure his family's future success in Canada.

Glenbow Archives ND-9-4

Crow's Nest Pass construction

Although jobs appeared to be available in a variety of coal mines around the Edmonton area, for some reason Anton made the decision to work with the railroad construction crews. As it so happens, the C.P.R was building the Crow's Nest Pass Railway in 1897 (the year of arrival of the Gurba's in Canada) . It is highly probable that Anton had heard that workers were required in the area while he and his family were making their way from New Brunswick to Alberta during the spring of 1897. Workers were scarce because the Klondike Gold Rush was in full swing. The C.P.R. had also decided not to hire Chinese workers for the Crow's Nest as they infamously did while building their main line a decade earlier. A ready source of cheap labour were the new immigrants from Europe. The C.P.R. obviously felt that these new immigrants were desperate for whatever money they could make. Many of the immigrants began to feel "used" and as a result, there was a great deal of labour strife on the construction site. In fact, the Federal Government had ordered a Federal Royal Commission to investigate the matter. This certainly coincides with the "Gurba" timeline. I ordered a copy of the Commission report with the hopes of finding a deposition given by Anton. I was disappointed not to find one but the report does paint a very interesting portrait of what life was like on the construction site and would certainly reflect the conditions that faced Anton during that first year in Canada.

On the 15th day of January, 1898 the Government of Canada, ordered 3 men, Calixte Aime Dugas, Francis Pedley and John Appleton to:

> make inquiry into certain matters....to the effect that immigrants from different parts of Great Britain and other countries, as well as other persons who have been and are engaged in the construction of the branch line of the Canadian Pacific Railway, known as The Crow's Nest Pass Railway, their contractors, or agents of contractors, on said railway, harsh and unjust treatment in the matter of wages, board, lodging, clothing and supplies, and also any other matters relevant to the purpose.

The Commission worked from 15 January 1898 until the 28th of March 1898. They traveled down most of the rail line and took depositions from 282 witnesses.

According to the Commission report, the "first principal cause of discontent" dealt with the wages the workers received and the costs incurred by said workers.

As of February 1ˢᵗ, there were 4,500 workers on the line, one of them being Anton Gurba. They were paid $1.50/day and charged $4.00/week for board. Other charges included "medical fees" of 50¢/month and mail fees of 25¢/month. It is interesting to note that very few of the workers used the mail service and that medical care was often many miles away from where the workers were located. (The 4 hospitals used by the workers were located in Nelson, B.C., St. Eugene, Fort McLeod and Lethbridge. There were no field hospitals or temporary hospitals.)

The workers were also required to pay premium costs for necessities as well. The Commission reported that supplies were only available at railway stores and that they often charged a premium that resulted in "20-40% profit" for the company. The report stated that the most commonly bought product were blankets. They would charge workers $4.50 but it cost the company $2.35. Other examples including cost to the worker and cost to the store (in brackets) are as follows:

    overalls...$1.25-$1.50 (63¢)

    tobacco.... 30-40¢ (26¢)

    underwear... $2.25 (85¢)

    shirts........$1.50 (53-71¢)

    soap.........20¢ (5¢)

    candles...... 30¢ (2¢)

    socks.........50¢ (25¢)

    mittens.......75¢ (50¢)

    boots.........$2.00 ($1.30)

The Commission included a chart that indicated that working for 1 year, a worker would receive $387 but have deductions and costs of $381.90 leaving $5.10 profit. A worker only working for 9 months would be out of pocket $22.40. It is no wonder that Anton had decided to stay at the work camps longer than first planned.

The workers were often paid in "time cheques" and these were very difficult to cash. (The Commission reported that many workers were owed back wages of over 2 months.) The Commission reported an incident where a man had a time cheque of $22 and that he desperately needed cash. He had to walk 75 miles to have it cashed and then had to walk 100 miles back so that he could settle in the Nelson area. Occasionally, the C.P.R. would be able to cash the cheques but would charge a "discount", much like the cheque cashing stores of modern day Alberta.

When an employee left (after giving 15 days notice), there was "no means of transportation home provided" although the workers were charged 1¢/mile to initially get to the worksite. The Commission reported that many workers had to walk back home, some as far as Ontario or Quebec. If the employee was "dismissed" for any reason (no notice required), they were "refused food" for the return trip and worksites along the rail line were forbidden from giving food to former employees. The Commission reported that many former employees relied on "remnants of food, orange peel, etc., thrown by passengers from passing coaches".

Construction crews at the Crow's Nest

Working and living conditions were obviously horrendous. The Commission admited that improvements were made IN ADVANCE of their visits but still found many of the workers "were all in a perfect state of destitution." The most prevalent diseases observed were coughs, mountain fever, rheumatism, diphtheria and physical injuries. The workers lived in either tents or box cars. The Commission reported:

tents had to be removed from point to point periodically, as the work

progressed and it happened that men, after quitting their work at six

o-clock, would have to pitch their own tent, on frozen earth, often covered

with snow and ice. The tents not being provided with stoves, the men's

suffering was intensified by their clothes being wet, after working

amidst snow and snow droppings from the trees, and having no means of

having them dried. A common result of this was suffering from

rheumatism and colds.

Some of the workers lived in box cars. Between 90-115 men would sleep in each car. The Commission described these cars as "not heated, filthy, intolerable, unhealthy, no washing facilities or lavatory facilities and not having sufficient drinking water". The bunks were 4 feet wide, 6 feet long and 2 feet above the next one. There would be 2 men per bunk with 3 levels on each side of the car. An aisle of almost 4 feet was between each side of the car.

Due to the closeness of the workers, lice was a very common and pervasive presence. Workers were not provided with lanterns or candles, so once the sun went down, the work camps were often in total darkness.

In some camps, the Commission reported that men were "entirely forbidden on pain of dismissal, to say a single word during work".

The workers were not allowed to bring their travel trunks with them to the job site. Many of the workers had to leave their trunks in Fort McLeod and when they returned to get them, they were nowhere to be found.

Workers at Crow's Nest Pass. Was one of these men Anton?

Even though the workers had paid for their "board", food was often meager. When questioned about the food situation, a foreman "acknowledged a certain deficiency in the food but there was enough in quality and quantity to permit the men to work." A cook that was interviewed disagreed. An interesting anecdote was related to the Commission about 2 Armenian workers that fellow Eastern European immigrants like Anton would no doubt have experienced as well. The 2 Armenians complained that the food that was being prepared for them was totally unfamiliar and they sought permission to acquire their own food and prepare it as they were accustomed. The powers that be allowed that request but soon "dismissed" the men when they bought their foodstuffs from a source other than the C.P.R. supply store or their approved subcontractors.

Although none of the above information specifically relates to Anton Gurba, we do know that he was working on the CPR lines during the time of the Commission and obviously was well acquainted with the horrendous conditions. He no doubt experienced them. Whether he lived in a tent or on one of the cramped railcars will probably never be known. The Commission reported that many of the "ringleaders" of discontent towards the C.P.R. were dismissed or immediately "discharged". It must have been very difficult for Anton to work in such condition but he knew that he couldn't forgo the money that was paid to him. Anton had been in the country for less than a year and desperately needed money for his young family and to get his farm started. Was he threatened with dismissal if he refused to work ? The pressure must have been immense. We probably will never know for sure.

The conclusion of this episode in Gurba history is certain. As stated earlier, Anton did not return to the homestead as scheduled in late spring of 1898. Semen, Tekla, her children and their neighbours' were able to clear some land on their own and planted a meager crop that spring. They then harvested that crop without Anton that fall. Shortly after the planting their crops in the spring of 1899, Anton hobbled up the path to the farmstead, somewhat lame, with a tiny horse name Yoshka. He had walked all the way home from southern Alberta doing odd jobs along the way to supplement whatever meager income he got from the C.P.R. Yoshka, (the horse), was obtained by Anton from an Indian that he had helped somewhere along his journey. There was a special untold bond between Anton and Yoshka. No one was ever allowed to ride Yoshka, nor was she allowed to do any work other than to have colts of her own. Yoshka received the freedom of the homestead and was never fenced in. Frances recalls that everyone in the settlement knew the horse because Yoshka would often visit neighbouring farms. She always returned back to Anton on her own. Although Yoshka was small of stature, all of her offspring were strong and hard-working horses. Yoshka lived a long life. Frances recalls that one day, Yoshka couldn't get up off the ground. Anton put Yoshka out of her misery with his rifle. It was the only time Frances saw her father cry.

Not to be overshadowed in this entire story is the strength and courage shown by Anton's wife, Tekla. While Anton was toiling in Southern Alberta, Tekla, with the help of her father-in-law Semen,

kept the family together and performed many of the labourious tasks
that needed to be done in the establishment of a homestead in the
unbroken land of east-central Alberta. It was initially through both of
their strengths that the Gurba family was able to prosper and become
what we are today.

CHAPTER 7

THE DEATH OF PAUL CZTERNASTEK
JANUARY 12, 1906

Friday night. January 12, 1906. The weather had been good for early January. In fact, The Edmonton Bulletin on January 11th had a report describing the "long continued mild winter and small amount of snow". On this night however, there would be a feel of snow in the air. The next days Edmonton Bulletin would proudly write, "there was a heavy fall of snow last night making sleighing fairly good". Snowfall was not going to stop Paul from carrying out his plan for the evening to socialize with his friends in the nearby village of Camrose. Paul had decided to dress warmly putting on his "fur coat, inside coat, vest, 2 shirts, drawers, pants, stockings and boots" (as reported in the coroners' report). He then said good-bye to his 40 year old

Camrose 1908 (Arlington Hotel on the extreme left)

Glenbow Archives PA-3486-1

wife, Rosalia (nee Gurba), his daughters, 16 year old Annie, 12 year old Mary (who had just celebrated her birthday earlier that week), 11 year old Kathleen, 8 year old Sylvia, 5 year old Francis and 2 year old Josephine. Leaving the homestead that he proudly applied for on

April 16, 1901 and received title to on November 4, 1904, he headed for the nearby town of Camrose.

He picked up "a pint" of moonshine from a local man, drank the contents after diluting it with a "pint of water" and then made his way to the newly built Arlington Hotel. It was there, according to family tradition, that Paul got into an argument with neighbours Anton Dragon and George Rakowski about shares in a grain binder. By midnight, Rosalia and the 6 young girls would be without their husband and father forever.

Five days later, on Wednesday, January 17, 1906, on the front page of The Evening Journal (a forerunner of the Edmonton Journal) the following article appeared:

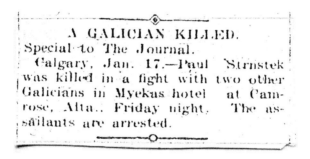

A GALICIAN KILLED.
Special to The Journal.
Calgary, Jan. 17.—Paul Strnstek was killed in a fight with two other Galicians in Myekas hotel at Camrose, Alta., Friday night. The assailants are arrested.

The Edmonton Daily Bulletin, on January 20, 1906, also reported Paul's death on their front page albeit by leaving his name out. It was a much more detailed report.

FOUND DEAD IN A CHAIR

A report reached the city yesterday of the sudden death of a Gallician at the hotel at Camrose on Monday night last, which will probably call for an investigation on the part of License Inspector W. H. Cooper,

According to the report, three Gallicians were drinking in the Camrose hotel on Monday night, and commenced wrestling in a friendly spirit, but the landlord, Oll Bakken, not appreciating their horseplay, ordered them out of the hotel. Later one of the Gallicians came back into the house and sat down on a chair, where he went to sleep. When it came time to lock up, the hotel people tried to awaken him, and

were shocked to discover that he had died in the chair.

An investigation was held on Tuesday afternoon, Dr. Robertson, of Wetaskiwin, conducting the inquiry. The verdict showed that the man died a natural death, and that no suspicion of wrong doing attached to anyone. The official report of the inquest has not yet reached the license inspector.

There are several contradictions between the 2 articles. What exactly happened to Paul? Did he die on the 12th as reported by The Journal or on the 14th as reported by The Bulletin? Did he die in a "fight" (The Journal) or in "a chair" (The Bulletin)? Was he "killed" (The Journal) or did he die as a result of "wrestling in a friendly spirit" (The Bulletin)? If he "died a natural death" (The Bulletin), why were 2 "assailants...arrested" (The Journal)?

On August 20, 2002, I went to the Provincial Archives in Edmonton to access the Attorney General records for the year 1906. In a matter of minutes, I had found that the *"Inquisition into the death of Pal Sternastke"* was part of the public records and I was able to read the original documents. (The record is ACC #66.166 Box 53 Item 404). The material found in that file resolved the contradictions between the 2 newspapers and gives us a very intriguing story.

Arlington Hotel Bar 1931

Robert Robertson convened the Inquest on 13 January 1906. The board of inquiry consisted of Mr. Robertson and 6 members of the community acted as jury: Duncan Sampson (storekeeper), Hiram Burger (merchant) ,D. Twombie (merchant) Andrew Leslie (farmer), Ed Langham (clerk), and W.J. Thompson (carpenter). The minutes of the inquiry reads as follows:

> .....*on viewing the body a slight abrasion was found under the left eye and blood oozing from mouth and nose otherwise no signs of violence. The body was that of a man about 35 years of age, fairly well nourished at 5'8"height, light hair, light moustache......His body was found lying in a room adjoining the public room of the Arlington Hotel. The jury after viewing the body returned to the barracks where the following witnesses were examined.*

On consideration the jury ordered a post mortem
to be held and the inquest was adjourned til
Tuesday the 16ᵗʰ of January at 4:30.

The witness list consisted of 8 men: V. Metejka, Thomas Kostakzy, Theo Skagen, H. Henrickson, Albert Sysens, Gunwald Hill, Frank Herman and T. M. Grunditen.

As ordered by the jury, Doctor W. Vernon Lamb performed the autopsy the next day (14 January 1906) at the Arlington Hotel. His extensive and detailed handwritten notes are included in the files at the Archives. Paul appeared to be a very healthy individual. There was no sign of illness and all of his organs were "normal" in appearance and weight. The autopsy gave a very detailed description of what Paul looked like:

5'8", 165 pounds, hair brown, eyebrows lighter, eyes hazel,

eyelashes color of hair. Moustache dark brown mixed with

gray. Beard about 3 days old, brown mixed with gray. Lips large.

His injuries did not seem to be outwardly severe:

Head: *no bruise about neck or scalp. Over his face is seen an*

abrasion over each eyebrow. Bruise on left temple. Marks of

blood about both nostrils. Moustache matted. Small puddle of

blood in ear,

> **Right shoulder** *shows a bruise about 2" in diameter.*
> *6-7ᵗʰ rib near sternum is swollen, another small bruise*
> *Back of right hand discoloured with blood.*

The finding of the autopsy was "death from causes unknown". (The doctor then submitted a bill for $10.00. Upon the conclusion of the

Inquiry, Mr. Robertson submitted a total bill of $71.70 for the Inquest which included paying each witness $1.00 and each jurist $2.00).

The file at the Provincial Archives contains witness statements from all of the eight witnesses. All witnesses basically agreed with each other with regards to the events of the evening. However, the statement from Valaclav Madjeka is the most detailed:

> *I, Valaclav Madjeka, hotel keeper, make oath and say that I am the keeper of the Arlington Hotel in Camrose and was in my hotel on the evening of January 12, 1906. At 7 PM Sternacsk, Draggin and Recowsky came into the bar and had drinks (4 in number) until I left the bar at 7:30 to get my supper. On returning, Sternacsk was leaning against the bar and was there when I returned to the office. The next I saw of him they were carrying him out to put him in the chair in the office. In about an hour I heard him fall out of the chair and at the same time somebody called my attention to it. I looked and saw him on his knees and elbow with his face near a spittoon. Then I with Tom Kustahurst dragged him into the baggage room while I was moving him he wakened enough to call me by name. I left him in the baggage room until 11:30 PM. Then I closed the bar and then went into see him and was going to put him in a bed upstairs. When I put him into the [baggage] room I left him on his side and when I returned he was on his stomach with his head turned to the right. I thought he was dead after I felt his pulse and heart and listened for his breath and then went to summon medical aid. I turned him on his back before going to the doctor. I saw a little blood on his face. Nobody went into the baggage room between my visits. Nobody has a key but Theodore and myself and it is a springlock. Sternacsk asked for more drinks and I refused him and gave him a cigar. I also ordered the bartender to refuse him any more drinks.*

Unfortunately, Mr. Madjeka didn't see the events that preceded Paul being carried out. Another witness, Frank Herman, a carpenter did witness a fight between Paul and two other men. His witness statement, in part, states:

> *Three Galicians were drinking together. Sternacsk and Draggen and Recowsky were their names. Sternacsk and Draggin were having a row and Recosky parted them and said he said he didn't want them to fight. After a while they started again and were parted. After another while, Sternacsk slapped Recowsky in the face and Recowsky slapped him back. Then Sternacsk caught hold of Draggin and they started wrestling. Then Sternacsk was put on the floor and Recowsky kicked him while Draggin held. I pulled Recowsky away and the two went off. I helped to sit the man on his feet and he leaned against the bar with his head down. About 5 minutes after, he fell back on the floor and I helped to carry him out to the sitting room and set him in a chair. There was little blood on his face and he opened his eyes when we carried him out. The man who is dead was very drunk.*

The other witness statements generally agree with the above facts. Theodore Skagen, the bartender at the hotel and presumably the "Theodore" mentioned in Mr. Madjeka's statement, also mentioned the fact that Sternacsk "could not have been kicked more than 2 or 3 times". He disagreed with Mr. Herman's above statement in that Mr. Skagen stated that Paul Czternastek slept at the bar for "about an hour" before he fell, not the 5 minutes stated by Mr. Herman. None of the witnesses knew what the men were fighting about because the "Galicians weren't speaking English".

Based on the witness statements, it does appear that both the Journal and the Bulletin were correct in their articles, both in their own ways. Paul Czternastek did die as a result of a fight but not immediately. He didn't die "in a chair" but rather on the floor of the baggage room of the hotel. It is also very clear that he died on a Firday as opposed to a Monday. The Journal refers to the Arlington Hotel as "Myekas" hotel. This probably refers to Valaclav Madjeka, the hotel keeper and witness to Paul's death. Mr. Madjeka purchased the hotel in 1905 from Oli Hakken, (the man mentioned in the Bulletin report), who built the hotel in 1904.

The story however, doesn't quite end there. The file in the Archives also contains a handwritten letter from the Police to H.H Cooper, License Inspector, in Edmonton. It is dated February 1, 1906 and provides more detail about what happened to Paul Czternastek's assailants, the ones referred to in the Edmonton Journal article.

> *I have the honour to report that on January 12 a fight occurred in the Arlington Hotel between three Galicians, A. Drageru, G. Rakowsky and P. Strenastik.*
>
> *These men were drunk and later in the evening, Strenastik died; a post mortem examination revealed that he died of concussion, no marks of violence being found on the body, the evidence at the coroners inquest that the fight led to a fall subsequent to blows as cause of death. Rakowsky and Drageru were arrested for common assault and sentenced to 2 months.*
>
> *In the evidence prisoners stated they had bought a pint of alcohol previous to going to the Arlington.*
>
> *Information was laid before Mr. Adams JP against Thompson + Dahl, wholesalers, under Sec 19 sub sec 3 of the Liquor License Ordinance. Defendant denied selling a pint of alcohol but admitted making a pint of alcohol and mixing it with a pint of water, thus making quart. The justice gave the benefit of the doubt and dismissed the case. The case against Matejka of disorderly conduct has been postponed until Mr. Lingham Esq. was gazetted a J.P.*

The fate of Paul Czternastek's assailants were further detailed in a letter sent to the Attorney General's office in Edmonton on February 19, 1906 by George Henwood, a lawyer from Wetaskiwin, who expressed his concern that the two assailants were only sentenced to 2 months:

Dear Sir,

I have been consulted this AM by Mrs. Rosalie Sternascky with reference to the circumstances surrounding the death of her husband, Paul Sternascky, at the Arlington Hotel, Camrose, on January 12th last. She has instructed me to take proceedings against the proprietor of the hotel under Section 79 of the Liquor License Ordinance. But it appears to me that a more thorough investigation should be made by your department or by the Office of the RNWMP of the facts of the case.

[Mr. Henwood relays the facts of the case and then continues his letter]

An inquiry was held and also an autopsy and a verdict of death from some cause unknown was returned. The 2 Galicians who were with Stenaszky were charged before Mr. Adams, J.P. at Camrose with assault and sentenced to 2 months imprisonment at Fort Saskatchewan, where they now are.

The woman tells me that these 2 Galicians, after the row, boasted a great deal about the treatment they had given Sternascky, and if what she says is true, it would seem that their intentions, according to what they said after the quarrel, was to injure him severely if not kill him. These boastful statements were made by them before they knew that Sternascky had died.

The Attorney General's office responded almost immediately, 3 days later on February 21, 1906. After stating numerous legal precedents, the Deputy Attorney General wrote that he doubts

..as to whether a more serious charge can be laid after the
accused have been tried and convicted and were in the
course of suffering the penalty for the lessor offense for
which they have been convicted.

I am of the opinion that an indictment for manslaughter
under the circumstances of this case---the deceased having
died before the accused were tried and convicted of assault —
would upon application be quashed.

The next day, February 22, 1906, (amazing how fast the mail moved in those days), the lawyer, Mr. Henwood, wrote back to the Attorney General concurring with his interpretation and the matter was apparently dropped.

It is interesting to note that Paul's "assailants" were charged, convicted and were already serving time in the Fort Saskatchewan jail within a few days of the incident. It is curious to see the quick rush to judgment compared to what we as a society are accustomed to seeing in today's world.

This story however, is still not completed. There remains in the Archives one more very important letter signed by Rosalia herself and sent to the Deputy Attorney General on April 12, 1906.

Dear Sir,

On January 12th last my husband was killed in Hotel
at Camrose by two men named George Rakoski and
Anton Dragon. It was put down as a drunken fight.
But I can prove that is was no such thing as these men
had been after him for some time before. Rakoski told
A. Makaviciki before the row that we would fix him.
These men are still annoying me saying that they will
fix me and my children same as they did my husband.
Anton Makako and [illegible] both heard these men say

they would do same to me as they had done to my husband.

Yours respectfully,

rosalija czternastek

The Deputy Attorney General replied to Rosalia on April 17, 1906 informing her that her "best course...to follow would be to lay the complaint before your nearest Justice of the Peace or Police authority." It is not known whether or not Rosalia followed that advice. There are no more documents in that file at the Provincial Archives.

Latter day picture of Rosalia (3rd from left)

It is known that Rosalia did fear for herself and her children. She probably achieved a certain degree of comfort and feeling of safety when she soon met and later married Anton Rombalski, a farmer/prospecter from Wisconsin. A few years earlier, on 27 December 1905, Anton applied for and got title to a 40 acre farm in

Trempealeau County in Wisconsin. Two short years later, for reasons unknown, he headed north to Canada where he met Rosalia. They would marry very quickly. Anton and Rosalia had a son Tony in 1908 and Clarence in 1910. By the 1910, Anton, Rosalia and 5 of their children (Katie, Frances, Josie "Stenastek" and Anton and Casmir Rombalski) were enumerated living on a farm near Great Falls, Montana.

By 1918, all of Rosalia's family, except for her eldest daughter Annie (who had married Anton Piontkowski and had already started her own family shortly after Paul's death) moved to Glanford, Ontario (near Hamilton) after their short stay in Montana. Tragedy once again hit Rosalia when her new husband, Anton died 2 years later on Feb 14, 1921. His death certificate indicated that the cause of death was "apoplexy". Two months later, in April of 1921 Rosalia and her family then moved to Albion, New York where she died in 1954.....48 years after the death of Paul Czternastek at the Arlington Hotel in Camrose Alberta.

Glenbow Archives NA-3403-1

Arlington Hotel 1930

CHAPTER 8
WANDERLUST

Rosalia was neither the first nor the last of Semen's children to leave Alberta and set up stakes in places far away from Alberta. As written in the previous chapter, 4 years after the tragic death of her first husband, Paul,   Rosalia, along with her new husband Anton and most of her family headed west to Ontario to farm in the area around Glandford.   A few years later, after Anton's death, Rosalia and her family moved to New York state where she would die in 1954. What was the draw to New York?   As it would turn out, many of her relatives would move to the area in the early part of the 1900's.

Rose Budynski-Mack, husband Wilford Mack and their children Florence, Carl, Nester and Verna and their 1914 Ford on their way to New York.

Jozef and Anna Budynski's oldest daughter Rose married Wilford Mack in Round Hill, Alberta on November 20, 1910. It appears that Wilford had no intentions to stay in the Round Hill area, nor even in

Alberta. In May 1910, before Wilford and Rose would marry, Wilford and a delegation of his current and "soon-to-be" relatives crossed the border at Sweet Grass, Montana. According to the border crossing records, Wilford, his brother John, and Wilford's soon to be father-in-law Jozef Budynski (who declared himself a carpenter) stated to officials that they were headed to Chester, Montana, which is just south of the Alberta border. Accompanying them were Jozef's brother Michael and two of his sons, Frank and William. (Michael's son, Mike Jr. would later marry Anton Gurba's daughter Tylda in 1912). It is not known why they all went to Chester. Perhaps, it was

May 1910 border crossing form indicating the arrival of the delegation from Camrose, including Jozef Budynski and his soon to be son-in-law, Wilford Mack.

to investigate homestead possibilities in the area? In any event, they didn't stay and soon returned to the Round Hill area. What the event does indicate however, is that the close familial ties between the Budynski's, the Gurba's and the Mack's pre-date the marriages between the families.

The next mention of Jozef Budynski in the border crossing information is not until August 12, 1919. He crossed into the United States at Niagara Falls. He listed his address as R.R. #1 Caledonia, Ontario and stated that he was going to visit his daughter Rosalia Mack in Albion, New York for a period of 3 days. Less than 2 years later, on April 8, 1921, he crossed the border again but this time he was accompanied by his wife, Anna, and their children. The back of the border crossing form (which is upside down in the records) stated that he had "never been

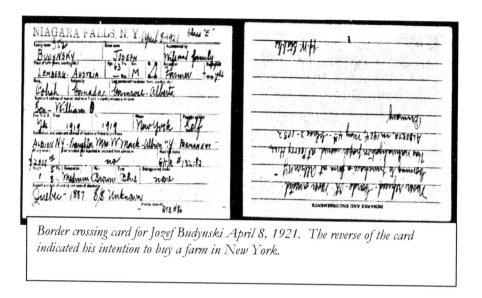

Border crossing card for Jozef Budynski April 8, 1921. The reverse of the card indicated his intention to buy a farm in New York.

arrested" and that the Budynski's were "coming to purchase a farm at Albion NY". The front of the card indicates that the Budynski's were bringing $2000 with them for that purpose. (The border crossing card for Anna gave a physical description stating that Anna was 5 ft 5 inches tall and had brown hair and blue eyes). The move from Alberta to New York was now complete for Semen's eldest daughter.

Anna and Jozef's niece, Tylda Gurba-Budynski (Anton's daughter) had arrived in New York a few months earlier. Her husband, Mike, had crossed into the United States at Buffalo, New York on June 14, 1920. Following him 3 months later, on September 27, 1920 were his wife Tylda, their 5 children and Tylda's sister, Annie. By then, Mike had bought a farm in Waterport, New York, ending his family's emigration from Canada.

Border crossing form October 1920 showing the arrival of Tylda Gurba-Budynski, her children and her sister, Anne.

The Gurba family member, however, with the greatest early travel history must be Rose Budynsky (daughter of Jozef Budynski and Anna Gurba). It appears that her family was the first to make the move to the United States. Although no formal border crossing records can be found for their immigration to the United States, it is known that their daughter, Verna, was born on May 30, 1917 in Colebrook, Ohio. Also, as required by law, Rose's husband Wilford, was to register as an alien during World War I. On June 5, 1917 he dutifully filled in his card as Vincent W. Mack and indicated that he was a farmer currently residing with his wife and four children in Colebrook. In the 1930 United States Census, the Mack family was registered as living in Ridgeway Town, Orleans county, New York. He listed his occupation as farmer and indicated that his family had arrived in the United States in 1917.

Wilford and Rose Mack with Florence, Carl, and Nester at their New York farm 1917

From Colebrook, the Mack's moved to New York state where they stayed until just before start of the depression in 1929. In the early 1920's, they lived on a farm near Lyndonville, New York, on Oak Orchard Creek, just south of Lake Ontario. Swimming and fishing in the creek was quite the past-time as Helen Mack Matwyshen (Rose Budynski and Vincent Mack's daughter) reminisces with Marylin Waingarten for her book *Small Farms, Big Dreams*. "we grew apples, cherries, plums and peaches in addition to raising horses, cows, pigs, sheep and chickens". Around this time, Rose and Vincent's other daughter Florence, who had developed diabetes 10 years earlier, had now contracted polio. In that same book , Marilyn Waingarten, quotes Adele Budinski Borawski (Anna's and Jozef's grandniece);

> *[the Mack's] moved to Texas to improve [Aunt Florence's] health,*
> *which is what they thought would help back then. When they came*
> *back from Texas in the early 1930's, Florence was half dead.*
> *They put her in a hospital, but they couldn't afford to pay*
> *the bill to get her out when she was better. So they had to*
> *sneak in and steal her!*

The Macks remained in Texas for only 2 or 3 years when they had to return to New York due to a combination of a hurricane and bad business dealings. They stayed in New York, mostly in the cities of Albion and Rochester. While living in Albion, they lived on Bank Street, which backed onto the Erie Canal.   Farming, however, must have remained in Wilford's blood because in the mid- 1940's, Wilford and Anna headed back to Texas where he bought 80 acres of land. At least 5 of Wilford and Anna's children soon followed and bought or leased more farm land in the Rio Grande Valley between San Benito and Brownsville, just a few kilometers from the Mexican border. They ended up farming over 1000 acres of cotton and sorgum. The Mack family would continue to farm the area until the year 2000. They continue to be our "Texas" cousins and many of them visited the Alberta area in 2005.

2005/05/28

Mack (aka Texas cousins) visit the homestead area and the Gurba cousins in Wetaskiwin in May 2005.

CHAPTER 9
THE YEAR 1911...THE GURBA FAMILY'S "ANNUS HORRIBILIS"

When retelling the history of ones family, we tend to focus on the stories of great joy, achievements, accomplishments or heroic deeds. In reality however, things don't always turn out in a positive light. The family of Queen Elizabeth have had their challenges. On 24 November 1992 while giving a speech on the occasion of her 40th Anniversary on her Accession to the throne, Her Majesty stated:

> *1992 is not a year on which I shall look back with undiluted pleasure.*
>
> *In the words of one of my more sympathetic correspondents, it has*
>
> *turned out to be an Annus Horribilis.*

The year 1911 could qualify as the Gurba family's "annus horribilis". It would be a year that would directly and dramatically affect 3 of Semen's children and their families: Anton's, Rosalia's and Sophia's. It would be a year when one of Semen's grandchildren would die under mysterious circumstances and several others would "run away" from home. Bodies would need to be exhumed from freshly dug graves. Marriages would disintegrate and criminal charges would be laid. People were physically and verbally threatened. There would be several visits to the Fort Saskatchewan Court House. A family member would become a resident of the Fort Saskatchewan Jail. It was definitely an annus horribilis.

Katie's story

Matvij Stecyk

Katie Danelko had been in Canada for almost 13 years. She arrived in Canada with her her young son Michael and her sister Rosalia Czternastek and her family during the 3rd and final voyage of the Gurba family from the old country. She would very soon give birth to a daughter, Mary, whose father we always assumed was Katie's missing husband Michal. (This would be confirmed by a statement given to the courts referred to later in this chapter.) We have yet to learn what had happened to Michal. (Was he deceased in the old country? Were they to meet here in Canada but he was a no show? Was she escaping from a miserable marriage?) She obviously believed him to be deceased as she would very quickly marry local farmer Matvij Stecyk in 1898. It was not to be a loving marriage. On May 2, 1911 after making a formal complaint with the authorities, the following criminal charge was laid against Katie's husband, Matvij:

without lawful excuse..did omit to provide necessities for his wife and 3 children, being head of a family and 3 children under 16 years of age. He failed his legal duty to provide necessities for them contrary to Section 242 of the Criminal Code.

Two days later, Matvij entered a Statement of the Accused which stated:

My wife does not want me. She has children from another man. She threw water at me. I never did anything to her.

On May 10, 1911 in front of a Justice of the Peace named John Ainsworth, two neighbours of Katie and Matvij's gave their depositions regarding the charges.

> .....*I know that the accused did not support his family for 3 ½*
> *years. I was at their home when she left. I was called over.*
> *When I got over there she told me that she was packing up*
> *and leaving. He gave her some potatoes and 1 cow for the baby....*
> *......I heard the accused say that he did not want his wife or*
> *feed the children.*
>
> deposition of Alex Litwin May 10, 1911

Another neighbour, Michael Halun, testified that Matvij,

> *is able to work if he wanted to. He did work when he had cattle,*
> *hay, etc. He has nothing now. He sold everything 3 – 4 weeks*
> *ago. He has 8 head of cattle. He also sold his plow, wagon*
> *and rake. I do not know what he got for it. He does not have*
> *the patience for the land.*

It is quite apparent that the Stecyk family was living in poverty and Sophia's life was far from the Canadian ideal that she had probably hoped for by immigrating to Canada. How unbearable her marriage and life had become is more dramatically described by her own deposition to the court on May 19, 1911.

> *I was married to the accused at Skaro 13 years ago. I lived with*
> *him till the fall of 1908. Then I went to work and with the money*
> *I made I bought clothes and flour etc for the children. I couldn't*
> *stay as my husbands mother stayed there and ill treated the children.*
> *I was with my husband for 6 years after we got married. Then I went*
> *to work for 6 months and then returned and lived with him again*

for 3 years. My husband told me go and take up a place and live there
as he had no use for me and the children. I left him. He promised me
½ the cattle if I left. I built a house but he would not give me the cattle
except for 1 and that died. I went to Edmonton and laid a complaint
against him. When there, my husband and interpreter went together
to the hotel and in court the interpreter stated that I left on my own
account which was not so. The case was dismissed. When living with
my husband he always refused to light a lamp or start a fire and told me
to go away. At that time, he threshed 1 acre of barley and that is what
we lived on. I have 4 children. The oldest, a boy working out, is 20 years
old and is from my first husband. So is the next, a girl about 13 years old.
Then I have 2 more, one about 7 years old, a boy, illegitimate from a farmer
where I was working. The smallest girl will be 5 next fall and is from
my husband. My husband did not give me anything at all. I did not ask
him for anything. I went to work to have bread etc for myself and the
children. My husband had a plow, wagon, mower and other implements
and sold everything about 3 weeks ago.

Upon hearing the evidence, the Justice of the Peace, John Ainsworth, adjudicated that the "matter should stand trial at the next sitting of the court of competent jurisdiction".

Unfortunately, we are unable to determine the final judgment of the matter as the Provincial Archive files make no reference of the final adjudication. What is known is that by the time of the 1911 census taken a few weeks after the trial, only Katie and her children Mike, Mary, Fred and Rose are listed. The son, Mike, is listed as the "head" of the family. Matvij is no where to be found although we know that he died on 29 March 1947 and is buried in Eldorena. It is also known that Katie and her family were taken under the wing of her brother, Anton, who looked after her up to her death on 18 May 1924. According to her niece, Frances Bezborodka, she died of cancer.

Anton also arranged for her burial at the Holy Cross Ukrainian Catholic Church in Skaro, as ever the big brother.

Sophia's story

Around the same time that Katie and her family were in turmoil, the family of Sophia were experiencing problems of their own. Sophia,

John and Sophie Dombrowsky's family. L to R: Cassie, John, Tillie, Sophie holding Bessie, Lillian

the youngest of Semen's children, arrived in Canada on April 8, 1897 with her father and her brother Anton and his family. She was 28 years old and unmarried. Shortly after arriving in Skaro, she met and soon married, the widowed John Dembrowsky, a former army colonel. Sophia instantly became a mother for John's 5 children: Jewka, John, Simon, Annie, and Mary. Katie would then have 10 children of her own (5 of which would live into adulthood). Sophia's biography written by her daughter Tillie Dziwenka for the book *By River and Trail: the history of Waskatenau and districts*, stated that "life was hard and did not fare too well for Sophie". Upon examining the events of 1911, we have a more complete understanding of how "hard" that life would become.

By mid January 1911, Sophia had left an abusive relationship and had sought refuge at the home of her brother Anton. She had done this several times earlier as confirmed by Anton's daughter, Frances Bezborodka, in interviews I had with her in 2007. On January 30, 1911, the situation had boiled over. On February 2, 1911, Anton Gurba signed an Information and Complaint form in Fort

Saskatchewan that resulted in the following charge being laid against John Dembrowski:

> ..that John Dembroski of Skaro on 30th January 1911 at Lamont in said Province of Alberta did threaten to assault Anton Gurba contrary to Chapter 146 Section 291 of the Criminal Code.

A deposition signed by Anton (with his mark) gives details as to what happened.

> I am Anton Gurba. I am brother in law to John Dembrowski. On 30 January last, John Dembrowski in Lamont came round to me when I was ready to go home and accused me of keeping his wife away from him. Dembrowski touched me with his hand and wanted to start a fight with me. He said to me I thought you were keeping a home for yourself but you are keeping whores at your place. Dembrowski was swearing at me and said he would catch me on the road.

Two witnesses were called, Paula and Annie Jankowski. They agreed with Anton's statement and added that "Dembrowski was so drunk he could not hitch up his team".

The case was formally heard on February 15 whereupon Justice of the Peace John Ainsworth convicted John Dembrowski and imposed "a fine of $1 and $3.40 costs to be paid within one week or in default to be imprisoned in the common goal at Fort Saskatchewan for a period of one month".

On the same day, the same Justice of the Peace also found John Dembrowski guilty of "assaulting [Sophia] his wife contrary to Chapter 146 Section 291 of the Criminal Code" and sentenced him

> to enter into his own recognizance to keep peace for a period of 12 months and to

give security of $100 and a surety of $100 and to pay costs amounting to $4.90

or in default to go to the common goal at Fort Saskatchewan for 3 months...

Essentially, John was told to behave for a period of one year. John's behaviour seemed to be well known throughout the community. At John's assault hearing, a neighbour, John Sachman, made the following observation...

> *I live near John Dembrowski and see most everything that goes on when I am*
>
> *home. I never go to John Dembrowski's place as he is never in good humour*
>
> *but I have seen his wife running away because she can not live with him.*

Another neighbour, Fedor Keenish [Kinash] testified..

> *Sophia came to ask me to go to the farm with her because she was afraid of him.*
>
> *When I got to the Dembrowski yard.......he started to go after his wife telling*
>
> *her that he did not want people to camp here. Then he threw a cup of tea at her*
>
> *and other things as well.*

The most poignant testimony however, is the one given by Sophia herself. It is indeed sad to read how the home situation had deteriorated so badly that the oldest children, Margaret (aka Anna) – aged 13 and Nancy –aged 11, had run away from home.

> *I am Sophia Dembrowski, wife of John Dembrowski. I ran away from my*
>
> *husband about 3 months ago. I was sick in bed for 2 weeks. When I came back*
>
> *from town he assaulted me 4 times. I have 7 children. Five are living with*
>
> *their father and 2 ran away from home. They are girls 11 and 13 years old. My*
>
> *other children are younger. When John Dembrowski come home he assaults*
>
> *me and the children. He has done this the past 9 years. Ever since he made up*
>
> *his mind that I was going with John Sachman he assaulted me many nights*
>
> *and I had to stay overnight in the neigbours bush. Every time he came home [I]*

was to go out and help him unhitch his team.. He would get right after me. I would runaway if I could but most of the time I would get beaten. He was good to me the first 5 years. Many times he was jealous of me and told me I was stinking in the house and he would throw a cup of tea or anything he could get his hands on at me. Two men were present when he told me to get away from him and give me a living. Most of the time when he assaulted me he hit me with his hands on my head. Once when he came home he tried to choke me. He was pounding me on the head.

As stated earlier, John was found guilty of the charge and ordered to enter a peace bond with conditions to be of good behaviour and keep the peace. However, things would not get easier for Sophia or her children.

Shortly after the above events transpired, Sophia had left the farmhouse, presumably for her own protection, and probably moved in with her brother Anton. Even though she feared for her own children's safety, she left them at the farm with her oldest daughter in charge (as indicated by Dr. Archer during an upcoming trial). One day, John was to return home from Lamont in a drunken state whereupon he beat his 10 month old son, Mike. He did this in front on his children. Mike suffered an injury and died a few weeks later. A formal Information and Complaint form was filed on 26 June 1911. A warrant for the arrest of John Dembrowski was issued on July 5, 1911 whereupon John was sent to the Fort Saskatchewan Jail. (It is interesting to note that John Dembrowski was enumerated for the 1911 census as one of several prisoners inhabiting the jail.)

There were 3 charges laid against John. Although the 3 charges are very similarly written they all relate that John:

did unlawfully and in disregard of his duty in that behalf, refuse, neglect and omit, without lawful excuse to provide necessities: to wit, sufficient

medical aid for his infant child, Mike Dembrowski, by means whereupon
the life of the said Mike Dembrowski was endangered.

The other two charges refer to John not providing the necessities of life resulting in death and assault causing bodily harm.

This was obviously a very dramatic event for the children of Sophia to witness. Not only did the children see the abuse, they had to care for the injured Mike, bury him and then witness the exhumation of the body so that Dr. Archer from Lamont could do a post mortem examination for the courts. They then had to testify against their father at the first trial on July 18, 1911. The first child to give her deposition was Annie (aka Margaret). She was about 14 at the time.

> *[father] came from Lamont and mother was gone. He said mother should*
> *have taken it [Mike] with her. He said he did not want the boy and took*
> *him and hit him on the chest with his fist. He was 10 months old at the*
> *time. I was home at the time he was born. I did not count the blows but*
> *there must have been about 8. The child was crying. The other children*
> *were there, some were asleep. Two others, Nancy and Rosie, saw it and*
> *took Mike to bed. They told him not to hit it. It was back in the cradle*
> *......I was about 3 feet away and saw every blow.*
> *.........when it died, it's chest had a mark and a lump on it. He was*
> *buried at the cemetery near home. I was there and saw it done.*
> *I did not see it taken out. I did see it after burial last Saturday in the*
> *shed when I was called. The doctor was there. He lived in Lamont.*
> *I could tell it was Mike's body by the clothes on it.*

When questioned by the Justice of the Peace, Annie indicated that her father, John, was "drunk".

Next to make a deposition was Rosie. Although only 12 years old, Rosie had already run away from home and was working as a servant in Edmonton. Sadly, Rosie would die a few years later in 1916.

I am Rosie. I am 12 years old. I have been working in Edmonton. I was home when Mike died. From the time father hit him he was sick. I was home when father hit him. Father went to Lamont and when he came home he beat Mike on

a Saturday. My sister had to unhitch the horses. Father sat down and drank whiskey from a quart jar....he was very drunk.....When she came back in the house he quarreled with us. He saw where Mike was. We were in the kitchen, father in the other room. When Mike was crying father took him and the cradle into the other room. He started to beat Mike. We took him and hid him under the bed. Then father beat all of us because Mike cried. He was crying bad afterwards and we sat up with him until morning. He beat Mike with his fist when Mike was in the cradle Father struck him all over. He struck him pretty hard not as hard as he could. If he had done so, he would have killed him. He said he beat him because mother would not take him with her. He said no more.

The next person to be questioned and deposed was Dr. Archer from

Dr. Archer

Lamont. He testified that he had been called to the Dombrowsky farm in the later part of March 1911 to examine a sick young boy. He noted that the household was in the charge of the "eldest girl" (Margaret). Mike had a temperature of 100, was "weak and thin and had the appearance of not having had good care". He had also noted that he observed a "swelling on the right side of the 6,7,and 8th rib and that it was hard". He concluded at the time that "the injury was the cause of it's illness" and that he prescribed a poultice that the girls in their deposition admitted to applying to Mike's chest.

Dr. Archer would not return to the Dombrowsky farm until after Mike's death. He was ordered to exhume Mike's body and perform a post mortem which he did in a shed on the Dombrowsky farm. Parts of his 7 page deposition are as follows:

> [Mike] was dressed in a white dress with black spots, white cap, his hands and feet wrapped in cotton clothes and in advanced stage of decomposition.........body markings and discoloration due to the decomposition process did not provide valuable information.....there was thickness to the ribs probably due to injury..... no indication of broken bones ......It is impossible to state from this post-mortem the immediate cause of death. There are still traces of injury but I can not state that this was the cause. I can not state whether the injury actually accelerated death. If the cause of death was other than injury however, there would be other symptoms that would have manifested themselves.

Even though Dr. Archer could not definitively determine that Mike's injuries were the cause of his death, the Justice of the Peace, Mr. Ainsworth felt that there was enough evidence to proceed to a full trial as he adjudicated that the "matter should stand trial at the next court of competent jurisdiction". He then ordered a Warrant of Commitment against John Dembrowsky indicating that he was to remain in the Fort Saskatchewan jail until his trial.

The formal trial was held on 17 October 1911 but it's findings are not known.

As a sad postscript to this story, 2 more of John and Sophia's children would die in the next few years. As already stated, Rosie, who gave such gripping testimony at her father's trial, would die 5 years later in 1916 at the age of 17. Her older sister, Nancy, who had "run away" from the homestead at the age of 11 to work in Edmonton, had returned by 1917 to marry a local farmer by the name of Michael Tychkowsky. Michael and Nancy would have 2 children, David (1918-1918) and Rose (1919-1919) but both would die very shortly after birth. Nancy herself, would die soon after giving birth to Rose. Michael would then quickly marry Nancy's younger sister, Ksenia (Cassie). Their first child, Marie would be born on 20 May 1920 but would die 6 months later. They would then have 8 more children who all lived into adulthood. It certainly was a tragic decade for Sophia's family.

Anton's story

The events described above would have had a profound effect on Anton. Only 5 years earlier, his brother in law, Paul Czternastek (Rosalia Gurba's husband) had been violently killed in Camrose. The resulting animosity between Rosalia and the family of the man accused of killing her husband, eventually forced her to move to Ontario and then to New York state. Now Anton was dealing with the messy dissolution of two other sisters' marriages. It is well known that as the older brother, Anton took serious interest in his sisters' well being and looked after them. Not only was his support emotional it ended up with legal ramifications as well.

As related earlier, John Dembrowsky was found guilty of "threatening to assault Anton Gurba" on January 30, 1911. A few months later, in April of 1911, John, obviously still angry at Sophia and Anton, laid complaints in Fort Saskatchewan which ended up in separate charges being laid against Sophia and Anton.

Sophia was charged with "taking away one gun (double barrel) from the house of complainant without colour of right". The case was heard before Justice of the Peace E.G. Holmes. After asking John 3 quick questions, he dismissed the case.

Q. Are you married?
    A. Yes
Q. Have you had a legal separation?
    A. No
Q. Is she still your wife?
    A. Yes
Case dismissed

The case was obviously dismissed very quickly as the judge held that since John and Anna were married, she could not have "stolen" his gun.

The next day, the charge against Anton was heard. He was accused with "possession of stolen property". For some unknown reason, the file at the archives contains very little detail about the incident and there are no depositions. The file only contains a "Conviction" form that finds Anton guilty of possession of stolen property and an order to return to John Dembrowsky his gun, and to pay a $1 fine and costs of $3.10. Was this the same gun that Sophia was found not guilty of stealing only the day before? We will probably never know. One also has to wonder how a person could be in possession of a stolen gun which, in a court the previous day, declared was not a stolen item.

Conclusion

The year 1911 was indeed an "annus horribilus" for the Gurba family. It is disconcerting to read about "family problems" and to bring up "dirty laundry". Events such as those described above are often hoped to be left in the past. Some may believe that they should be forgotten and ignored. I believe that they give us a better understanding of where we come from and of who we are. It can also explain the strength of character that we have seen in many Gurba ancestors. Many of the older generations of the Gurba family remember "Auntie Sophia" as a very tough, strong willed, hard working woman, who, with the valuable help of her brother and her nephew Lucas, cleared the land and raised a family by herself. After learning about what she went through in 1911, is it any wonder how she became so independently strong? It can also explain why many of us have a strong sense of family after we learn about the strong and protective filial bond that Anton had for his sisters. What Semen's children went through only strengthens my resolve to honour them and remember them.

CHAPTER 10
THE SPANISH FLU CLAIMS A GURBA

John, with his sisters Mary and Anne

"He knew that he was going to die," Baba told me. "While he was sitting on the chair in the kitchen waiting for Mother and Father to get the wagon to take him to the hospital, he looked at me and said in a feeble voice, 'Franka, I will probably never see you again'"

Baba paused for a moment, tears even then welling up in her eyes 90 years later. "He knew. I never did see him again". John Gurba, son of Anton and Tekla Gurba and brother to Baba, died shortly thereafter on November 15, 1918 of the Spanish flu, one of the 30,000 – 50,000 fellow Canadians to perish the same way.

I asked Baba to tell me as much as she could remember about how the flu had affected the Gurba family. "I vividly remember all of it," was her response. Although my grandmother, Frances Bezborodka (nee Gurba), was nearing her 100th birthday, her memories of her brother John were crystal clear as she related the tragic story of his battle with the Spanish flu in 1918. This is her story.

It was autumn of 1918. The first World War was mercifully getting close to an armistice. A good crop was being harvested. After nearly 2 decades of living in their newly adopted country, life was finally starting to get easier. The Gurba family was beginning to prosper on their 160 acre farm. The community of Skaro had several churches. Transportation was becoming much easier. The children were going to school to learn to read and write, a privilege the Gurba family could only dream about a few years earlier when they immigrated from the village of Skoloszow, Galica in 1897. The 1912 Svoboda school register listed 3 Gurba children in attendance: Rosie (age 8 and Grade 1), Mary (age 10 and Grade 4) and John (age 14 and also in Grade 4). See Chapter 12 for a copy of that school register.

John was just beginning to start life as a young man. "He was such a handsome man", Baba recalled. "He was always so good to us younger children. He even had a girl friend whose name was Marcella Mandryk."

"He was very smart," continued Baba with her recollections. "I think that if he had lived, he would have left the farm and done really well. He would buy seed from the big companies and then sell it to the farmers. He always made money. Farming really wasn't in his blood. He would probably have been a business man."

Whether or not he wanted to eventually go into business or not , John made an Application for Homestead Patent on May 28, 1914. He claimed the SE section of Section 8, Township 61, Range 19, a piece of land near his oldest brother, Lukas, and directly south of his other brother, Dmytro's homestead near the settlement of Hollow Lake. In the spring of 1916, with the help of his carpentry talented brother, Lukas, he built a 18' by 24' log house, 2 log barns, a hen house and a granary (with a value of $1650). In 1916, he cleared 2 acres of land and in 1917, he cleared another acre. No more land would be cleared until 3 years after John's death (although the land was transferred to his father, Anton, on Feb 5, 1919 by virtue of the fact that John had died intestate.)

It was while attending school at Svoboda in the fall of 1918 when Baba first started to feel ill. She had just turned 12 years old a month previously and was one of the oldest children still in school. In fact, she had already "finished" all of the work available to children in those early days of the 20th century but both of her parents insisted that she stay in school as long as she could as education was deemed essential for the younger group of the Gurba children. Although Tekla could both read and write in Ukrainian and Polish, Anton could not and desperately wanted his children to "better themselves." While at school, Baba was required to help the teacher with the younger students. During the course of the day at school, Baba recalls that she developed a little sniffle and that her back began to ache. By the time she walked the ½ mile back to the homestead after school, she was violently ill. Every bone in her body ached, she shook uncontrollably and couldn't get warm.

"Mother put me to bed and covered me with blankets. She told me and my brothers and sisters NOT to say anything about me being ill because the threshing crew was working at the Gurba's that day and any indication of flu in the house would frighten the crew and they would leave thereby jeopardizing the completion of the harvest. I was assured that it was just a cold."

Albertans' wearing mask during the Flu Epidemic

Privately, Tekla was probably very concerned. Rumours had been rife about a serious illness spreading across the country, indeed the world. On September 8, a few weeks earlier, the first outbreak of this illness began in Victoriaville College in Quebec, when 2 students got sick, followed alarmingly quickly by 398 more. It struck Edmonton on October 19 when the first 41 cases were reported. Within days, hundreds of people in Northern Alberta were dead. Tekla didn't want to needlessly alarm the threshing crew and the community. It was a moot point. The flu spread quickly. Baba wasn't the only child to get sick that day in Skaro or indeed, across the province. Immediately, precautions were taken throughout Alberta. Schools were closed, as were movie houses and many businesses. Public meetings were banned. Many towns in Alberta surrounded themselves with barbed wire, essentially quarantining themselves. On October 25th, citizens throughout Alberta were ordered to wear gauze masks while outside their homes.

Miraculously, Baba was ill for only one day. She recalls that she couldn't get warm until her mother covered her with her father Anton's buffalo fur coat. She recalls falling asleep with "that animal fur wrapping me up from head to toe."

Waking up the next day, exhausted and weak, but feeling much better, Baba quickly realized that she would not be the only one to fall victim to this rapidly spreading virus. In a few short days, every member of the Gurba family got sick, save for Mother Tekla. Since Baba was the first "recovered", it fell to both her and mother Tekla to nurse everyone back to health.

Baba recalls that everyone was burning up with fever. There wasn't much that could be done. With no antibiotics to rely on, people could only turn to their time-honoured cures; rest, liquids, a lot of hope, and prayer. Baba and her mother were constantly trying to cool the family down with cold, wet rags. Baba spent much of her time washing clothes and trying to keep the house properly aired out. It was while washing clothes that Baba recalls glancing over at her mother and seeing her pray. At this point, the doctors and nurses assigned to the area by the provincial government were much too busy in makeshift hospitals tending to the most needy and were unable to make house calls.

The flu had also affected John and Baba's cousins in Round Hill as well. Their cousins Kathleen and Josephine Czternastek were working as hotel maids in 1918. They made $20 per month and had to clean spittoons, carry hot and cold water to rooms, clean the chambers, scrub the floors and make beds. This would have put them at great risk. In her wonderful family history, *Small Farms, Big Family- A Collective Memoir* (a book describing the Mack family, a family related to the Gurba's through Anna Gurba and Jozef Budynski), Marilyn Waingarten quotes Kathleen Czternastek-Rombalski Maxwell:

Me and my sister Josephine were working in a hotel in
Camrose during the great flu of 1918. People started
getting awful sick, and you couldn't hardly get a doctor.
People in the hotel got sick and Josephine got so sick
she didn't know who I was. I took care of her for three
or four weeks, but I never got it. Finally we got a
doctor and he helped Josephine. She had such a high
fever she didn't remember me. I was afraid she was
going to die. Later on there were more sicknesses too,
lots of typhoid fever once. But I must be strong
because I never got any of it.

It is interesting to read an editorial in the Edmonton Bulletin by
A.F.A. Coyne encouraging the businessmen of the Edmonton area to
help the citizens, especially those in "foreign settlements" which
would have included the Edna-Star area, where the Gurba's lived.

[the people are] God fearing religious people. Sympathize
with their manner and custom. Go in fearlessly. Show them
by example. They simply don't know what to do other than
lie with their rosary in their hands, pleading with their God
for help.......they are at a loss what to do. What is wanted
is direction. You can give that......BE BRITISH.....In
entering a house, open the windows and let them know that
fresh air is a prime requisite. Tell them to keep the windows
open and keep the fire going for heat. Keep the patient well
covered. Take their temperature with a thermometer....Give
patient Aspirin tablets—one or two for headaches. Two
quinine caplets always one in morning and one at night. See
that the bowels are kept moving; use cathartic pills; two to a

dose. If necessary, wash up the dishes, sweep the floors, and
generally show your good heart. For sick patients, only
liquid food, milk, Bovril, soup, water hot or cold.
For convalescent patients, some toast, little chicken,
avoid over eating. Don't antagonize the religious
instincts in the old folks. Where danger in the head of
the family take a piece of paper and make out his will….

Obviously, Baba and her mother did what was best as all of the Gurbas eventually got well….except for John.

Lamont Hospital c 1918

"John had been out working somewhere…I can't remember where…. but it closed down due to the flu so he had come to live with us at the homestead," Baba recalled. "When he came, he was already pretty sick."

John never showed any signs of getting better. He progressively got worse until pneumonia set in as it often did with this flu. Anton knew that his son was not doing well and made the decision to take him to the nearest hospital in Lamont after a public health official had visited the Gurba home and strongly encouraged him to do so. Baba watched from the window and waved as John left the homestead lying in the back of a wagon, bundled up in the same buffalo robe that covered Baba earlier. It was a 10 mile trip to Lamont. Mother Tekla and Father Anton came home that night.

On November 18, the Honourable A.G. MacKay, Alberta Minister of Health, reported to the Edmonton Journal that since early October, there had been "7000 cases in Edmonton with 332 deaths"...and in Whitford, a town not too far from Skaro, there have been "2856 cases with 109 deaths". On November 19, a headline in the Edmonton Journal declared "Austrians Are Health Menace During the Flu". It reported that "large numbers of Galicians were brought in by the police .....in a dying state, having been sick and without attention for days". The article continued..... "owing to the hostility of the local people at Shandro [a small community near Skaro] the hospital [in Lamont] was invaded by a mob, who lifted sick people out of bed and carried them off" concerned that so many sick people were in a single ward. In response, Dr. Archer was able to arrange for an isolation ward with 12 beds but had to increase it to 30 beds by the next day. The flu was certainly taking its toll. It was during these events at the Lamont Hospital that John Gurba had passed away.

(At this point it is worth noting that another member of the Gurba family passed away from the flu. Nancy Tychkowsky (Sofia Gurba-Dombrowsky's daughter) had recently married her husband, Michael. They had a son, David who died shortly after birth. Nancy would deliver another child a year later, Rose. It would be a very difficult birth, leaving Nancy in a very weakend state. She quickly caught the flu virus and was too weak to fight it, dieing shortly thereafter. Michael had difficulty in looking after baby Rose alone and would soon marry Nancy's sister, Ksenia. Unfortunately, baby Rose would die 6 months after her mother. Ksenia and Michael would then have 9 children of their own.)

Dr. Archer signed the Registration of Death (shown below). He stated

that the cause of death was "influenza". He also indicated that John had been in the hospital for 1 day.

Mother Tekla and Father Anton left the next morning for Lamont as they received word that John had died that night. Baba recalls John coming home in a "simple wooden coffin" that Anton "picked up along the way to Lamont". Tradition would normally call for his body to lay in repose in the main room of the Gurba home. The family would be visited by friends and family to pay their respects. However, these were not normal times.....no one came calling. John's body lay in one of the out buildings on the farm. The settlement of Skaro was in a virtual quarantine as 13 other Skaro residents had died between September 17 and November 26, 1918, Most of the deaths were due to the flu and most victims were in their late teens or early 20's.   John's casket remained closed.

The next day, with the temperatures hovering in the mid 20 degrees Fahrenheit and with light flurries falling from the sky, Baba watched from the window as Anton and Tekla Gurba, accompanied by the priest and neighbours Mr. and Mrs. Nimchuk, transported John's coffin to the church cemetery. There would be no other mourners in attendance, not even John's brothers and sisters, as they were forbidden to go to say their final farewells.

"It was so very, very sad," Baba whispered.

John's grave at Skaro

CHAPTER 11
CHURCH LIFE

SKARO AREA

Faith has always played an important role in the Gurba family. Frances recalls very clearly her mother, Tekla, reading almost daily from the Polish Bible that she brought with her from Skoloszow. Religion also played a very important role for many of the original settlers in the Skaro area. It is not possible to travel in the Skaro area without constant reminders of the religious history of the area. The Gurba family's home church, Exaltation of the Holy Cross Ukrainian Catholic Church, is one of 7 historic churches within a few kilometers of each other. A dispute over the ownership of a neighbouring church ended up being decided in 1907 when the Privy Council in London, England, gave possession and ownership of the church to the Orthodox Church. The famous Grotto of Our Lady of Lourdes (Skaro Shrine) is only a few kilometers down the road from the Gurba homestead.

At the family reunion in 2007, the family gathers infront of the Gurba "ancestral" church.

On August 6, 1898, the 40 acres where the Gurba family church now stands was blessed by Father Paul Tymkevych. This was only a few months after the arrival of the Gurba family but Anton and his family took an immediate role in the establishment of the church. Anton Gurba is listed among the 29 founding members of the parish. It would take several more years until a building was actually erected on the site. The cemetery was used almost immediately. One of the first people buried there was Semen Gurba who died on December 1, 1901.

A battle line would soon develop as the Russian Orthodox Church and the Ukrainian Catholic community claimed the same land to build their respective churches. The county refused to divide the property. The two parties appealed to the government. Part of the argument used by the Catholic delegation was that there were 45 member families for the Catholic Church but only 8 families belonged to the Orthodox church. As a result of the appeal, the Catholics were given the southern half of the parcel of land and the Orthodox was given the northern portion. Their 2 respective churches remain today, a cemetery on the property line beween the 2 churches.

The parish linked with the Gurba family was initiated on May 25, 1900. A building fund to build the Catholic Church was finally established in 1911 but it wasn't until 1917 that a church was finally built under the title Ruthenian Greek Catholic Church of Czesnoho Kresta at Skaro. The estimated cost of all the building material and labour was $1500.00. Each founding member was expected to donate $50.00, which in itself was a considerable amount.

Yearly membership dues were $1.00 per family. Each family was also expected to contribute $1.00 for the cost of the priest's lodging and members were also expected to pay $1.00 each year for Kolady Christmas Carolling. Marriages would cost $2.00 and there would be a collection taken at each wedding mass. By October 13, 1913, the parish had collected a sum of $2,128.40 but expenses totaled $2,133.45.

The funeral of Anton Gurba at the original church, 1927.

The church would be serviced by the Basilian Fathers. Fr. Anthony Strotsky would be the first to serve in the newly built church. Tragically, the church burned down in 1942. It was replaced with the current church that was built in 1945 at a cost of $46, 190.92. The bell tower adjacent to the church, built in 1926 at a cost of $912.05 (the bell itself cost an additional $1,040.10), survived the fire.

The following members of Semen's family join him in final repose in the church cemetery: his son Anton (1858-1927) and his daughter in law Tekla (1866–1944), his daughter Katie Stecyk (1865–1924), his grandsons Dmytro (1894–1974), Ivan (1895-1918), Steve (1909-1978) with his wife Sophie (1914-2005), his granddaughters Katie (1905-1978) and Victoria (1913-1923), and his great grandsons Anthony (1934-1938) and Michael (1952-1996).

Blessing of the Centennial plaque (2002) to be mounted on the back of Semen's headstone. The service was conducted by Father Janko Herbut.

Located just a few kilometers east of the church is the Grotto of Our Lady of Lourdes, locally known as the Skaro Shrine. Although not intimately related to the Anton Gurba family, it did play an important role in the Gurba family history. In the fall of 1918, Father Anthony Sylla proposed the building of a small grotto which was a very common religious site in the Polish areas of Galicia. He felt that this would be a link between the new immigrants and the homeland that they left behind. He consulted with Father Phillip Ruh, who was doing missionary work in the area. Father Ruh was very familiar with the Grotto of Lourdes in France and was quite excited about building a similar structure in the Skaro area. He agreed to make plans and supervise the construction of the grotto with 2 conditions. Firstly, the people of the area would need to supply the labour and the materials and secondly, he stated that the monument must be big or he couldn't be bothered. His exact words apparently were "If I build it, it must be big, otherwise, I do not start at all". In June of 1919, the work commenced. It took two back-breaking months of construction using 600 loads of rock and 300 bags of cement.

Photo OB8648 appears courtesy of the Missionary Oblates, Grandin Collection (Provincial Archives of Alberta)

Photo OB2173 appears courtesy of the Missionary Oblates, Grandin Collection (Provincial Archives of Alberta)

Building of the Skaro Shrine in 1919. Although none of the pictures definitely show any members of the Gurba family, they do give us an insight into the "appearance" of the community; how they dressed, the types of tools they used, their modes of transportation, etc. We also know for a fact that members of the Gurba family helped with the community efforts in building of the Shrine. The man at the far left in the front row of the top photo, however, certainly has the appearance and body language of a young Metro Gurba. Could the man beside him be his father, Anton??

On August 14, 1919, pilgrims arrived at sunset to offer their special prayers at the completed grotto. Anton's daughter, Frances, vividly recalls how the construction of the Grotto was very much a community effort. Although the Gurba family were not members of that parish, or even considered themselves "Roman Catholic" Anton spent many hours hauling rocks from neighbouring farms and even up from the North Saskatchewan River to be placed in a spot determined by Father Ruh. The building of the Shrine was seen to be in the public interest of the community and community involvement was a strong tenet in the Gurba family belief system. Pilgrimages to the Grotto and Shrine became a yearly event and continue to this day. Frances has very fond memories of family members from Round Hill, (the remaining Czternastek-Budynski's), coming to Skaro every year for the event. These were to be the first of the Gurba family reunions.

ROUND HILL AREA

St. Stanislaus Church as it appears today.

Another church in Alberta with deep early Gurba family roots is the St. Stanislaus Church in Round Hill. It is the oldest existing Polish church in Alberta. Shortly after arriving in Canada, Semen's daughter Anna, her husband Jozef Budynski and their children (Wladek, Rosalia, and Lawrence) moved to the Round Hill area near present day Camrose where they established their homestead. As the early settlers had done in Skaro, the immigrants in the Round Hill area quickly moved to establish a place of worship. After an arduous journey by horse and wagon, Father Francis Olszewski celebrated Mass in the home of Michael Budynski, Jozef's brother. A year later, on January 6, 1904 Father Paul Kulawy would celebrate another Mass at the Budynski home. The community gathered shortly afterwards to build a church and a rectory. They called upon Frank Mack to design the church. Frank would soon be the father-in-law of Rose Budynski (Jozef and Anna Gurba's daughter.) The steeple created a problem for Frank and in late spring of 1904, when the church was almost complete, a strong prairie wind levelled the church because it had not been properly braced. The farmers blamed Frank but they were not discouraged. The following spring, construction began on the current church. They cut the studs shorter so that the ultimate height of the church would be smaller and lower but much stronger. It was built at a total cost of $710.00. The first mass said in the new church was on Easter Sunday, April 23, 1905.

St. Stanislaus Church in Round Hill on the Patron Saints Day 1910 (Photo OB2432 appears courtesy of the Missionary Oblates, Grandin Collection Provincial Archives of Alberta)

Among the original 43 families listed as members of the congregation were 2 "Gurbas" and their families. These included Jozef Budynski and his wife Anna Gurba and Paul Czternstek and his wife Rosalia Gurba. Also of note is that the first Baptism to be held by the Parish (but not in the church) was held on July 8, 1902 for Frances Budynski (the daughter of Jozef Budysnki and Anna Gurba). Another early event would be the marriage of Rosalia Budynski (Jozef and Anna's daughter) to Vincent Mack on November 20, 1910. They would be married by Father Kulawy. Father Kulawy would serve as parish priest until 1921 when he returned to Poland for a visit. He would not return and would eventually perish in the Auschwitz concentration camp on August 21, 1941. Members of Semen's immediate family who rest in the church's cemetery are his son in law Paul Czternastek (1864-1906), Semen's granddaughter Anna Budynski (1917-1934), his granddaughter Anna Pointkowski (1890-1969) with her husband Anton (1885-1943), his great-grandsons Clarence Pointkoski (1908-2003) and Edward Piontkowski (1914-2005) and his great-great grandsons Donald (1948-1948) and Ray (1955-1987) and great-great granddaughter Lorraine (1946-46).

DARLING AREA

Darling Church as it appears today.

Although it does not fall into the time line of this book, it would be remiss to not mention another church intimately connected with the Gurba family. The Darling Ukrainian Catholic Church began construction in 1936 very close to the farm that Anton and Tekla's son Lucas homesteaded after he got married in 1917. Lucas was an excellent, self taught carpenter. (According to my Baba, Frances, their father Anton could "barely pound a nail. Lucas learned it all by himself.") Lucas played in integral role in the physical construction of the church and his family continues to be members of the church today.

CHAPTER 12
SCHOOLING IN CANADA

Once the essentials of beginning a new life in Canada had become stable, the Ukrainian settlers in the Skaro area decided to build a school to educate their children. Education was a rare experience for many of the early children who immigrated from the old country. The only Gurba child who received any education in Skoloszow was Tylda, Anton and Tekla's oldest child. Once in Canada, formal education was not possible in Skaro until early 1906.

On April 10, 1906 the Svoboda School District #1479 was established. Mr. John Figol was the first secretary. It was his responsibility to name the school and he chose the word "Svoboda" meaning freedom in the Ukrainian language. A school was originally to be built on Sec 6- Township 56- Range 18 W4, just slightly north of the Gurba homestead. It was eventually built on the SW ¼ of Section 6 in the 57th Township. The land was owned by John Dombroski, the husband of Sophia Gurba. It would then be sold to Mr. Pasemko when the Dombroski family moved to Edmonton. A second room was built in 1928. At it's peak, there were 70 students attending the school in two rooms. The school would eventually close in 1949; it's students transferred to the nearby Jaroslaw school.

On the next page is an attendance roster for August of 1912. Pupils #1 and #2 are 14 year old John Gurba and his 10 year old sister Mary. Both are listed as Grade 4 students. Student #15 is 6 year old Rosie Gurba (Grade 1). Three Gurba cousins were also members of this class. Pupil # 5 was Rose Dembroski, student #16 was Cassie Dembroski and student #19 was Tekla (Tille) Dembroski. These were the children of Sophia Gurba (Anton's sister). Student #9 is 7 year old

Nick Bezborodka, who would later marry Frances Gurba. Frances would become a student at Svoboda in the following year, 1913.

Svoboda school attendance record for August 1912

The teacher of the class was Michael Luczkovec (Luchkovich) who would eventually become the first person of Ukrainian descent to be elected to the Parliament of Canada. He would run as a United Farmers of Alberta candidate in the Vegreville constituency in 1926. He would be reelected in 1930 but was defeated in 1935. He would

Michael Luchkovich Oct 13 , 1917 at a Ukraininan teachers conference

also be the translator of several Ukrainian books into English, including the famous *Sons of the Soil* by Ilia Kiriak. He was born in November of 1892 in Shamokin, Pennsylvania. He spoke "po Rus'kiy with a Lemko accent" and according to his memoirs , before he arrived in Winnipeg in 1907 to register at Manitoba College to do his high school, his "knowledge of Ukrainian was limited to a few words like 'khata' (house), 'stil' (table), 'krislo' (chair), hovoryty' (speak), 'yisty' (eat) and 'pyty' (drink), but I lacked the ability to combine them into grammatical sentences." It was while in Manitoba that he met many "Ukrainians" and quickly picked up the language.

It is important at this point in the story to quote once again from Luchkovich's memoirs:

If I were to credit any single person with bringing me to Alberta I would not hesitate in naming Ivan Nimchuk of Skaro, Alberta. It was in the springtime of the year 1912. I was faced with the grim problem of not only earning a livelihood but in scrapping up enough money to get through my first year of university. In those early days the main source of revenue for students was

to go out teaching during the summer months somewhere in
Saskatchewan or Alberta.

Thus a few weeks before the end of my 1912 school term, I had
inserted an ad in one of our Ukrainian newspapers stating that
I would be able to take over some school in the west starting at
the beginning of June. My first and only answer was from John
Nimchuk, secretary of the newly organized school district "Svoboda"
at Skaro, accepting my application. I was overjoyed at this turn
of events, but there was one hitch to it: I couldn't rake up enough
money to pay my fare to Lamont which was the nearest railway
station to the place called Skaro. I accepted on the basis my fare
to Lamont would be paid. I thought for sure that this would write
finis to my trip to Lamont. To my great surprise however, a few
days later I received a registered letter from Mr. Nimchuk
enclosing more than enough money to pay for my fare to the
above destination.

My readers will excuse me for feeling that this must have been
a divine act of Providence for I was completely broke at the time
and the receipt of the money was a real God-send.

Later I learned that Mr. J Nimchuk had sent this railway fare to
me over the objections of the rest of the school board which
contended that it was taking a chance in sending money to an
unknown person.

Thus it was because of this act of faith shown towards me by
this man that I came to a province that was to be my home for
the next 50 years. This unusual gesture of trust left an indelible
imprint on my mind; It not only fixed my belief in the goodness
of the common man, but it drew me like a magnet to Alberta .

The above mentioned John Nimchuk was literally "an across the road" neighbour to the Gurba's and they were considered to be best friends. As related in other chapters of this book about the Gurba family, this was the same John Nimchuk whom Tekla would ask about her husband's missing status in the late 1890's. It was the same Nimchuk family who were the only people allowed at the funeral of John Gurba in 1918. They were also the Nimchuks that Anton would visit on an almost daily basis to listen to John read the newspapers and to talk about current events. Utlimately, it will also be the same John Nimchuk who attended to Anton at his bedside as he lay dying in 1927. (See Chapter 14). It is not a stretch then to believe that one of the first people to learn about the arrival of this soon to be famous Canadian, was the Gurba family nor is it beyond the realm of possibility that Anton and Tekla helped John Nimchuk "choose" this man to be their children's teacher.

It is interesting to note that four of the Gurba children, 3 cousins and a future brother-in-law, were all part of Michael Luchkovich's first class in Canada.

Education was a priority for both Anton and his wife Tekla, although this was not a common belief amongst the first immigrants from Eastern Europe. Most parents saw their best chance of improvements in their lives in farm ownership and not in education. In the March 8, 1911 issue of *Ukrainskiy Holos*, (a newspaper that Tekla read religiously), an article claimed that "90%" of immigrants opposed the formation of school districts. In the same paper, a farmer is quoted as saying , "If we feed freeloaders (teachers) to play with our children, we will never make our farms here". Another settler is quoted in *Kanadyiskiy farmer*, "We came here to plough not to build schools." Although both papers took editorial stands in favour of education, only 1/3 of the Ukrainian population in Canada had formed school divisions by 1911.   Bring the avid reader that Tekla was, these quotes from fellow settlers must have provoked some interesting conversions at home and with their Nimchuk neighbours. Anton received no formal education, something that he regretted for his entire life. Tekla had gone to school in Skoloszow and was in fact, quite literate. It was part of Anton's Canadian dream that his children would become educated. Both of them believed very strongly in the value of an education. To them, education was the road away from poverty.

Svoboda School --Boys 1914. Nick Bezborodka is in the rear 4ᵗʰ from the left.

Frances has some vivid memories of her years at Svoboda. She would attend the school until Grade 8, which at that time was the farthest one could get at Svoboda. She initially did not want to go to school. She was afraid because she could only speak Ukrainian and the language of instruction was English. So determined with the thought she would not go to school, she ran off to the barn to hide. Her mother, Tekla, searched high and low for her until her hiding place was betrayed by her younger brother Steve. Tekla came after Frances with a switch of willow twigs. Frances recalls how her mother commenced to hit her about the legs with the switch, chasing her down the road towards the school. Once at the school however, Frances became enamored with the place in part with the educational possibilities but more so "to get out of doing the chores". By the time Frances finished her schooling at Grade 8, she opted to do an additional year of Grade 8 to help out the teacher. "It was either that or stay at the farm and do work", Frances recalled.

Frances has no recollection of Michael Luchkovich but she has very fond memories of Mr. John Hackett and his wife Clara. John was the teacher at the neighbouring Jaroslaw school and Clara taught at Svododa. They would reside at the teacherage during the week (a building Frances recalls was more of a "shack") and would return to their more permanent home in Lamont for the weekend. She also has very fond memories of Mr. Holman. He was an elderly gentleman with very long whiskers. The girls in the class would love to pull his whiskers and Mr. Holman always obliged. He would always play with the kids at recess time, often playing soccer with them. They only had one ball and it would invariably become flat by the end of the day. One of the boys would take it home at the end of the day to repair it. Frances also lovingly recalls the "big" playground that was part of the school property.

Of Anton and Tekla's 12 children, only Lucas, Dmytro and Anne received no formal early education. Dmytro had developmental difficulties and in the early years of the 20th century, there was no educational opportunities for him. According to Frances, my grandmother, Lucas, Tylda and Anne felt that they were too old to begin schooling once Svoboda school opened. Eventhough John was older than Anne, father Anton insisted that John had no choice. He HAD to attend eventhouhg he was by fat the oldest in class; further proof of the high regard Anton had for education. Why Anton allowed Anne the option of NOT attending is not known, although Frances says that her sister, Anne, was always "stubborn" and "always did what she wanted to do". It is worth noting however, that once Anne emigrated to New York with her sister Tylda, she eventually enrolled in adult education night classes and soon learned to read and write. Frances recalls…"I still remember getting that first letter from her that was written in her own handwriting. It was such a wonderful surprise! She didn't tell anyone that she was learning how to read and write." Frances and Anne corresponded by letters on a regular basis for decades.

CHAPTER 13
TEKLA STORIES

Tekla Gurba

Family histories tend to focus on the achievements of the males. While it is true that the Gurba family has had many strong male members,

one of the most strong, enduring and memorable people of the "early" Gurba family was the matriarch of our family in Canada, Tekla. Barely 5 feet tall, she was an incredibly brave, smart and determined individual who most of the current family know little. It is important to acknowledge the person she was and to honour the contributions she made to the establishment of our successful family. Just who was Tekla?

Tekla Albert was born in Skoloszow, Galicia in 1866 to Jozef Albert and Zofia Blonarowicz. Although we are not certain, it is believed that she had a brother as she often told her daughter, Frances, my grandmother, that Tekla had left a brother and his family back in the old country. As a young girl, Tekla attended school where she learned to read and write in Polish, quite the accomplishment for a poor rural girl in Galicia at the time. It is believed that in the late 1880's , Tekla met and married Anton Gurba after he had completed his mandatory military service.

They immediately started their family and within 5 years had 4 children, (Tylda, Lucas, Dmytro and Ivan). By 1897, Tekla and her husband, Anton, had made the major decision to immigrate to Canada. Upon arriving in Edmonton in early 1897, they took out a homestead near Edna-Star. For the next 2 decades, Tekla and Anton worked extremely hard in developing their homestead and building their family. In addition to the 4 children born in Galicia, they had 8 more children in Canada (Anne, Mary, Rose, Kate, Frances, Steve, Peter and Victoria). Tekla was widowed in 1927. She would remain on the homestead for another 17 years until she died at the age of 78 on March 1, 1944. In addition to her husband, she outlived her son, John, who died of the Spanish Flu on November 15, 1918 and her youngest daughter Victoria, who died at the age of 10 on July 27, 1923. She is buried near her husband (and several of her children) at The Exaltation of the Holy Cross Ukrainian Catholic Church at Skaro.

Those are the facts of Tekla's life, but they really don't convey the type of person she was. It goes without saying that she must have been an extremely hard working woman. Consider the fact that she immigrated to Canada with virtually no money nor personal or household effects. She along with her husband and 4 children endured an arduous journey across an ocean and then across a largely untamed continent to eventually begin the backbreaking job of clearing land for a new homestead. During the next 16 years, Tekla would bear 8 more children for a total of 12. One can only imagine what it must have been like for the diminutive Tekla to assist her husband with the physical aspects of beginning a homestead but then, compound that with the responsibilities of managing a household filled with young children. Her home was small, un-insulated, lacked electricity, had no running water and almost none of the modern conveniences we take for granted today. In this day of Pampers, microwaves, baby formula, washing machines, and DVD's, I wonder how the farm wives of those days managed. Child raising required constant vigilance and obviously a lot of hard work.

To go beyond the obvious and to uncover the complex person Tekla was, I was determined to learn about some of the specific aspects of her daily life; to probe people's minds about what they might have heard or actually experienced by their interactions with Tekla. What follows are some vignettes of Tekla's life.

THE VOICE

As I write this, there is only one person alive who remembers Tekla as

a young lady...and a mother. Frances, my grandmother, was the 9th child born to Tekla and Anton. The source of most of the following vignettes is from Frances. Though her 102 year old body is frail, her mind is active, vivid and filled with many memories. When I asked her what her favourite memory of her mother is, she replied instantly, "Her voice!". Frances vividly recalls how much her mother loved to sing. She would often be caught in the kitchen singing songs from Galicia. Apparently, Anton loved to listen to his wife sing. On Sundays, Tekla would lead the congregation in singing the responses in church. She was one of the few that could read the hymn book and would ensure that everyone else would sing the correct words. She loved to sing.

Tekla at the wedding of her grand-daughter, Pauline, on 24 Nov 1936.

THE SNUFF

Tekla's grandson, Robert Broda, has a very vivid image of his grandmother. He sees the diminutive woman opening the oven door of the wood burning stove, checking to make sure it was relatively cool, and then she would make herself comfortable by sitting on the door. She would then open a hockey puck shaped cardboard container of Copenhagen snuff which she always kept close by in her apron pocket. Deftly putting a pinch of snuff between her thumb and forefinger, she would then place the snuff beneath her nostril and inhale deeply. This was quite the scene for the young Robert. According to Tekla's daughter, Frances, her mother's addiction to snuff came quite late in life. At one point in time, Tekla was suffering from severe eye pain. The doctor prescribed snuff. The eye pain eventually went away but Tekla's addiction to snuff would last until the end of her life.

THE ACCIDENT

Tekla was a tough lady. Few things would slow her down but Frances recalled an event that resulted in a trip to the hospital in Lamont. It was winter time, probably around 1915 as Frances was "about 10" when it happened. Tekla required some supplies that were only available in the town of Bruderheim, 10 kilometers from the homestead. Tekla's daughter, Mary was asked to accompany Tekla on her errand. As she often did, Tekla would harness up the horse to the sleigh and drive to Bruderheim. On this particular day, Mary took the reins. Somewhere along the way, they encountered another sleigh on the road that was moving a bit too slowly for Mary's liking. Mary decided to pass the slow moving sleigh. This slow moving sleigh had a canvas covering attached to it. While in the process of passing the sleigh, the covering moved, spooking the horse pulling the Gurba sleigh. The horse bolted, tearing one of the reins out of Mary's hand. Trying to control the quickly moving sleigh with one rein was futile. The sleigh soon began to sway on the snow covered roadway and tumbled into the ditch. Tekla and Mary were thrown from the sleigh. Mary was badly bruised but Tekla was unable to move. The sleigh that Mary tried to pass came to the rescue. Realizing that Tekla was seriously injured, the driver loaded both Mary and Tekla onto his sleigh, turned it around and transported mother and daughter to the hospital in Lamont. It was determined the Tekla had broken her leg. A message was sent back to Anton on the homestead. By the time he arrived at the hospital, Tekla's leg was in a cast but she was ready to go back home. Tekla did not take well to using crutches but moved about the house by pushing a chair in front of her wherever she went. Tekla removed the cast by herself when she felt that her leg has sufficiently healed, but according to Frances, her leg never went back to normal again.

Tekla feeding the ducks

THE SINGLE PARENT

As related in a previous chapter in this collection of stories about the Gurba family, Anton spend much of the family's first year in Canada working on the railroad in the Crows Nest Pass area of southern Alberta. This left Tekla alone on the homestead with her four children, Tylda (7), Lucas (5), Metro (3) and baby John (2). One can only imagine what that would have been like and the strength of character one would have to possess to survive those first few months. The Gurba's arrived too late in the year to plant any crops. They barely had enough time to build a house. The weather that fall and winter was much colder than normal. In fact, on December 16, 1897 the temperature that night reached -41.7 degrees Celsius. I'm sure that it never reached temperatures like that in Skoloszow! One could only guess whether Tekla had second thoughts about leaving Skoloszow a few months previously. In January of 1898, Inspector P.C.H. Primrose of the North West Mounted Police was instructed by Major Griesbach, the officer in command at Fort Saskatchewan, to visit the families in the settlement of Edna-Star and to report on their conditions. He reported that the Gurba family had "1 cow, 1 calf, 20 bs potatoes, 15 lb flour, 2 bags Bran, 1 bag wheat". A few months later, the Gurba family was visited by an immigration supervisor by the name of Thomas Bennett. In his report on the Gurba family, he noted that they had "5 acres broken, a log house and a cook stove". He granted them relief to the amount of $10,00. These were the conditions that Tekla lived with while Anton was striving to make more money on the railroads. Anton did not return that spring, leaving Tekla to seed those 5 acres by herself. She probably also relied on the assistance of her neighbours and of course her father in law, Semen. Although Tekla spoke primarily in Polish, many of her neighbours were "Ukrainian". It was during these first few months in Canada, that Tekla learned to read, write and converse in the Ukrainian language in addition to her native Polish. In the first few months of Anton's absence, he would send Tekla letters that he dictated to a scribe. The letters stopped coming in the spring of 1898 and rumours spread that Anton had been murdered. Tekla never gave up hope. She maintained the homestead and looked after her young family virtually by herself until Anton's return a year later in the spring of 1899. With the money Anton made on the railway and Tekla's hard work maintaining the early beginnings of the homestead, the Gurba family were finally able to strengthen their toehold in their new land...and as they say, the rest is history.

THE KIND AND COMPASSIONATE GRANDMOTHER

Tekla with her daughter, Frances, and grandsons, Robert, Walter and Raymond

Joe Gurba, Tekla's grandson by her son Lucas, has some tender memories of his grandmother. They indicate that Tekla was a kind, caring but firm grandmother who certainly understood that boys will be boys. Joe shared some of his memories of Tekla with me in July 2008. He recalls that:

Grandmother Tekla was small in stature at almost five feet but she was huge as the kind, intelligent, and sensible matriarch of the family especially after Anton died in 1927. Tekla was left with a farm and home to operate, and five children, including Dmytro

who was mentally handicapped. At age 18 Steve gradually took
over the farm operation but Tekla remained the general manager.
I remember one incident that illustrates the relationship: as an
8 year old I spent about one month in 1930 at the Skaro
farm, taking a Catechism course at the Sloboda school in preparation
for First Communion. Uncle Steve had bought me a fancy straw
hat which I proudly wore to school. Several big boys, probably
envious, threw the hat on the floor and tramped on it in a most
un-Christian like manner. I carried the smashed hat home, and
Uncle Steve was furious. Without asking for an explanation,
he threw me over his knee, ready to discipline me, when
Grandma Tekla intervened. She asked me about the hat and I
tearfully told about the big boys. I was grateful for the missed
thrashing and realized who was the kind, fair boss.
Tekla had an interesting habit of putting Copenhagen snuff up
her nose. She would sneeze several times and claim it was good
for her health. She often sat and talked with Uncle Dmytro while
he ate his favorite rye bread and pork-lard sandwich. Grandma
enjoyed her grandchildren and asked about my activities: catching
gophers with twine snares, climbing trees to examine bird nests,
eating raw chicken eggs until I chanced on a partly hatched one,
or chasing the young pigs around the hog pasture and through
the 30 foot tunnel in the straw stack.
Grandma was kind but had firm rules. At the 2 ½ hour mass
for my First Communion, we stood since there were no pews.
She reminded me to keep my hands folded in front and not
akimbo my hips since this wasn't a Kozak dance. After mass
there was a picnic and Tekla bought me a double ice cream cone.
Many other well–wishers got me ice cream until I probably
had ten, got horribly sick to my stomach, and lost a bundle.
I didn't eat ice cream again for about five years.

Granma Tekla died in March 1944 while I was stationed at the
RCAF station in North Battleford, Sask. Sister Pauline phoned me
about the funeral at Skaro and I requested compassionate leave
to attend. However the Air Force claimed "grandmother funerals"
were poor excuses unless I had proof. I couldn't prove a phone call so
I missed the chance to pay my respects for this wonderful, little old
lady who was a role model for us of the next generation.

Tekla's grandson Joe at about the
time of the "straw hat" incident

AVID READER and LIFELONG LEARNER

Tekla was an avid reader. She had gone to school in the old country and was quite literate. She read Polish fluently and learned to read Ukrainian once she immigrated to Canada. She would read whatever she could get her hands on. Her daughter Frances, recalls that she especially enjoyed reading *Ukrainskyi Holas* and *Ukrainskyi visti*. It was very important to Tekla that she knew "what was happening around the world" and she would often read the newspapers to her husband Anton. Anton, conversely, would love to be read to. Quite often, he would walk to the Nimchuk farm across the road, where Mr. Nimchuk would read the papers to him. This was a tradition from the old country where non-literate farmers would go to the local reading club (called chytalni), where the more educated of the community would inform the rest about events from around the world.

St. John's Nursing class in Skaro. Tekla is the small woman under the left window. Her daughter Mary, is the woman with glasses under the middle window.

Tekla took great pride in saving every issue of the newspapers that she would receive. As her daughter, Frances, demonstrated to me, Tekla would lovingly and carefully fold each issue and stuff them between the shelves around the house. Tekla's mind would work much like a modern day computer data base and she would often return to a particular issue of a newspaper to "prove a point" to a neighbour. "I knew I read about it a long time ago," she would often say.

Keeping abreast on current events and new ways of doing things was also a passion of Tekla. She would often tell her daughter, Frances, that since they were now in Canada, they had to do things in the Canadian way. In the old country, they would celebrate religious events the traditional way. Christmas for example, was celebrated on January 7 but after a few years in Canada, Tekla insisted that they celebrate on the same day as the Canadians. When a nursing instructor came to the Skaro area to teach the women about new ways of nursing to the ill, Tekla was a member of the class. The event was photographed and Tekla can be seen in the front row, the smallest woman there (and probably the oldest as well).

Tekla's daughter, Frances, recalls that her mother also loved to write. Her daughter Tylda kept in touch with Tekla through the mail after she moved to the United States and the communication went both ways. By looking at Tekla's signature at the beginning of this chapter, she must have had incredible penmanship, although according to Frances, she never wrote in English...only in Polish. Frances also recalls that Tekla's handwriting was "very big" and that she would often use 2 lines, unlike Frances who would write on only one.

In her 78 years, Tekla achieved no widely heralded great deeds. Nor will she be mentioned in the history books describing the building of the great province of Alberta. Nonetheless, her contribution to the world was significant. Through good times and bad, she stood firm, gave life to, loved and nurtured twelve good, moral men and women. She, with her husband, came to this yet to be named province of Alberta and met the harsh, virgin parkland on its own terms, refused to be defeated by it, and in fact, co-existed with it. Through learning some of the circumstances of her life and times, I feel that I know her better now, and I count it a privilege. She was a brave, determined, intelligent and compassionate lady.

CHAPTER 14

VICTORIA

They say a picture is worth a thousand words. There are so very few pictures of the Gurba family pre-1920's. We know for a fact that there are no pictures of Anton as he refused to have his picture taken. Finding the one known picture of John (shown in Chapter 9) was a thrill as were the series of pictures taken at the funeral of Anton in 1927. (See pages 113, 145, 146) There is one picture however that has a somewhat haunting feel to it.

It is a picture of a young girl, perhaps 6 or 7 years old. She is standing in the middle of a promising field of wheat on land which was cleared

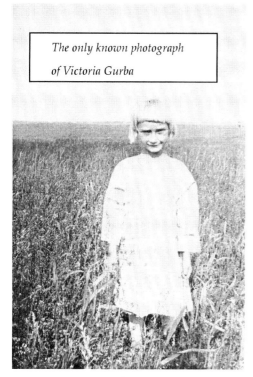

The only known photograph of Victoria Gurba

by her parents over a decade earlier. Her one piece smock is old, worn and probably a hand-me-down from her older sisters. Her blonde hair is closely cropped, somewhat unevenly. Her mischievous smile, makes us wonder what she was thinking. She has the unmistakable features of a young female Gurba. This is the only photo known to exist of young Victoria, the last child born to Anton and Tekla. She was born on November 18, 1913. She died at the young age of 9 ½ on July 27, 1923.

She had been visiting her older brother Lucas, and his family at the Hollow Lake farm. It was summer holidays and she no doubt looked forward to seeing her brother and play with her very young nieces and nephew, Pauline, Lily and Joseph. Perhaps she would even help her sister-in-law Pearl with the babies. While there, she passed away from what her death certificate originally stated was "stomach trouble". This was crossed out and changed to "mumps".

Victoria's older sister, Frances, was back on the homestead when Victoria passed away. She vividly recalls that she was outside helping her mother, Tekla. A flock of crows were creating a racket nearby and Tekla remarked that "the crows are trying to tell us something". She explained to Frances, that the cawing of crows foretold of a bad event, often a death. A few hours later, they received a visit from their neighbour, John Nimczuk. He had just received a phone call from Lucas, who had journeyed down to Waskatenau to use the phone there. The Nimczuk's had a telephone installed on their farm but the Gurba's had not. The message was that Victoria had fallen ill and that Anton and Tekla should come down to Hollow Lake to pick up Victoria. Victoria being ill was not an unusual occurrence. According to Frances, Victoria was always a very weak child. From birth, she was listless and suffered from a multitude of illnesses. In fact, she had not started school until she was 8 years old due to many illnesses. "I'm sure she had heart truble that doctors could probably fix today," sister Frances said in 2007. This visit to Lucas' farm was her first journey away from home, a visit she insisted on taking because "she was feeling really good". In any event, Anton and Tekla decided that it was too late in the day to journey all the way to Hollow Lake to pick her up and they made the decision to spend the night at home and leave in the morning to go pick up Victoria.

Victoria's grave at Skaro

While preparing to leave the next morning, Anton and Tekla heard Lucas's wagon coming down the road. He appeared to be alone. Upon arriving at the homestead, the family had discovered that the body of Victoria lay in the back of the wagon, lovingly wrapped in a blanket. According to Lucas, the previous morning Victoria had awoken saying that she was ill. While Lucas was making the phone call in Waskatenau, Victoria simply collapsed as she was sitting in the bed and quickly died.

As can be expected, the death of a child was traumatic for the parents. Frances recalls that her father was devastated but Tekla was stoic. Victoria was laid to rest in the church cemetery in a handmade coffin built by her brother Lucas.

CHAPTER 15

THE DEATH OF ANTON

In the course of researching family history one comes across copies of many documents. Often these documents are seen on a computer screen or a microfilm reader. The thrill of finding an old document with an ancestors name on it can be truly exciting. Seeing copies of the marriage record for Daniel Gurba and Ewa Blonarowicz dated November 10, 1799 was a moment I'll not soon forget. But they are none the less only copies. All that pales in comparison to finding an original document describing a momentous, although sad, moment in the Gurba history. While browsing through the Alberta Archives, I found the original, handwritten will of Anton Gurba, dictated to John Nimczuk. It was written on a small yellowed scrap of paper. Anton signed it with his mark, a rather feeble X. What was emotional for me was realizing that it was written <u>mere hours</u> before his death. I was transfixed, rubbing my fingers over his X... a definite no-no from an archivist perspective. A copy of the original will, as it was written, follows this chapter.

A story emerges from its existence. Anton was ill for many days before his death. His daughter, Frances, claims that it was double pneumonia, something that could probably be cured with today's antibiotics. It is clear that Anton knew that he was dying and he summoned his neighbours, John Nimczuk and Thomas Wachowicz. Not only were these two men very close friends with Anton, they were also literate. Anton dictated his will to John who translated it into English using the legal skills he obviously picked up as one of the few "educated" men of the community. This was probably not the first time that Mr. Nimczuk would have been called upon by his community to write such a document. The will was written, as indicated at the bottom of the document, "in the house of Anton Gurba on the 10th of March 1927". Anton died the next day at the age of 69.

Joe Gurba, Anton's grandson through Lucas, has a vivid memory of the funeral that he shared with me in July 2008:

I really don't remember Grandfather Anton but I remember his funeral in March of 1927. We had traveled for about 10 hours with a team of horses and sleigh to cover the 30 miles to Skaro. On the evening before the funeral the Gurba house was filled with family, neighbours and friends. There were no funeral parlors in rural areas then so family and friends gathered to build the coffin, prepare and dress the deceased, bring food, drinks and comfort for grandmother Tekla and family; today this type of gathering would be viewed as a wake, viewing, or vigil.

I remember Anton's body laid out on the dining room table with various people praying, singing hymns and comforting each other. As a 4 ½ year old I soon lost interest and wandered upstairs where about 30 people had gathered. Someone said "Joe, sing us a song" and gave me a few coins. So I sang a number of Ukrainian funny, somewhat raunchy songs, that I had learned on my maternal grandfather Stefan Zarusky's knee. There was much clapping and laughter, and my pockets were filing with nickels and dimes. Suddenly my mother came up the stairs. "Yoseph", she said, "What are you doing? This is your Grandfather's funeral!" She took me to the woodshed and warmed my seat hard enough that I couldn't sit for a week. So I don't remember Grandpa Anton but I remember his funeral !

The next morning I remember probably 50 horse/sleigh teams pulling out of the farmyard as the funeral procession traveled the 1 ½ miles to the Skaro Ukrainian Catholic church. What a tribute and show of love and respect for this pioneer, hard worker, good neighbor and worthy ancestor of many of us!

Photographs from the funeral of Anton Gurba March 1927

Burial of Anton Gurba in the church graveyard

Several aspects of Anton's will are interesting. Even though near death, Anton was very clear in his instructions. He was specific enough for example, to bequeath 2 sleighs and one gang plow to his son Stephen. He even made provisions for his mentally challenged son, Metro, by asking Stephen "to look after and take care of" his brother. He willed each of his daughters (except for Tylda and Anne) a sum of $500 upon their marriages (probably considered by Anton to be his girl's dowry). Tylda was already married and living in the United States. Perhaps she already received her dowry. His other daughter, Anne had also already moved to the States and Anton probably felt that she wasn't entitled to a full dowry, hence willing her only $300. Maybe he had already given Anne some money to begin her new life in the United States. We will never know his reasoning. He also promised his remaining daughters that if they were to remain unmarried, they could stay at the homestead as long as they wished. Anton's final thoughts were obviously of his family and the safe well being of his daughters. (He may well have remembered that 2 of his sisters required a safe haven in their lives.)

Frances recalls that none of the girls ever received their $500 in cash. The cash just simply wasn't available. However, they received goods in kind. Frances, for example, said that she got all the wood she needed to build her house on the Radway farm, where she and her husband Nick had just moved with their young family. Frances recalls that the wood came from Lucas, but Lucas owed money to Steve. Steve offered to forgo the debt if Lucas would give Frances $500 worth of wood. She also remembers that Rosie got some farm equipment to begin her married life after she married George years later.

The 2 lots in the village of Uncas and the property near Hollow Lake referred to in the will came from the estate of Anton's son, John who died intestate in 1918. John had obviously acquired the 2 town lots in one of his business transactions that he made in his short life. Frances did say that John was more of a business man than a farmer.

When the will was probated, the value of Anton's estate was determined to be $15,457.00. When one considers, that only 25 years earlier, the North West Mounted Police declared the family near destitute, Anton and his family had begun to make great strides in their new home.

A copy of Anton's will follows on the next 2 pages. It is printed exactly as it was written. Pages 1 and 3 are on one side of the sheet and the second page of the will appears as a full page.

Scaro P.O.
Alberta

March the 10th 1927

In the matter of my Last Will

Being in possession of all my senses and knowing what I am about to do, I hereby revoke all my former wills, and I hereby bequeath all my personal and real property after payment of just debts and funeral expences

To: my wife Tekla the North half of North West (Quarter) of section 30 #
T.56 R.19 W.4 Mer. And all buildings on this section quarter (namely the North half), as also all personal and real property in the house. And also five cows. And also all the money as asset or on current.

3

The two lots which are at Luscar I give to my son Peter.

To my daughter Annie I bequeath three hundred dollars

And all the rest of the property real or personal which has not been named in this will, I leave to my wife Tekla who is to dispose of it as she will deem proper.

Anton x Gurba
    mark

Witnesses { John Minozuk
Thomas Washuruk

Made in the house of Anton Gurba on the 10th March 1927 P.O. Scaro.

TO : Stephen the South half of the West quarter of section 30, T 56, R 19 W. of 4ᵗʰ mer, and five horses, and five head of Cattle, and two wagons, two sleighs, and one Gang plow. And binder, mower & rake, Drill & packer and harrows.

It is my wish also that Stephen help Peter and Peter must help Stephen in farming for five years from date of this will.

And to Peter I bequeathe the South East quarter, section 24; T 56, R 20; and five horses, five head of Cattle, Gang plow, sulky plow, one sleigh and one wagon and disks.

And to my son Dmytro I bequeathe the North west quarter, sect. 9, T. 61, R 19, which property is to be held in Trust by Stephen who is to look after and take care of the above named Dmytro.

The North half of the South East Quarter sect 8 T. 61. R 19 I bequeath to Peter and the other half to Lucas.

TO My daughters: Mary, Rosie, Catharine and Francis I bequeathe five hundred dollars to each one of them. Which money is to be paid out by my wife from the money which are as rent or on account and this same money is to be paid out to the above named daughters when getting married

And it is also my wish that should any one or all of the above named daughters not wish to get married, then they may remain at this home if they so desire and as long as they wish.

CHAPTER 16
FAMILY TREE

The next 94 pages show the most up-to-date listing of the descendants of Daniel Gurba, up to his 5th great grandchildren. The list shows that there are 755 DIRECT LINE descendents of Daniel.....and the family tree is no where near complete as the reader will note. Additions, corrections, deletions, etc are always an ongoing project in maintaining a family tree. The author of this book always appreciates any input into the tree.

This report starts with Daniel and then moves forward through his descendents. Each direct line descendent is given a number. Children with an upcoming main entry are displayed with a "+" to the left of the child's number. For example, on the first page Daniel is assigned number 1. His son, Stefan, is assigned #2. The "+" sign indicates that Stefan had children. Going to the next page, one sees a more detailed report on Stefan and his family. Notice that Stefan had 8 children, one of whom was named Semen (assigned #8). We can tell that Semen had children, indicated by the "+" sign. Following Semen into the 3rd generation, we see that he had 6 children. As one progresses through the descendent report, a line of decendentcy appears, following the name of the direct descendent. It is written in italics. For example, finding person #103 (Robert Broda), we can determine his descendentcy from Daniel by reading the names in italics.

Descendants of Daniel Gurba

First Generation

1. Daniel Gurba, son of **Unknown** and **Unknown**, was born in 1772 in Skoloszow, Galicia and died on 11 Feb 1827 in Skoloszow, Galicia aged 55.

Daniel married **Ewa Blonarowicz** on 10 Nov 1799 in Skoloszow, Galicia. Ewa was born in 1783 in Skoloszow, Galicia and died on 27 Nov 1842 in Skoloszow, Galicia aged 59.

Children from this marriage were:

+ 2 M i. **Stefan Gurba** was born on 6 Jan 1808 in Skoloszow, Galicia and died on 28 Apr 1857 in Skoloszow, Galicia aged 49.

3 F ii. **Tatiana Gurba** was born on 1 Jan 1805 in Skoloszow, Galicia and died on 24 Jan 1805 in Skoloszow, Galicia.

4 F iii. **Pelagia Gurba** was born on 6 May 1811 in Skoloszow, Galicia.

5 M iv. **Basilius Gurba** was born on 27 Jul 1813 in Skoloszow, Galicia and died on 6 Sep 1818 in Skoloszow, Galicia aged 5.

+ 6 M v. **Simeon Gurba** was born on 10 May 1817 in Skoloszow, Galicia.

7 M vi. **Basilius Gurba** was born on 9 May 1822 in Skoloszow, Galicia and died on 10 Jul 1822 in Skoloszow, Galicia.

Second Generation (Children)

2. Stefan Gurba *(Daniel 1)* was born on 6 Jan 1808 in Skoloszow, Galicia and died on 28 Apr 1857 in Skoloszow, Galicia aged 49.

Stefan married **Maria Kosteczko** in Nov 1829 in Skoloszow, Galicia, daughter of **Elias Kosteczko** and **Anastasia Boruch**. Maria was born on 16 Feb 1810 in Skoloszow, Galicia and died on 30 Jan 1854 in Skoloszow, Galicia aged 43.

Children from this marriage were:

+ 8　M　i.　**Semen Gurba** was born on 10 Sep 1832 in Skoloszow, died on 1 Dec 1901 in Skaro, Alberta aged 69, and was buried in Exhaltation of the Holy Cross Ukrainian Catholic Church cemetery at Skaro.

　9　M　ii.　**Pantelemno Gurba** was born on 8 Aug 1830 in Skoloszow, Galicia and died on 27 May 1855 in Skoloszow, Galicia aged 24.

　10　M　iii.　**Gregorz Gurba** was born on 17 Jan 1835 in Skoloszow, Galicia.

　11　F　iv.　**Salomea Gurba** was born on 7 Sep 1837 in Skoloszow, Galicia.

　12　F　v.　**Ewa Gurba** was born on 29 Jan 1840 in Skoloszow, Galicia and died on 11 Dec 1840 in Skoloszow, Galicia.

　13　M　vi.　**Elias Gurba** was born on 3 Oct 1841 in Skoloszow, Galicia.

　14　M　vii.　**Izydor Gurba** was born on 14 Feb 1844 in Skoloszow, Galicia.

　15　F　viii.　**Anastasia Gurba** was born on 1 Jan 1847 in Skoloszow, Galicia and died on 16 Apr 1850 in Skoloszow, Galicia aged 3.

6. Simeon Gurba *(Daniel 1)* was born on 10 May 1817 in Skoloszow, Galicia. Simeon married **Franciska Kolanko**, daughter of **Unknown** and **Unknown**.

Children from this marriage were:

　16　M　i.　**Lukasz Gurba** was born on 9 Oct 1859 in Skoloszow, Galicia.

　17　M　ii.　**Jan Gurba** was born on 4 Aug 1862 in Skoloszow, Galicia.

+ 18　M iii.　**Michal Gurba** was born on 30 Oct 1864.

　19　F iv.　**Katarzyna Gurba** was born on 18 Jul 1867 in Skoloszow, Galicia.

　20　F v.　**Maria Gurba** was born on 8 May 1870 in Skoloszow, Galicia.

　21　M vi.　**Antoni Gurba** was born on 20 Sep 1871 in Skoloszow, Galicia.

+ 22   M   vii. **Jan Gurba** was born on 4 Mar 1874 in Skoloszow, Galicia.

  23   M   viii. **Mikolaj Gurba** was born on 10 May 1879 in Skoloszow, Galicia.

Third Generation (Grandchildren)

8. Semen Gurba *(Stefan 2, Daniel 1)* was born on 10 Sep 1832 in Skoloszow, died on 1 Dec 1901 in Skaro, Alberta aged 69, and was buried in Exhaltation of the Holy Cross Ukrainian Catholic Church cemetery at Skaro.

Semen married **Pelagia Chomik** on 29 Sep 1857 in Skoloszow, Galicia, daughter of **Mathias Chomik** and **Tatiana Dutko**. Pelagia was born on 17 Apr 1835 in Skoloszow, Galicia and died on 29 Jun 1863 in Skoloszow, Galicia aged 28. Another name for Pelagia was Pelagia Gurba.

Children from this marriage were:

+ 24　M　i. **Antoni Gurba** was born on 17 Oct 1858 in Skoloszow, Galicia, died on 11 Mar 1927 in Skaro, Alberta aged 68, and was buried in Exhaltation of the Holy Cross Ukrainian Catholic Church cemetary at Skaro.

+ 25　F　ii. **Anna Gurba** was born on 7 Feb 1861 in Skoloszow, Galicia, died on 14 Sep 1937 in Albion, New York, United States aged 76, and was buried in St. Joseph's Cemetery, Albion, Orleans, New York.

26　M　iii. **Jan Gurba** was born on 25 Jun 1863 in Skoloszow, Galicia and died on 26 Jun 1863 in Skoloszow, Galicia.

Semen next married **Marina Didicz** circa 1864. Marina was born on 12 Jun 1823 in Skoloszow, Galicia and died about 1880 in Galicia aged about 57. Another name for Marina was Marina Gurba.

Children from this marriage were:

+ 27　F　i. **Kate Gurba** was born in 1865 in Skoloszow, Galicia, died on 18 May 1924 in Skaro, Alberta aged 59, and was buried in the Exhaltation of the Holy Cross Ukrainian Catholic Church cemetery at Skaro.

+ 28　F　ii. **Rozalia (Rose) Gurba** was born on 24 Dec 1866 in Skoloszow, Galicia, died on 25 May 1954 in Albion, New York aged 87, and was buried in St. Joseph's Cemetery Albion, New York in the same plot with her daughters Mary Adams and Kathleen Mexwell.

+ 29　F　iii. **Sofia Gurba** was born on 12 Jan 1869 in Skoloszow, Galicia, died on 16 Dec 1956 in Canfield, Ontario aged 87, and was buried in the Blackheath United Cemetery, Binbrook, Wentworth, Ontario under the name of Sofia Dembonski..

18. Michal Gurba *(Simeon 2, Daniel 1)* was born on 30 Oct 1864.
Michal married **Katerina**.

Children from this marriage were:

+ 30 M i. **John Gurba** was born on 26 Dec 1919 in Radymno, Ukraine.

+ 31 M ii. **Walter Gurba** was born on 16 Jun 1924 in Radymno, Poland.

22. Jan Gurba *(Simeon 2, Daniel 1)* was born on 4 Mar 1874 in Skoloszow, Galicia. Jan married **Maria Jaromie**. Maria was born in 1880.

Children from this marriage were:

+ 32 M i. **John Gurba** was born in Brandon, Manitoba.

33 M ii. **Michael Gurba** was born in 1902.

34 F iii. **Katarina Gurba** was born in 1903.

35 M iv. **Wadislav Gurba** was born in 1905.

36 M v. **Miron Gurba** was born in 1909.

37 F vi. **Sofia Gurba** was born in 1911.

Fourth Generation (Great-Grandchildren)

24. Antoni Gurba *(Semen 3, Stefan 2, Daniel 1)* was born on 17 Oct 1858 in Skoloszow, Galicia, died on 11 Mar 1927 in Skaro, Alberta aged 68, and was buried in Exhaltation of the Holy Cross Ukrainian Catholic Church cemetary at Skaro.

> Antoni married **Tekla Olber** in Galicia, daughter of **Jozef Albert** and **Zofia Blonarowicz**. Tekla wasborn in 1866 in Skoloszow, Galicia, died on 1 Mar 1944 in Skaro, Alberta aged 78, and was buried in Exhaltation of the Holy Cross Ukrainian Catholic Church cemetary at Skaro. Another name for Tekla was Tekla Gurba.
>
> Children from this marriage were:

> + 38　F　i.　**Tylda Gurba** was born on 20 Aug 1890 in Skoloszow, Poland, died on 18 Apr 1960 in Gaines, New York aged 69, and was buried in Mt. Albion Cemetery, Albion, Orleans, New York.

> + 39　M　ii.　**Lucas Gurba** was born on 17 Oct 1893 in Skoloszow, Galicia, died on 25 Feb 1968 in Darling, Alberta aged 74, and was buried on 29 Feb 1968 in Holy Spirit Ukrainian Catholic Church cemetery, Darling, Alberta.

> 40　M　iii.　**Dmytro Gurba** was born on 21 Oct 1894 in Skoloszow, Galicia, died on 26 Sep 1974 in Skaro, Alberta aged 79, and was buried in Exhaltation of the Holy Cross Ukrainian Catholic Church cemetery at Skaro.

> 41　M　iv.　**Ivan Gurba** was born in 1895 in Skoloszow, Galicia, died on 15 Nov 1918 in Lamont, Alberta aged 23, and was buried in Exhaltation of the Holy Cross Ukrainian Catholic Church cemetary at Skaro.

> 42　F　v.　**Anne Gurba** was born on 22 Dec 1899 in Edna, Alberta, died on 17 Jan 1976 in Rochester New York aged 76, and was buried in Mt. Albion Cemetery, Albion, Orleans, New York.

> 43　F　vi.　**Mary Gurba** was born in Nov 1901 in Skaro, Alberta and died on 21 Apr 1955 in New Westminster, B.C. aged 53. Other names for Mary were Mary Robertson, and Mary Vanbrienen.
>
> > Mary married **Alex D. Mckeracke Robertson** in 1926. Alex died in Oct 1942 in Sexsmith (Emerson Trail Cem), Alberta.
> > Mary next married **Tony Vanbrienen**. Tony was born in 1881 and died on 15 Dec 1953 in Essendale, British Columbia aged 72.

> + 44　F　vii.　**Rose Gurba** was born on 26 Jun 1903 in Skaro, Alberta, died on 10 Apr 1990 in Radway, Alberta aged 86, and was buried on 17 Apr

1990 in Holy Ghost Ukrainian Catholic Church Cemetery, Waskatenau, Alberta.

45 F viii. **Kate Gurba** was born in May 1905 in Skaro, Alberta, died on 23 Mar 1978 in Skaro, Alberta aged 72, and was buried in Exhaltation of the Holy Cross Ukrainian Catholic Church cemetery at Skaro.

+ 46 F ix. **Francesca Gurba** was born on 1 Sep 1906 in Skaro, Alberta.

+ 47 M x. **Steve Gurba** was born on 1 Jan 1909 in Skaro, Alberta, died on 6 Oct 1978 in Redwater, Alberta aged 69, and was buried on 10 Oct 1978 in Exhaltation of the Holy Cross Ukrainian Catholic Church cemetary at Skaro.

48 M xi. **Peter Gurba** was born on 10 Jun 1910 in Skaro, Alberta, died on 10 Jul 1976 in Edmonton, Alberta aged 66, and was buried in St. Michael's Cemetery, Edmonton, Alberta.

Peter married **Emilie Chmilar**, daughter of **Harry Chmilar** and **Maria Chmilar**. Emilie was born on 18 Aug 1918 in Mundare, Alberta, died on 28 Aug 2002 in Edmonton, Alberta aged 84, and was buried on 3 Sep 2002 in St. Michael's Cemetery, Edmonton, Alberta. Another name for Emilie was Emilie Gurba.

49 F xii. **Victoria Gurba** was born on 18 Nov 1913 in Skaro, Alberta, died on 27 Jul 1923 in Skaro, Alberta aged 9, and was buried in Exhaltation of the Holy Cross Ukrainian Catholic Church cemetery at Skaro.

25. Anna Gurba *(Semen 3, Stefan 2, Daniel 1)* was born on 7 Feb 1861 in Skoloszow, Galicia, died on 14 Sep 1937 in Albion, New York, United States aged 76, and was buried in St. Joseph's Cemetery, Albion, Orleans, New York. Another name for Anna was Anna Budynski.

Anna married **Jozef Budynski**, son of **Unknown** and **Unknown**. Jozef was born on 19 Mar 1858, died on 12 Mar 1953 in Arnold Gregory Memorial Hospital, Albion, Orleans, New York aged 94, and was buried on 16 Mar 1953 in St. Joseph's Cemetery, Albion, Orleans, New York.

Children from this marriage were:

+ 50 M i. **Wladek (William) Budynski** was born on 26 Sep 1888, died on 1 Jan 1958 in Victoria, British Columbia aged 69, and was buried in Royal Oak Burial Park, Victoria, British Columbia.

+ 51 F ii. **Rose Budynski** was born on 15 Apr 1893 in Skoloszow and died on 25 Dec 1977 in San Benito, Cameron, Texas aged 84.

+ 52 M iii. **Lawrence Boden** was born on 3 Aug 1896 and died on 10 Apr 1993 in Rochester, Monroe, New York aged 96.

+ 53 F iv. **Frances A. Budynski** was born on 2 May 1902 and died on 29 Apr 1995 in Lockport, Niagara, New York aged 92.

54 F v. **Josephine (Jackie) Budynski** was born on 23 Aug 1904 and died in May 1974 in Rochester New York aged 69. Another name for Josephine was Josephine (Jackie) Temp.

Josephine married **Irving Temp**. Irving was born on 6 Feb 1914 and died 3 May 3, 1994 in Las Vegas, Nevada.

+ 55 F vi. **Florence Elizabeth Budynski** was born on 2 Feb 1907, died on 12 Sep 1993 in Medina, New York aged 86, and was buried in St. Joseph's Cemetery, Albion, Orleans, New York.

27. Kate Gurba *(Semen 3, Stefan 2, Daniel 1)* was born in 1865 in Skoloszow, Galicia, died on 18 May 1924 in Skaro, Alberta aged 59, and was buried in the Exhaltation of the Holy Cross Ukrainian Catholic Church cemetery at Skaro. Other names for Kate were Kate Danelko, and Kate Stecyk.

Kate married **Michal Danelko** before 1890, son of **Jakub Danelko** and **Maria Wolos**.

Children from this marriage were:

56 M i. **Mike Danelko** was born in Aug 1891.

+ 57 F ii. **Mary Danelko** was born on 30 Oct 1898 in Skoloszow, Galicia.

Kate next married **Matvij Stecyk** after 1900. Matvij was born in 1863, died on 29 Mar 1947 in Eldorena, Alberta aged 84, and was buried in Eldorena Ruthenian Greek Catholic Cemetery, Eldorena, Alberta.

Children from this marriage were:

58 M i. **Fred Stecyk** was born in 1904 and died in 1920 in Eldorena Ruthenian Greek Catholic Cemetery, Eldorena, Alberta aged 16.

+ 59 F ii. **Rosalia (Rosa) Stecyk** was born on 21 Sep 1906 in Skaro, Alberta, died on 10 Jul 2004 in Radway, Alberta aged 97, and was buried on 14 Jul 2004 in Protection of the Blessed Virgin Mary Ukrainian Catholic Cemetary, Eldorena, Alberta (aka Elderena Ruthernian Gr. Catholic Cemetery).

28. Rozalia (Rose) Gurba *(Semen 3, Stefan 2, Daniel 1)* was born on 24 Dec 1866 in Skoloszow, Galicia, died on 25 May 1954 in Albion, New York aged 87, and was buried in St. Joseph's Cemetery Albion, New York in the same plot with her daughters Mary Adams and Kathleen Mexwell. Other names for Rozalia were Rose Czternastek, and Rose Rombalski.

Rozalia married **Paul Czternastek** about 1889. Paul was born on 22 Jul 1864, died on 12 Jan 1906 aged 41, and was buried in St. Stanislaus Roman Catholic Cemetery, Round Hill, Alberta (in unmarked plot 07, 05).

Children from this marriage were:

+ 60 F i. **Annie Czternastek** was born on 10 Jun 1890, died on 10 Oct 1969 aged 79, and was buried in St. Stanislaus Roman Catholic Cemetery, Round Hill, Alberta.

+ 61 F ii. **Mary Czternastek** was born on 6 Jan 1894, died in 1971 aged 77, and was buried in St. Joseph's Cemetery, Albion, New York in the same plot as her mother Rozalia and her sister Kathleen Maxwell..

+ 62 F iii. **Kathleen P. Czternastek** was born on 4 May 1895, died on 12 May 1996 in Fairport, Monroe, New York aged 101, and was buried in St. Joseph's Cemetery, Albion, New York in the same plot as her mother Rozalia and sister Mary Adams..

63 F iv. **Sylvia H. Czternastek (Stenask)** was born on 1 Jun 1900, died in Jun 1981 in Albion, New York aged 81, and was buried in St. Joseph's Cemetery, Albion, New York in the same plot as her brother Clarence and sister Josephine Clarke.

+ 64 F v. **Francis Czternastek** was born on 8 May 1901 and died in 1970 aged 69.

65 F vi. **Josephine Czternastek** was born on 18 Jul 1903 and died on 10 Feb 1996 in Lockport, Niagara, New York aged 92. Another name for Josephine was Josephine Clarke. Josephine married **Oliver Clarke.**

Rozalia next married **Anton Rombalski** about 1907, son of **Unknown** and **Unknown.** Anton was born on 14 Dec 1857 in Prussia, died on 14 Feb 1921 in Glanford, Ontario aged 63, and was buried on 16 Feb 1921 in Blackheath United Cemetery, Binbrook, Wentworth, Ontario.

Children from this marriage were:

+ 66 M i. **Anthony Joseph Romball** was born on 1 Apr 1908 and died on 7 Jul 1989 in Mesa, Arizona aged 81.

+ 67 M ii. **Clarence B. Romball** was born on 3 Feb 1910, died in Mar 1981 in Rochester, New York aged 71, and was buried in St. Joseph's Cemetery, Albion, Orleans, New York in the same plot as his sisters Sylvia and Josepehine.

29. Sofia Gurba *(Semen 3, Stefan 2, Daniel 1)* was born on 12 Jan 1869 in Skoloszow, Galicia, died on 16 Dec 1956 in Canfield, Ontario aged 87, and was buried in the

Blackheath United Cemetery, Binbrook, Wentworth, Ontario under the name of Sofia Dembonski.. Another name for Sofia was Sofia Dombrosky.

Sofia married **John Dombrosky**. John was born in 1856, died on 17 Jul 1933 aged 77, and was buried on 20 Jul 1933 in St. Joachim's Cemetery, Edmonton (in unmarked plot 01A, 055B).

Children from this marriage were:

68 F i. **Margaret Dombrosky** was born on 3 Apr 1895 and died in Aylmer, Ontario. Another name for Margaret was Margaret Showolter.

Margaret married **Patrick Showolter**.

+ 69 F ii. **Nancy Dombrosky** was born on 24 Aug 1899, died on 1 Feb 1919 aged 19, and was buried in St. Mary's Ruthenian Greek Catholic Cemetery, Star, Alberta.

70 F iii. **Rosie Dombrosky** was born in 1901 and died in 1916 aged 15.

+ 71 F iv. **Ksenia (Cassie) Dombrosky** was born in 1903 and died in 1990 in Dunville, Ontario aged 87.

+ 72 F v. **Tillie Dombrosky** was born on 25 Apr 1905, died in 2003 aged 98, and was buried in Evergreen Cemetery, Edmonton.

+ 73 F vi. **Bessie Dombrosky** was born in 1907.

74 M vii. **Michael Dombrosky** was born in Aug 1910 and died in Jun 1911.

75 F viii. **Pearl Dombrosky** was born in 1912 and died in 1912.

76 F ix. **Lillian Dombrosky** was born in 1914. Other names for Lillian are Lillian Burick, Lillian Becker, and Lillian Dryer.

Lillian married **John Burick**.

Lillian next married **Harry Becker**

Lillian next married **Ed Dryer**.

77 F x. **Stephanie Dombrosky** was born in 1910 and died in 1910.

30. John Gurba *(Michal 3, Simeon 2, Daniel 1)* was born on 26 Dec 1919 in Radymno, Ukraine.

John married **Hilda Zerbst**. Hilda was born on 11 Oct 1924 in Sarbia, Poland. Another name for Hilda is Hilda Gurba.

Children from this marriage were:

+ 78 M i. **Alexander John Gurba** was born on 14 Sep 1954 in Edmonton, Alberta.

79 M ii. **Andry Steven Gurba** was born on 9 Jan 1957 in Edmonton, Alberta.

80 F iii. **Katharine Marie Gurba** was born on 8 Jul 1958 in Edmonton, Alberta.

31. Walter Gurba *(Michal 3, Simeon 2, Daniel 1)* was born on 16 Jun 1924 in Radymno, Poland.
Walter married **Henrietta Kaminska** on 11 Oct 1962 in Gdansk, Poland. Henrietta was born on 19 Jan 1930 in Todz, Poland.

The child from this marriage was:

81 M i. **Alexander Gurba** was born on 31 Mar 1963.

32. John Gurba *(Jan 3, Simeon 2, Daniel 1)* was born in Brandon, Manitoba.

John married someone
His child was:

+ 82 M i. **James Gurba**.

Fifth Generation (Great Great-Grandchildren)

38. Tylda Gurba *(Antoni 4, Semen 3, Stefan 2, Daniel 1)* was born on 20 Aug 1890 in Skoloszow, Poland, died on 18 Apr 1960 in Gaines, New York aged 69, and was buried in Mt. Albion Cemetery, Albion, Orleans, New York. Another name for Tylda was Tylda Budynski.

> Tylda married **Michael Budynski** in 1912, son of **Mike Budynski** and **Anna Kontek**. Michael was born in 1890, died on 18 Jan 1958 in Albion, New York aged 68, and was buried in Mt. Albion Cemetery, Albion, Orleans, New York.
>
> Children from this marriage were:
>
> 83   M   i.   **Victor Budynski** was born on 5 Jan 1912, died on 16 Apr 1969 in Albion, New York aged 57, and was buried in Mt. Albion Cemetery, Albion, Orleans, New York.
>
> 84   M   ii.   **Carl Budynski** was born on 28 Feb 1913, died on 21 Jul 1965 in Albion, New York aged 52, and was buried in Mt. Albion Cemetery, Albion, Orleans, New York.
>
> + 85   F   iii.   **Jean Budynski** was born on 5 May 1915 and died on 23 Apr 1968 in Niagara Falls, New York aged 52.
>
> 86   M   iv.   **Burnett Budynski** was born on 30 Apr 1916, died on 18 Jun 1956 in Buffalo, New York aged 40, and was buried in Mt. Albion Cemetery, Albion, Orleans, New York.
>
> + 87   F   v.   **Mildred Budynski** was born on 15 Oct 1917, died on 12 Jan 1995 in Albion, New York aged 77, and was buried in Mt. Albion Cemetery, Albion, Orleans, New York.
>
> + 88   M   vi.   **Earl Budynski** was born on 2 Mar 1922 in Waterport, N.Y., died on 3 Nov 1997 in Medina, Orleans, New York aged 75, and was buried in Mt. Albion Cemetery, Albion, Orleans, New York.

39. Lucas Gurba *(Antoni 4, Semen 3, Stefan 2, Daniel 1)* was born on 17 Oct 1893 in Skoloszow, Galicia, died on 25 Feb 1968 in Darling, Alberta aged 74, and was buried on 29 Feb 1968 in Holy Spirit Ukrainian Catholic Church cemetery, Darling, Alberta.

> Lucas married **Pearl Zarusky** on 3 Jun 1917 in St. Onufrey Ukrainian Catholic Church, Smoky Lake, daughter of **Stefan Zarusky** and **Palahia Strychar**. Pearl was born on 14 Oct 1898 in Sosnytsia, Jaroslaw, died on 1 May 1992 in Radway, Alberta aged 93, and was buried on 4 May 1992 in Holy Spirit Ukrainian Catholic Church cemetery, Darling, Alberta. Another name for Pearl was Pearl Gurba.
>
> Children from this marriage were:
>
> + 89   F   i.   **Pauline Gurba** was born on 23 Apr 1918 in Hollow Lake, Alberta.

+ 90 F ii. **Lily Gurba** was born on 9 Sep 1920 in Hollow Lake, Alberta, died on 10 Sep 2005 in Radway, Alberta aged 85, and was buried on 15 Sep 2005 in Nativity BV Mary Ruthenian Greek Catholic Cemetery, Newbrook (nearby Darling, Alberta).

+ 91 M iii. **Joseph Gurba** was born on 8 Nov 1922 in Hollow Lake, Alberta.

+ 92 M iv. **Bill Gurba** was born on 20 Mar 1925 in Hollow Lake, Alberta.

+ 93 F v. **Nettie Gurba** was born on 24 Dec 1926 in Hollow Lake, Alberta.

94 M vi. **Walter Gurba** was born in 1931 in Hollow Lake, Alberta, died in 1932 aged 1, and was buried in Holy Spirit Ukrainian Catholic Church cemetery, Darling, Alberta.

+ 95 F vii. **Olga Tillie Gurba** was born on 16 Oct 1932 in Hollow Lake, Alberta.

+ 96 M viii. **Paul Bohdan Gurba** was born on 11 Sep 1937 in Hollow Lake, Alberta, died on 1 Jul 1991 in Edmonton, Alberta aged 53, and was buried on 7 Jul 1991 in St. Michael's Cemetery, Edmonton, Alberta.

+ 97 M ix. **Peter Roman Gurba** was born on 11 Sep 1937 in Hollow Lake, Alberta.

+ 98 M x. **Maurice Gurba** was born on 19 Jan 1942 in Radway, Alberta.

44. Rose Gurba *(Antoni 4, Semen 3, Stefan 2, Daniel 1)* was born on 26 Jun 1903 in Skaro, Alberta, died on 10 Apr 1990 in Radway, Alberta aged 86, and was buried on 17 Apr 1990 in Holy Ghost Ukrainian Catholic Church Cemetery, Waskatenau, Alberta. Another name for Rose was Rose Wenger.

Rose married **George Wenger** on 28 Jul 1937, son of **Fred Wenger** and **Mary Wenger**. George was born on 18 Apr 1899 in Malniw, Galicia, died on 25 May 1987 in Radway, Alberta aged 88, and was buried in Holy Ghost Ukrainian Catholic Church Cemetery, Waskatenau, Alberta.

Children from this marriage were:

+ 99 M i. **Nester F. Wenger** was born on 21 Feb 1938 in Danube, Alberta.

100 F ii. **Ann Wenger** was born on 28 Jul 1940 in Danube, Alberta. Another name for Ann is Ann McPherson.
Ann married **Angus McPherson** on 5 Aug 1972 in Edmonton, Alberta. Angus was born on 22 Jan 1943 in Spy Hill, Saskatchewan.

+ 101 F iii. **Rose Wenger** was born on 11 Apr 1942 in Danube, Alberta.

46. Francesca Gurba *(Antoni 4, Semen 3, Stefan 2, Daniel 1)* was born on 1 Sep 1906 in Skaro, Alberta. Another name for Francesca is Francesca Bezborodka.

Francesca married **Nick Bezborodka** on 19 May 1928 in Edmonton, Alberta, son of **Michael Bezborodka** and **Pearl Rozka**. Nick was born on 7 Jun 1905 in Edmonton, Alberta, died on 15 Jun 1956 in Radway, Alberta aged 51, and was buried on 19 Jun 1956 in Holy Ascension Ukrainian Orthodox Cemetery, Radway, Alberta.

Children from this marriage were:

+ 102　F　i.　**Helen Bezborodka** was born on 24 Apr 1928 in Edmonton, Alberta, died on 1 Feb 1979 in Edmonton, Alberta aged 50, and was buried on 5 Feb 1979 in St. Michael's Cemetery, Edmonton, Alberta.

+ 103　M　ii.　**Peter Robert Broda** was born on 12 Jul 1929 in Edmonton, Alberta.

+ 104　F　iii.　**Mae Mary-Pearl Bezborodka** was born on 22 Jun 1931 in Radway, Alberta.

47. Steve Gurba *(Antoni 4, Semen 3, Stefan 2, Daniel 1)* was born on 1 Jan 1909 in Skaro, Alberta, died on 6 Oct 1978 in Redwater, Alberta aged 69, and was buried on 10 Oct 1978 in Exhaltation of the Holy Cross Ukrainian Catholic Church cemetary at Skaro.

Steve married **Sophie Wenger** on 4 May 1934, daughter of **Teodor Wenger** and **Annie Kozoway**. Sophie was born on 25 Jul 1914 in Radway, Alberta, died on 20 Sep 2005 in Redwater Lamont, Alberta aged 91, and was buried on 23 Sep 2005 in Exhaltation of the Holy Cross Ukrainian Catholic Church c emetery at Skaro. Another name for Sophie was Sophie Gurba.

Children from this marriage were:

105　M　i.　**Anthony Gurba** was born in 1934 in Lamont, Alberta, died in 1938 in Skaro, Alberta aged 4, and was buried in Exhaltation of the Holy Cross Ukrainian Catholic Church cemetery at Skaro.

+ 106　M　ii.　**Walter Gurba** was born on 29 Jun 1935 in Lamont, Alberta.

+ 107　M　iii.　**Raymond Gurba** was born on 12 Feb 1938 in Lamont, Alberta.

+ 108　M　iv.　**Eugene Adolf Gurba** was born on 4 Dec 1940 in Lamont, Alberta.

+ 109　F　v.　**Sylvia Gurba** was born on 11 Jun 1942 in Lamont, Alberta, died on 18 Nov 1992 in Edmonton, Alberta aged 50, and was cremated on 23 Nov 1992 in Edmonton, Alberta.

+ 110   M   vi.   **Sylvester Gurba** was born on 6 Dec 1943 in Lamont, Alberta.

111   M   vii.   **Michael Gurba** was born on 3 Nov 1952 in Skaro, Alberta, died on 19 Apr 1996 in Edmonton, Alberta aged 43, and was cremated on 23 Apr 1996 in Edmonton, Alberta but interred at Exhaltation of the Holy Cross Ukrainian Catholic Church Cemetery at Skaro.

Michael married **Barbara Temple** on 9 Nov 1985. Barbara was born on 14 Oct 1953 in New Westminister, British Columbia. Another name for Barbara is Barbara Gurba

.
50. Wladek (William) Budynski *(Anna Gurba 4, Semen 3, Stefan 2, Daniel 1)* was born on 26 Sep 1888, died on 1 Jan 1958 in Victoria, British Columbia aged 69, and was buried in Royal Oak Burial Park, Victoria, British Columbia.

Wladek married **Sally (Salomina, Sylvia) Plachner**. Sally was born on 20 Jun 1895 and died on 21 Jun 1955 in Saanich, British Columbia aged 60. Another name for Sally was Sally Budynski.

Children from this marriage were:

+ 112   M   i.   **Louie Budynski** was born in 1911 and died in 1981 aged 70

+ 113   M   ii.   **Kaizer (Clarence) Budynski** was born on 29 Jul 1915, died on 19 Jun 1967 in Victoria, British Columbia aged 51, and was buried in Royal Oak Burial Park, Victoria, British Columbia.

114   F   iii.   **Anna Budynski** was born in 1917 and died in 1934 aged 17.

+ 115   F   iv.   **Marie Budynski** was born on 26 Mar 1919.

+ 116   F   v.   **Joan (Josie) Budynski** was born on 25 Apr 1921, died on 16 Jan 1996 aged 74, and was buried in French Creek Cemetery, Parksville, British Columbia.

+ 117   M   vi.   **Joseph Lawrence Budynski** was born in 1913, died on 30 Dec 1975 in Victoria, British Columbia aged 62, and was buried in Royal Oak Burial Park, Victoria, British Columbia.

+ 118   F   vii.   **Virginia (Ginnie) Budynski** was born on 7 Sep 1926.

51. Rose Budynski *(Anna Gurba 4, Semen 3, Stefan 2, Daniel 1)* was born on 15 Apr 1893 in Skoloszow and died on 25 Dec 1977 in San Benito, Cameron, Texas aged 84. Another name for Rose was Rose Mack.
Rose married **Vincent Wilford Mack** on 20 Nov 1910 in Round Hill, Alberta, son of **Francizek (Frank) Mack** and **Elzbieta Bartnick**. Vincent was born on 17 Apr 1889 in Galicia and died on 4 Aug 1983 in SanBenito, Cameron, Texas aged 94.

Children from this marriage were:

119   F   i.   **Florence Mack** was born on 15 Sep 1911 in New York and died on 3 Oct 1988 in Harlingen, Texas aged 77. Another name for Florence was Florence Fay.

         Florence married **Ed Fay**. Ed was born in 1904 and died on 8 Feb 1991 aged 87.

+ 120   M   ii.   **Carl Anthony Mack** was born on 22 May 1913 and died on 7 Feb 1997 in Spokane, Washington aged 83.

+ 121   M   iii.   **Nestor Mack** was born on 10 Jun 1915 in New York and died on 29 Feb 1984 in Harlingen, Texas aged 68.

+ 122   F   iv.   **Verna Mack** was born on 30 May 1917 in Colebrook, Ohio and died on 6 Jan 1998 in Harlingen, Texas aged 80.

+ 123   F   v.   **Helen Mack** was born on 17 Jul 1919.

+ 124   M   vi.   **Wilfred (Will) Barney Mack** was born on 28 Feb 1920 and died on 22 Mar 1999 in Harlingen, Texas aged 79.

+ 125   F   vii.   **Stella Bernice Mack** was born on 7 Feb 1923 in New York and died on 2 Feb 1993 in Harlingen, Texas aged 69.

+ 126   M   viii.   **Edward A. Mack** was born on 22 Jan 1924.

+ 127   M   ix.   **Florian Sy Mack** was born on 22 Feb 1926 in Ridgeway, New York and died on 15 Sep 2006 aged 80.

+ 128   F   x.   **Gloria Mack** was born on 8 Jan 1930 and died on 18 Dec 1967 in San Antonio, Texas aged 37.

52. Lawrence Boden *(Anna Gurba 4, Semen 3, Stefan 2, Daniel 1)* was born on 3 Aug 1896 and died on 10 Apr 1993 in Rochester, Monroe, New York aged 96.

Lawrence married **Annie Brenda**. Annie was born on 22 Dec 1901 and died in Sep 1984 in Rochester, Monroe, New York aged 82.

Children from this marriage were:

129   M   i.   **Lawrence F. (Bud) Budynski** was born in 1924.

+ 130   F   ii.   **Adele Boden** was born in 1926.

53. Frances A. Budynski *(Anna Gurba 4, Semen 3, Stefan 2, Daniel 1)* was born on 2 May 1902 and died on 29Apr 1995 in Lockport, Niagara, New York aged 92. Another name for Frances was Frances Britt.

Frances married **Thomas F. Britt** on 21 Apr 1927. Thomas was born on 5 Aug 1900 and died on 24 Jul 1989 in Lockport, Niagara, New York aged 88.

Children from this marriage were:

131 F i. **Marcia Fay Britt** was born on 15 Dec 1927.

+ 132 F ii. **Mary Anne Britt** was born on 11 Apr 1929.

133 M iii. **Franklin Britt** was born on 25 Jul 1933 and died on 27 Feb 2002 in Gasport. Niagara, New York aged 68.

+ 134 F iv. **Elizabeth Loretta Britt** was born on 21 Sep 1935.

135 M v. **William Britt** was born on 25 May 1937.

55. Florence Elizabeth Budynski *(Anna Gurba 4, Semen 3, Stefan 2, Daniel 1)* was born on 2 Feb 1907, died on12 Sep 1993 in Medina, New York aged 86, and was buried in St. Joseph's Cemetery, Albion, Orleans, New York.

Florence married **Jim Ciesielski-Schultz**, son of **Casmir (Mike) Ciesielski** and **Frances Romanowski**. Jim was born on 6 Dec 1902, died on 5 Aug 1984 in Medina, New York aged 81, and was buried in St. Joseph's Cemetery, Albion, Orleans, New York.

The child from this marriage was:

136 M i. **Joseph James Ciesielski** was born on 6 Jun 1927 and died on 3 Jun 2007 in Gasport, Niagara, New York aged 79.

57. Mary Danelko *(Kate Gurba 4, Semen 3, Stefan 2, Daniel 1)* was born on 30 Oct 1898 in Skoloszow, Galicia.

Mary married **? Darby.**

Children from this marriage were:

137 M i. **Donald Darby** died in 1942.

138 F ii. **Pearl Darby.**

59. Rosalia (Rosa) Stecyk *(Kate Gurba 4, Semen 3, Stefan 2, Daniel 1)* was born on 21 Sep 1906 in Skaro, Alberta, died on 10 Jul 2004 in Radway, Alberta aged 97, and was buried on 14 Jul 2004 in Protection of the Blessed Virgin Mary Ukrainian Catholic Cemetary, Eldorcna, Alberta (aka Elderena Ruthernian Gr. Catholic Cemetery). Another name for Rosalia was Rosalia Boychuk.

Rosalia married **Fred Boychuk** in 1924. Fred was born in 1890 in Slobodzia, Czernowitz, Austria, died on 6 May 1966 in Eldorena, Alberta aged 76, and was buried in Protection of the Blessed Virgin Mary Ukrainian Catholic Cemetery, Eldorena, Alberta (aka Elderena Ruthernian Gr. Catholic Cemetery).

Children from this marriage were:

+ 139 M i. **John Boychuk** was born on 16 Jun 1925 in Hardyville.

+ 140 F ii. **Antonia Boychuk** was born in 1927 in Radway, Alberta, died in 2007 aged 80, and was buried in Evergreen Cemetery, Edmonton, Alberta.

+ 141 M iii. **Steve Boychuk** was born in 1928, died on 23 Jan 2004 in Edmonton, Alberta aged 76, and was cremated on 28 Jan 2004 in with inurnment at St. Michael's Cemetary, Edmonton, Alberta.

+ 142 F iv. **Mary Boychuk** was born in 1930.

+ 143 F v. **Winnie Boychuk** was born in 1932.

+ 144 M vi. **Paul Boychuk** was born in 1935.

+ 145 M vii. **George Boychuk** was born in 1938.

+ 146 M viii. **Sandy Boychuk** was born in 1940.

+ 147 F ix. **Alexandra Boychuk** was born in 1942.

+ 148 F x. **Gloria Boychuk** was born in 1946.

149 M xi. **Doug Boychuk** was born in 1948.

+ 150 F xii. **Elizabeth Boychuk** was born in 1951.

60. Annie Czternastek *(Rozalia (Rose) Gurba 4, Semen 3, Stefan 2, Daniel 1)* was born on 10 Jun 1890, died on 10 Oct 1969 aged 79, and was buried in St. Stanislaus Roman Catholic Cemetery, Round Hill, Alberta. Another name for Annie was Annie Piontkowski.

Annie married **Anton Piontkowski**. Anton was born on 12 Jan 1885, died on 8 Jul 1943 aged 58, and was buried in St. Stanislaus Roman Catholic Cemetery, Round Hill, Alberta.

Children from this marriage were:

+ 151 F i. **Julia Piontkowski** was born on 11 Jun 1907 and died on 15 May 1990 aged 82.

152　M　ii.　**Clarence Pointkoski** was born on 14 Jul 1908, died on 3 Mar 2003 in Round Hill, Alberta aged 94, and was buried on 7 Mar 2003 in St. Stanislaus Roman Catholic Cemetery, Round Hill, Alberta.

+ 153　M　iii.　**John Piontkowski (Point)** was born on 12 Dec 1909.

154　F　iv.　**Florence Piontkowski** was born in 1912 and died in 1951 aged 39.

+ 155　M　v.　**Edward Piontkowski** was born on 27 May 1914 in Round Hill, Alberta, died on 24 Jul 2005 in Camrose, Alberta aged 91, and was buried on 29 Jul 2005 in St. Stanislaus Roman Catholic Cemetery, Round Hill, Alberta.

156　F　vi.　**Helen Piontkowski** was born on 15 Feb 1916. Other names for Helen are Helen Steer, and Helen Kosinski.

Helen married **Sam Steer**. Sam was born on 4 Jan 1903 and died on 17 Jan 1980 aged 77.

Helen next married **Stan Kosinski**. Stan was born on 5 Aug. 1924.

+ 157　M　vii.　**Frederick Paul Pointkoski** was born on 17 Mar 1918, died on 24 Nov 2004 in Edmonton, Alberta aged 86, and was buried on 26 Nov 2004 in Camrose Cemetary, Camrose, Alberta.

+ 158　M　viii.　**Walter Piontkowski** was born on 5 Aug 1919 and died on 3 Mar 2000 aged 80.

+ 159　F　ix.　**Margaret Piontkowski** was born on 24 Nov 1920.

160　M　x.　**Joseph Piontkowski** was born on 23 Nov 1924.

Joseph married **Sophie Bayron**. Sophie was born on 13 Oct 1926.

+ 161　F　xi.　**Bernice Piontkowski** was born on 20 Dec 1928.

---

61. Mary Czternastek *(Rozalia (Rose) Gurba 4, Semen 3, Stefan 2, Daniel 1)* was born on 6 Jan 1894, died in 1971 aged 77, and was buried in St. Joseph's Cemetery, Albion, New York in the same plot as her mother Rozalia and her sister Kathleen Maxwell.. Another name for Mary was Mary (Adamoski) Adams.

Mary married **Mike (Adamoski) Adams**. Mike was born in 1889.

Children from this marriage were:

+ 162   M   i.   **Carl (Adamoski) Adams** was born on 7 Apr 1913, died in Jan 1984 in Batavia, Genesee, New York aged 70, and was buried in St. Joseph's Cemetery, Albion, Orleans, New York.

163   M   ii.   **Stanley (Adamoski) Adams** was born in 1914 and died in 1922 in Hillyard, Alberta aged 8.

+ 164   M   iii.   **Steve E. (Adamoski) Adams** was born on 2 Sep 1916 and died on 11 Aug 2002 in Spencerport, Monroe, New York aged 85.

62. Kathleen P. Czternastek *(Rozalia (Rose) Gurba 4, Semen 3, Stefan 2, Daniel 1)* was born on 4 May 1895, died on 12 May 1996 in Fairport, Monroe, New York aged 101, and was buried in St. Joseph's Cemetery, Albion, New York in the same plot as her mother Rozalia and sister Mary Adams.. Another name for Kathleen was Kathleen Maxwell.

Kathleen married **Clark Maxwell**.

The child from this marriage was:

+ 165   M   i. **J ohn Maxwell** was born in 1928

.

64. Francis Czternastek *(Rozalia (Rose) Gurba 4, Semen 3, Stefan 2, Daniel 1)* was born on 8 May 1901 and died in 1970 aged 69. Another name for Francis was Francis Johnson.

Francis married **Percy Johnson**.

Children from this marriage were:

+ 166   F   i.   **Marlene Johnson**.

167   F   ii.   **Patricia Johnson**.

Patricia married **Steinhorst**.

66. Anthony Joseph Romball *(Rozalia (Rose) Gurba 4, Semen 3, Stefan 2, Daniel 1)* was born on 1 Apr 1908 and died on 7 Jul 1989 in Mesa, Arizona aged 81.

Anthony married **Mary Francis Langowski**. Mary was born on 12 May 1916 and died on 3 Dec 1988 in   Winnona, Minnesota aged 72. Another name for Mary was Mary Francis Romball.

Children from this marriage were:

+ 168   M   i.   **James Phillip Romball** was born on 6 May 1945.

+ 169 M ii. **Tony Jr. Romball** was born on 20 Sep 1947, died on 7 Apr 1976 in South Minneapolis, Minnesota aged 28, and was buried on 12 Apr 1976.

170 F iii. **Patricia Anne Romball** was born on 20 Apr 1951 in Winona, Minnesota and died in Mesa, Arizona. Another name for Patricia was Patricia Anne Nowak.

Patricia married **Nowak**.

67. Clarence B. Romball *(Rozalia (Rose) Gurba 4, Semen 3, Stefan 2, Daniel 1)* was born on 3 Feb 1910, died in Mar 1981 in Rochester, New York aged 71, and was buried in St. Joseph's Cemetery, Albion, Orleans, New York in the same plot as his sisters Sylvia and Josepehine.
Clarence married **Mary Brenda ??**. Mary was born on 19 Jul 1909.

Children from this marriage were:

171 F i. **Brenda Romball** was born on 3 Sep 1940. Another name for Brenda is Brenda Stringfield.

Brenda married **William Stringfield**.

172 F ii. **Carol Romball** was born on 27 Sep 1942. Another name for Carol is Carol Weigle.

Carol married **William Weigle**.

69. Nancy Dombrosky *(Sofia Gurba 4, Semen 3, Stefan 2, Daniel 1)* was born on 24 Aug 1899, died on 1 Feb 1919 aged 19, and was buried in St. Mary's Ruthenian Greek Catholic Cemetery, Star, Alberta.

Nancy married **Michael Tychkowsky**. Michael was born in 1892, died on 23 Feb 1987 aged 95, and was buried in Old Fort Saskatchewan Cemetery, Fort Saskatchewan, Alberta.

Children from this marriage were:

173 M i. **David Tychkowsky** was born in 1918 and died in 1918.

174 F ii. **Rose Tychkowsky** was born 1919 ?, died 1919 ?, and was buried in St. Mary's Ruthenian Greek Catholic Cemetery, Star, Alberta in a plot that is next to Nancy (with the inscription "daughter of M & N Tychkowski").

71. Ksenia (Cassie) Dombrosky *(Sofia Gurba 4, Semen 3, Stefan 2, Daniel 1)* was born in 1903 and died in 1990in Dunville, Ontario aged 87.

Ksenia married **Michael Tychkowsky**. Michael was born in 1892, died on 23 Feb 1987 aged 95, and was buried in Old Fort Saskatchewan Cemetery, Fort Saskatchewan, Alberta.

Children from this marriage were:

175 F   i. **Marie Tychkowsky** was born on 30 May 1920, died on 27 Nov 1920, and was buried in St. Mary's Ruthenian Greek Catholic Cemetery, Star, Alberta.

+ 176 M ii. **Walter Tychkowsky** was born in 1922 and died in Warspite, Alberta.

+ 177 F iii. **Lena Tychkowsky** was born in 1924.

+ 178 M iv. **George Tychkowsky** was born in 1926.

+ 179 M v. **Adam Tychkowsky** was born in 1928.

180 M vi. **Russel Tychkowsky** was born in 1929 and died in 1971 in Wentworth, Ontario aged 42.

181 F vii. **Emily Tychkowsky** was born in 1932.

+ 182 F viii. **Francis Tychkowsky** was born in 1933.

+ 183 M ix. **Nestor Tychkowsky** was born in 1937 and died in 1984 aged 47.

72. Tillie Dombrosky *(Sofia Gurba 4, Semen 3, Stefan 2, Daniel 1)* was born on 25 Apr 1905, died in 2003 aged 98, and was buried in Evergreen Cemetery, Edmonton.

Tillie married **Stanley Frank Dziwenka**. Stanley was born in 1900, died on 4 Feb 1990 in Edmonton, Alberta aged 90, and was buried in Evergreen Cemetery, Edmonton.

Children from this marriage were:

+ 184 M i. **Eddie Dziwenka** died in Sep 1999 in Edmonton, Alberta and was buried on 1 Oct 1999 in Evergreen Cemetery, Edmonton.

+ 185 F ii. **Emma Dziwenka** was born in 1930.

73. Bessie Dombrosky *(Sofia Gurba 4, Semen 3, Stefan 2, Daniel 1)* was born in 1907.

Bessie married **Bill McNee**.

Children from this marriage were:

+ 186 F i. **Pat McNee**.

187   F   ii.   **Judy McNee**.

78. Alexander John Gurba *(John 4, Michal 3, Simeon 2, Daniel 1)* was born on 14 Sep 1954 in Edmonton, Alberta.

Alexander married **Sheila Martha Zieper**. Sheila was born on 3 Dec 1956 in Edmonton, Alberta. Another name for Sheila is Sheila Martha Gurba.

Children from this marriage were:

188   M   i.   **Lucas Kevin Gurba** was born on 6 Mar 1985 in Edmonton, Alberta.

189   F   ii.   **Nadya Lina Gurba** was born on 14 Sep 1986 in Edmonton, Alberta.

82. James Gurba *(John 4, Jan 3, Simeon 2, Daniel 1)*.

James married someone

His child was:

190   F   i.   **Sue Gurba**.

Sixth Generation (3rd Great-Grandchildren)

85. Jean Budynski *(Tylda Gurba 5, Antoni 4, Semen 3, Stefan 2, Daniel 1)* was born on 5 May 1915 and died on 23 Apr 1968 in Niagara Falls, New York aged 52. Another name for Jean was Jean Prosser.

> Jean married **George Keymel**. George was born on 29 Mar 1915 and died on 1 Jun 1988 aged 73.
>
> The child from this marriage was:
>
> + 191   F   i.   **Joy Keymel** was born in Jun 1941.
>
> Jean next married **Elmer Prosser**. Elmer was born on 22 Nov 1910 and died in Sep 1983 in Lockport, Niagara, New York aged 72.

87. Mildred Budynski *(Tylda Gurba 5, Antoni 4, Semen 3, Stefan 2, Daniel 1)* was born on 15 Oct 1917, died on 12 Jan 1995 in Albion, New York aged 77, and was buried in Mt. Albion Cemetery, Albion, Orleans, New York.

> Mildred married **Ralph Eibl** on 12 Aug 1939 in Albion, New York, son of **John Eibl** and **Katherine**. Ralph was born on 24 May 1915, died on 31 May 1999 in Brockport, Orleans, New York aged 84, and was buried in Mt. Albion Cemetery, Albion, Orleans, New York.
>
> Children from this marriage were:
>
> 192   M   i.   **Roger Eibl**.
>
> 193   F   ii.   **Gail Eibl**.
>
> 194   M   iii.   **Allan Eibl** was born in 1951, died on 31 Dec 1979 in Yates, New York aged 28, and was buried in Mt. Albion Cemetery, Albion, Orleans, New York.

88. Earl Budynski *(Tylda Gurba 5, Antoni 4, Semen 3, Stefan 2, Daniel 1)* was born on 2 Mar 1922 in Waterport, N.Y., died on 3 Nov 1997 in Medina, Orleans, New York aged 75, and was buried in Mt. Albion Cemetery, Albion, Orleans, New York.

> Earl married **Laura Kokoszka** on 30 Oct 1948. Laura was born on 4 Jul 1921, died on 17 Aug 1989 in Medina, Orleans, New York aged 68, and was buried I n Mt. Albion Cemetery, Albion, Orleans, New York.
>
> Another name for Laura was Laura Budynski.
>
> Children from this marriage were:

195   M   i.   **Michael Budynski** was born in 1950.

196   M   ii.   **Gary Budynski** was born in 1951.

197   F   iii.   **Laura Budynski** was born in 1956.

Laura married **Rodney Daniels** on 30 Nov 1984 in Hawaii.

89. Pauline Gurba *(Lucas 5, Antoni 4, Semen 3, Stefan 2, Daniel 1)* was born on 23 Apr 1918 in Hollow Lake, Alberta. Another name for Pauline is Pauline Gordash.

Pauline married **John Gordash** on 24 Nov 1936 in Garden Park, Alberta. John was born on 14 Sep 1913 in Winnipeg, Manitoba, died on 8 Dec 1989 in Redwater, Alberta aged 76, and was buried on 13 Dec 1989 in Darling Catholic Cemetery, Darling, Alberta.

Children from this marriage were:

+ 198   F   i.   **Evelyn Marie Gordash** was born on 3 Jul 1938 in Radway, Alberta.

199   M   ii.   **Maurice David Gordash** was born on 14 Jan 1941 in Darling, Alberta.

+ 200   M   iii.   **Joseph John Gordash** was born on 14 Sep 1942 in Darling, Alberta.

+ 201   F   iv.   **Betty Lorraine Gordash** was born on 28 Jan 1946 in Radway, Alberta.

90. Lily Gurba *(Lucas 5, Antoni 4, Semen 3, Stefan 2, Daniel 1)* was born on 9 Sep 1920 in Hollow Lake, Alberta, died on 10 Sep 2005 in Radway, Alberta aged 85, and was buried on 15 Sep 2005 in Nativity BV Mary Ruthenian Greek Catholic Cemetery, Newbrook (nearby Darling, Alberta). Another name for Lily was Lily Horyn.

Lily married **Fred Horyn** on 15 Oct 1935. Fred was born on 10 May 1916, died on 7 Aug 1990 aged 74, and was buried in Nativity BV Mary Ruthenian Greek Catholic Cemetery, Newbrook (nearby Darling, Alberta).

Children from this marriage were:

+ 202   F   i.   **Phyllis Helen Horyn** was born on 18 Nov 1938 in Darling, Alberta.

203   M   ii.   **Bobby Horyn** was born in 1939, died in 1944 aged 5, and was buried in Nativity BV Mary Ruthenian Greek Catholic Cemetery, Newbrook (nearby Darling, Alberta).

204 M iii. **Orest Vernon Horyn** was born on 23 Mar 1942 in Radway, Alberta, died on 17 Nov 2001 in Thorhild, Alberta aged 59, and was cremated on 23 Nov 2001.

+ 205 M iv. **Edward Victor Horyn** was born on 14 May 1943 in Radway, Alberta.

+ 206 M v. **David Horyn** was born on 30 May 1949, died on 23 Sep 1984 aged 35, and was buried in Nativity BV Mary Ruthenian Greek Catholic Cemetery, Newbrook (nearby Darling, Alberta).

+ 207 M vi. **Donald Frederick Horyn** was born on 5 Oct 1951.

+ 208 F vii. **Cynthia Lillian Horyn** was born on 13 Dec 1956 in Radway, Alberta.

91. Joseph Gurba *(Lucas 5, Antoni 4, Semen 3, Stefan 2, Daniel 1)* was born on 8 Nov 1922 in Hollow Lake, Alberta.

Joseph married **Ramona Zenko** on 14 Jul 1951 in Vegreville, Alberta. Ramona was born on 10 May 1930 in Vegreville, Alberta. Another name for Ramona is Ramona Gurba.

Children from this marriage were:

+ 209 M i. **Gerald Gurba** was born on 8 Jul 1952 in Myrnam, Alberta.

210 M ii. **Wayne Gurba** was born on 3 Nov 1953.

Wayne married **Georgina Simmons**.

+ 211 F iii. **Monica Gurba** was born on 9 Apr 1955.

212 F iv. **Mary Jo Gurba** was born on 25 Oct 1956. Other names for Mary are Mary Jo Flanigan.

Mary married **Luke Flanagan** on 19 Oct 1991. Luke was born in 1951.

213 F v. **Karen Gurba** was born on 11 Jan 1960. Another name for Karen is Karen Gabriel.

Karen married **Michael Gabriel** on 21 Jun 2003. Michael was born on 29 Apr 1960.

+ 214 F vi. **Rose Marie Gurba** was born on 7 Feb 1962 in Edmonton, Alberta.

92. Bill Gurba *(Lucas 5, Antoni 4, Semen 3, Stefan 2, Daniel 1)* was born on 20 Mar 1925 in Hollow Lake, Alberta.

Bill married **Lillian Helen Elizabeth Dziwenka** on 6 Nov 1948 in Thorhild, Alberta, daughter of **John Dziwenka** and **Doris Wozniak**. Lillian was born on 6 Jun 1925 in St. Michael, Alberta. Another name for Lillian is Lillian Gurba.

Children from this marriage were:

+ 215   M   i.   **Robert William Gurba** was born on 8 Sep 1949 in Radway, Alberta.

+ 216   F   ii.   **Judith Ann Gurba** was born on 24 Jul 1951 in Radway, Alberta.

+ 217   M   iii.   **Theodore Wayne Gurba** was born on 13 Jun 1953 in Radway, Alberta.

+ 218   F   iv.   **Carol Lynn Gurba** was born on 8 Dec 1956 in Radway, Alberta.

+ 219   M   v.   **Bernard James Gurba** was born on 1 Feb 1959 in Radway, Alberta.

   220   M   vi.   **Anthony Steven Gurba** was born on 8 Jun 1960 in Radway, Alberta and died on 18 Nov 1960 in Darling, Alberta.

+ 221   M   vii.   **Zenon Lester Gurba** was born on 1 Apr 1963 in Radway, Alberta.

93. Nettie Gurba *(Lucas 5, Antoni 4, Semen 3, Stefan 2, Daniel 1)* was born on 24 Dec 1926 in Hollow Lake, Alberta. Another name for Nettie is Nettie Wosnack.

Nettie married **Joe Wosnack** on 4 Jun 1949 in Hollow Lake, Alberta, son of **John Wosnack** and **Martha Ravache**. Joe was born on 11 Jan 1925 in Redwater, Alberta.

Children from this marriage were:

+ 222   M   i.   **Randy Joseph Wosnack** was born on 5 Jan 1952 in Edmonton, Alberta.

+ 223   M   ii.   **Sidney Wosnack** was born on 29 Jul 1953 in Edmonton, Alberta.

+ 224   F   iii.   **Linda Mae Wosnack** was born on 24 Nov 1962 in Edmonton, Alberta.

95. Olga Tillie Gurba *(Lucas 5, Antoni 4, Semen 3, Stefan 2, Daniel 1)* was born on 16 Oct 1932 in Hollow Lake, Alberta. Another name for Olga is Olga Toronchuk.

Olga married **Russell John Toronchuk** on 15 Oct 1955 in Darling, Alberta, son of **Onufrey Toronchuk** and **Victoria Turchin**. Russell was born on 13 Aug 1929 in Radway, Alberta.

The child from this marriage was:

+ 225 M i. **Jerome Russell Toronchuk** was born on 26 Jan 1958 in Edmonton, Alberta.

96. Paul Bohdan Gurba *(Lucas 5, Antoni 4, Semen 3, Stefan 2, Daniel 1)* was born on 11 Sep 1937 in Hollow Lake, Alberta, died on 1 Jul 1991 in Edmonton, Alberta aged 53, and was buried on 7 Jul 1991 in St. Michael's Cemetery, Edmonton, Alberta.

Paul married **Henrietta Zatelny**. Henrietta was born on 27 Nov 1940 in Lamont, Alberta. Another name for Henrietta is Henrietta Gurba.

Children from this marriage were:

226 M i. **Stuart Paul Gurba** was born on 23 Oct 1964 in Edmonton, Alberta.

227 F ii. **Carrie Lynn Gurba** was born on 12 Oct 1967 in Edmonton, Alberta. Another name for Carrie is Carrie Lynn Dunn.

Carrie married **Matthew Paul Dunn** on 22 Sep 2001 in Whistler, British Columbia. Matthew was born on 4 Oct 1966 in Burlington, Ontario.

+ 228 F iii. **James Bradley Gurba** was born on 29 Oct 1968 in Edmonton, Alberta.

97. Peter Roman Gurba *(Lucas 5, Antoni 4, Semen 3, Stefan 2, Daniel 1)* was born on 11 Sep 1937 in Hollow Lake, Alberta.

Peter married **Frances Lynn Burkosky** on 28 Aug 1965. Frances was born on 8 Mar 1945 in Prince Albert, Saskatchewan. Another name for Frances is Frances Lynn Gurba.

Children from this marriage were:

229 M i. **Patrick Craig Gurba** was born on 19 Dec 1965 in Smoky Lake, Alberta.

230 M ii. **David Brian Gurba** was born on 29 Jul 1968 in Edmonton, Alberta.

+ 231 M iii. **Richard Joseph Gurba** was born on 23 Nov 1969 in Norman Wells, NWT.

98. Maurice Gurba *(Lucas 5, Antoni 4, Semen 3, Stefan 2, Daniel 1)* was born on 19 Jan 1942 in Radway, Alberta.

Maurice married **Pat Zatelny** in 1964. Pat was born on 23 May 1945 in Radway, Alberta. Another name for Pat is Pat Gurba.

Children from this marriage were:

232 F i. **Valerie Gurba** was born on 12 Nov 1964 in Smoky Lake, Alberta. Other names for Valerie are Valerie McKinlay, and Valerie Boulet.

Valerie married **Barry McKinlay** on 12 Aug 1989. Barry was born on 8 Aug 1967 in Smoky Lake, Alberta.

Valerie next married **Greg Boulet**.

+ 233 M ii. **Jason Maurice Luke Gurba** was born on 5 Jun 1976 in Athabasca, Alberta.

99. Nester F. Wenger *(Rose Gurba 5, Antoni 4, Semen 3, Stefan 2, Daniel 1)* was born on 21 Feb 1938 in Danube, Alberta.

Nester married **Gladys Duniec** on 23 Feb 1963. Gladys was born on 27 Jan 1943 in Prosperity, Alberta and died in 1970 aged 27. Another name for Gladys was Gladys Wenger.

Children from this marriage were:

+ 234 F i. **Sheryl Lynn Marie Wenger** was born on 11 Jun 1963 in Smoky Lake, Alberta

235 M ii. **Brian Dion Michael Wenger** was born on 15 Jun 1964 and died on 16 Jun 1964 in Darling, Alberta.

Nester next married **Pauline Welsh** on 1 Jul 1977. Pauline was born on 20 May 1932 in Hampton, Saskatchewan. Another name for Pauline is Pauline Wenger.

101. Rose Wenger *(Rose Gurba 5, Antoni 4, Semen 3, Stefan 2, Daniel 1)* was born on 11 Apr 1942 in Danube, Alberta. Another name for Rose is Rose Sawchuk.

Rose married **Mike Sawchuk** on 16 May 1959. Mike was born on 16 Mar 1933 in Waskatenau, Alberta.

Children from this marriage were:

236   M   i.   **Richard Sawchuk** was born on 27 Jul 1959 in Smoky Lake, Alberta.

+ 237   M   ii.   **Randolph Sawchuk** was born on 10 Oct 1961 in Smoky Lake, Alberta.

102. Helen Bezborodka *(Francesca Gurba 5, Antoni 4, Semen 3, Stefan 2, Daniel 1)* was born on 24 Apr 1928 in Edmonton, Alberta, died on 1 Feb 1979 in Edmonton, Alberta aged 50, and was buried on 5 Feb 1979 in St. Michael's Cemetery, Edmonton, Alberta. Another name for Helen was Helen Mykytiuk.

Helen married **William Mykytiuk** on 1 May 1954 in Edmonton, Alberta. William was born on 29 Dec 1931 in Wabamun, Alberta, died on 28 May 1981 in Edmonton, Alberta aged 49, and was buried in St. Michael's Cemetery, Edmonton, Alberta.

Children from this marriage were:

+ 238   F   i.   **Katherine Anne Mykytiuk** was born on 8 Feb 1955 in Edmonton, Alberta.

239   F   ii.   **Nancy Jean Mykytiuk** was born on 22 Apr 1967 in Edmonton, Alberta.

103. Peter Robert Broda *(Francesca Gurba 5, Antoni 4, Semen 3, Stefan 2, Daniel 1)* was born on 12 Jul 1929 in Edmonton, Alberta.

Peter married **Lillian Joyce Kozak** on 12 Jul 1957 in Willingdon, Alberta, daughter of **Nick Kozak** and **Helen Moshuk**. Lillian was born on 22 Jul 1935 in Mundare, Alberta. Another name for Lillian is Lillian Joyce Broda.

Children from this marriage were:

240   M   i.   **Brian Nicholas Broda** was born on 9 Apr 1958 in Edmonton, Alberta.

241   F   ii.   **Penny Joan Broda** was born on 22 Mar 1960 in Edmonton, Alberta.

104. Mae Mary-Pearl Bezborodka *(Francesca Gurba 5, Antoni 4, Semen 3, Stefan 2, Daniel 1)* was born on 22 Jun 1931 in Radway, Alberta. Another name for Mae is Mae Mary-Pearl McMurdo.

Mae married **Lloyd McMurdo** on 18 Feb 1956 in Edmonton, Alberta. Lloyd was born on 29 Oct 1929 in Lloydminster, Alberta.

Children from this marriage were:

242 F i. **Lynn McMurdo** was born on 24 Apr 1957 in Red Deer, Alberta.

+ 243 M ii. **Ryan Nicholas McMurdo** was born on 6 Jun 1961 in Red Deer, Alberta.

106. Walter Gurba *(Steve 5, Antoni 4, Semen 3, Stefan 2, Daniel 1)* was born on 29 Jun 1935 in Lamont, Alberta.

Walter married **Alvina Romaniuk** on 19 Oct 1957, daughter of **Jack Romaniuk** and **Mary**. Alvina was born on 13 Sep 1937 in Chipman, Alberta, died on 3 Nov 2007 in Edmonton, Alberta aged 70, and was buried on 9 Nov 2007 in St. Michael's Cemetary, Edmonton, Alberta. Another name for Alvina was Alvina Gurba.

Children from this marriage were:

+ 244 F i. **Gwen Gurba** was born on 11 Dec 1961 in Edmonton, Alberta.

+ 245 M ii. **George Walter Gurba** was born on 18 Apr 1964 in Edmonton, Alberta.

+ 246 M iii. **Gordon Gurba** was born on 7 Apr 1966 in Edmonton, Alberta.

+ 247 M iv. **Gary Gurba** was born on 7 Jan 1972 in Edmonton, Alberta.

107. Raymond Gurba *(Steve 5, Antoni 4, Semen 3, Stefan 2, Daniel 1)* was born on 12 Feb 1938 in Lamont,Alberta.

Raymond married **Vicky Melnyk**. Vicky was born on 26 Dec 1942 in Skaro, Alberta. Another name for Vicky is Vicky Gurba.

Children from this marriage were:

248 M i. **Kelly Schenley Stephen Gurba** was born on 28 Feb 1963 in Manning, Alberta.

249 F ii. **Shelly Lynn Gurba** was born on 13 Mar 1964 in Stony Plain, Alberta.

108. Eugene Adolf Gurba *(Steve 5, Antoni 4, Semen 3, Stefan 2, Daniel 1)* was born on 4 Dec 1940 in Lamont,Alberta.

Eugene married **Adeline Skitsko** on 15 Jun 1968 in Skaro, Alberta, daughter of **Mike Skitsko** and **Mary Woitas**. Adeline was born on 16 Jul 1939 in Bruderheim, Alberta. Another name for Adeline is Adeline Gurba.

Children from this marriage were:

+ 250   F   i.   **Brigitte Marie Gurba** was born on 8 Nov 1968 in Lamont, Alberta.

   251   M   ii.   **Bradley Gurba** was born on 20 Aug 1970 in Lamont, Alberta.

   Bradley married **Marielynne Carmen Roberge** on 11 May 2002 in Edmonton, Alberta. Another name for Marielynne is Marielynne Carmen Gurba.

   252   F   iii.   **Barbara Sofia Gurba** was born on 14 Nov 1972 in Lamont, Alberta.

109. Sylvia Gurba *(Steve 5, Antoni 4, Semen 3, Stefan 2, Daniel 1)* was born on 11 Jun 1942 in Lamont, Alberta, died on 18 Nov 1992 in Edmonton, Alberta aged 50, and was cremated on 23 Nov 1992 in Edmonton, Alberta. Another name for Sylvia was Sylvia Pietz.

Sylvia married **Harold Pietz** on 28 Dec 1963. Harold was born on 16 Aug 1942 in Posin, Germany.

Children from this marriage were:

+ 253   M   i.   **William Pietz** was born on 13 Sep 1963 in Edmonton, Alberta.

   254   M   ii.   **Wesley Pietz** was born on 4 Sep 1964 in Edmonton, Alberta.

   255   F   iii.   **Lorraine Pietz** was born on 30 May 1968 in Edmonton, Alberta. Another name for Lorraine is Lorraine Talbot.

   Lorraine married **Kevin Talbot** on 9 Sep 2000 in Victoria, British Columbia. Kevin was born on 11 Dec 1967.

   256   F   iv.   **Heidi Pietz** was born on 11 May 1969 in Edmonton, Alberta.

   257   F   v.   **Angel Pietz** was born on 10 Oct 1974 in Edmonton, Alberta. Another name for Angel is Angel Madu.

   Angel married **Keith Madu** on 16 Mar 2002. Keith was born on 3 May 1973.

110. Sylvester Gurba *(Steve 5, Antoni 4, Semen 3, Stefan 2, Daniel 1)* was born on 6 Dec 1943 in Lamont, Alberta.

Sylvester married **Marilyn Sumka** on 12 Oct 1968. Marilyn was born on 25 Mar 1946 in Radway, Alberta, died on 7 Jan 1994 in Edmonton, Alberta aged

47, and was buried on 11 Jan 1994 in St. Michael's Cemetery Edmonton, Alberta. Another name for Marilyn was Marilyn Gurba.

Children from this marriage were:

+ 258   F   i.   **Brenda Gurba** was born on 5 Mar 1969 in Edmonton, Alberta.

259   M   ii.   **Richard Gurba** was born on 19 Sep 1970 in Edmonton, Alberta

.

112. Louie Budynski *(Wladek (William) Budynski 5, Anna Gurba 4, Semen 3, Stefan 2, Daniel 1)* was born in 1911 and died in 1981 aged 70.

Louie married **Rose Lubomski**. Rose was born on 19 Sep 1923. Another name for Rose is Rose Budynski.

Children from this marriage were:

260   M   i.   **Leonard Budynski** was born in 1943.

+ 261   M   ii.   **Wayne Budynski** was born in Jul 1945 and died on 5 Jul 1994 aged 49.

+ 262   M   iii.   **Ken Budynski** was born on 10 Jan 1947.

113. Kaizer (Clarence) Budynski *(Wladek (William) Budynski 5, Anna Gurba 4, Semen 3, Stefan 2, Daniel 1)* was born on 29 Jul 1915, died on 19 Jun 1967 in Victoria, British Columbia aged 51, and was buried in Royal Oak Burial Park, Victoria, British Columbia.

Kaizer married **Bonnie Rindahl**. Bonnie was born in 1914. Another name for Bonnie is Bonnie Budynski.

Children from this marriage were:

+ 263   F   i.   **Anna Mae Budynski** was born on 16 May 1937.

264   M   ii.   **Wayne Budynski** was born on 14 Sep 1938.

Wayne married **Anne**. Another name for Anne is Anne Budynski.

Wayne next married **Dinah**. Another name for Dinah is Dinah Budynski.

115. Marie Budynski *(Wladek (William) Budynski 5, Anna Gurba 4, Semen 3, Stefan 2, Daniel 1)* was born on 26 Mar 1919. Another name for Marie is Marie Doulis.

Marie married **George Doulis**. George was born on 16 Oct 1909.

Children from this marriage were:

265 M i. **Alexander Doulis** was born on 5 May 1939.

+ 266 M ii. **Chester Doulis** was born on 23 Apr 1948.

116. Joan (Josie) Budynski *(Wladek (William) Budynski 5, Anna Gurba 4, Semen 3, Stefan 2, Daniel 1)* was born on 25 Apr 1921, died on 16 Jan 1996 aged 74, and was buried in French Creek Cemetery, Parksville, British Columbia. Another name for Joan was Joan (Josie) Leakey.

Joan married **Len Leakey**. Len was born in 1911, died in 1980 aged 69, and was buried in French Creek Cemetery, Parksville, British Columbia.

Children from this marriage were:

267 F i. **Marcia Leakey**.

268 M ii. **Andy Leakey**.

269 F iii. **Cindy Leakey**.

270 M iv. **Rod Leakey**.

117. Joseph Lawrence Budynski *(Wladek (William) Budynski 5, Anna Gurba 4, Semen 3, Stefan 2, Daniel 1)* was born in 1913, died on 30 Dec 1975 in Victoria, British Columbia aged 62, and was buried in Royal Oak Burial Park, Victoria, British Columbia.

Joseph married **Evelyn Cornelius**. Evelyn died in 1988 and was buried in Royal Oak Burial Park, Victoria, British Columbia. Another name for Evelyn was Evelyn Budynski.

Children from this marriage were:

+ 271 M i. **Orville Budynski** was born on 25 Mar 1937 in Dinant, Alberta.

272 M ii. **Jack Budynski**.

273 M iii. **Arnold Budynski**.

274 F iv. **Violet Adelia Budynski** was born in 1946, died on 23 Dec 1959 in Vancouver, British Columbia aged 13, and was buried in Royal Oak Burial Park, Victoria, British Columbia.

275 F v. **Evie Budynski**.

+ 276 M vi. **Daniel Budynski** died in 1988 in Kitchner, Ontario and was buried in Royal Oak Burial Park, Victoria, British Columbia.

118. Virginia (Ginnie) Budynski *(Wladek (William) Budynski 5, Anna Gurba 4, Semen 3, Stefan 2, Daniel 1)* was born on 7 Sep 1926.

> Virginia married **Bill Rossell**. Bill was born on 25 Aug 1927 and died on 22 Jun 1991 aged 63.

> Children from this marriage were:

> + 277 F i. **Norma Rossell.**

> + 278 F ii. **Judy Rossell.**

120. Carl Anthony Mack *(Rose Budynski 5, Anna Gurba 4, Semen 3, Stefan 2, Daniel 1)* was born on 22 May 1913 and died on 7 Feb 1997 in Spokane, Washington aged 83.

> Carl married **Barbara Ciesielski Russell** on 1 Sep 1939, daughter of **Unknown** and **Unknown**. Barbara was born on 24 Feb 1913 and died on 20 May 1978 aged 65. Another name for Barbara was Barbara Mack.

> Children from this marriage were:

> + 279 M i. **Carl David Mack** was born on 24 Sep 1941.

> + 280 F ii. **Barbara Sis Mack** was born on 30 May 1943.

> + 281 F iii. **Sandra Mack** was born on 21 Aug 1944.

121. Nestor Mack *(Rose Budynski 5, Anna Gurba 4, Semen 3, Stefan 2, Daniel 1)* was born on 10 Jun 1915 in New York and died on 29 Feb 1984 in Harlingen, Texas aged 68.

> Nestor married **Estelle Agnes Kaczmarek** on 11 Jun 1936 in Rochester, New York. Estelle was born on 2 Nov 1914. Another name for Estelle is Estelle Agnes Mack.

> Children from this marriage were:

> 282 M i. **Raymond Nester Mack** was born on 15 Jun 1937 and died on 9 Mar 1959 aged 21.

> + 283 M ii. **Nestor Robert Mack** was born on 24 Nov 1942.

122. Verna Mack *(Rose Budynski 5, Anna Gurba 4, Semen 3, Stefan 2, Daniel 1)* was born on 30 May 1917 in Colebrook, Ohio and died on 6 Jan 1998 in Harlingen, Texas aged 80. Another name for Vernawas Verna Russel.

Verna married **Joseph Ciesisielski Russell**. Joseph was born on 15 Mar 1912 and died on 10 Dec 1945 in Rochester, New York aged 33.

Children from this marriage were:

+ 284 F i. **Constance Rose Russell** was born on 22 Sep 1942 in Rochester New York.

+ 285 M ii. **Kenneth Joseph Russell** was born on 3 Oct 1940 in Rochester, New York.

123. Helen Mack *(Rose Budynski 5, Anna Gurba 4, Semen 3, Stefan 2, Daniel 1)* was born on 17 Jul 1919. Another name for Helen is Helen Matwyshen.

Helen married **John Matwyshen** on 26 Apr 1941. John was born on 7 May 1915 and died on 4 Jun 1977 in Rochester New York aged 62.

The child from this marriage was:

+ 286 M i. **Richard Dick Matwyshen** was born on 3 Sep 1948.

124. Wilfred (Will) Barney Mack *(Rose Budynski 5, Anna Gurba 4, Semen 3, Stefan 2, Daniel 1)* was born on 28 Feb 1920 and died on 22 Mar 1999 in Harlingen, Texas aged 79.

Wilfred married **Mary Bonnie Pukish**, daughter of **John Pukish** and **Melania Pukish**. Mary was born on 13 Mar 1923 in Rochester, New York, died on 20 Mar 2005 in Harlingen, Texas aged 82, and was buried on 24 Mar 2005 in Restlawn Memorial Park, La Feria, Cameron, Texas. Another name for Mary was Mary Bonnie Mack.

Children from this marriage were:

+ 287 M i. **Gary Mack** was born on 21 Oct 1952.

+ 288 F ii. **Paula Mack** was born on 27 Jun 1954.

125. Stella Bernice Mack *(Rose Budynski 5, Anna Gurba 4, Semen 3, Stefan 2, Daniel 1)* was born on 7 Feb 1923 in New York and died on 2 Feb 1993 in Harlingen, Texas aged 69. Another name forStella was Stella Bernice Demeret.

Stella married **George Max Demmert**. George was born on 23 Apr 1922 in New York and died on 2 Jun 1983 in Harlingen, Texas aged 61.

Children from this marriage were:

+ 289 M i. **Michael Demmert** was born on 16 Aug 1948 and died on 17 Nov 2004 in Lady Lake, Florida aged 56.

+ 290　F　ii.　**Judi Demmert** was born on 10 Jun 1952 in Rochester New York.

+ 291　M　iii.　**Robert (Bobby) Demmert** was born on 27 Feb 1954.

126. Edward A. Mack *(Rose Budynski 5, Anna Gurba 4, Semen 3, Stefan 2, Daniel 1)* was born on 22 Jan 1924.

Edward married **Rose Borseth** on 27 Aug 1955. Rose was born on 27 Dec 1936. Another name for Rose is Rose Mack.

Children from this marriage were:

+ 292　M　i.　**Eddy Mack** was born on 31 Mar 1956.

+ 293　M　ii.　**Wilfred D. Mack** was born on 4 Apr 1957.

+ 294　M　iii.　**Joseph M. Mack** was born on 18 Apr 1960.

+ 295　F　iv.　**Linda Mack** was born on 10 Sep 1961.

　　296　M　v.　**James Mack** was born on 4 Mar 1967 and died on 2 Jul 1968 aged 1.

+ 297　F　vi.　**Betty Mack** was born on 8 Sep 1968.

+ 298　M　vii.　**Jerry Mack** was born on 25 Aug 1970.

+ 299　F　viii.　**Rosie Mack** was born on 31 Jul 1971.

127. Florian Sy Mack *(Rose Budynski 5, Anna Gurba 4, Semen 3, Stefan 2, Daniel 1)* was born on 22 Feb 1926 in Ridgeway, New York and died on 15 Sep 2006 aged 80.

Florian married **Mary Lanelle West** on 23 Dec 1950. Mary was born on 30 Sep 1930 in San Saba, Texas. Another name for Mary is Mary Lanelle Mack.

Children from this marriage were:

+ 300　F　i.　**Marilyn K. Mack** was born on 3 Feb 1952 in San Benito, Texas.

　　301　M　ii.　**John Franklin Mack** was born on 10 Sep 1954 in San Benito, Texas and died on 11 Nov 1975 in Tucson, Arizona aged 21.

+ 302　F　iii.　**Michelle Marie Mack** was born on 29 Nov 1962 in Tucson, Arizona.

128. Gloria Mack *(Rose Budynski 5, Anna Gurba 4, Semen 3, Stefan 2, Daniel 1)* was born on 8 Jan 1930 and died on 18 Dec 1967 in San Antonio, Texas aged 37. Another name for Gloria was Gloria Jordan.

> Gloria married **Monty Jordan**.
>
> Children from this marriage were:
>
> + 303 M i. **James Jimmy Jordan** was born on 6 Aug 1950 and died on 2 Mar 1993 in Harlingen, Texas aged 42.
>
> 304 F ii. **Sharon Louise Jordan** was born on 29 Dec 1951 and died on 29 Dec 1951.
>
> 305 M iii. **Leroy Jay Jordan** was born in 1953 and died in 1953.
>
> + 306 M iv. **Stephen Jordan** was born on 31 Mar 1955.
>
> + 307 F v. **Margaret Jordan** was born on 12 Aug 1957.
>
> 308 F vi. **Patricia Ann Jordan** was born in 1958 and died in 1958.

130. Adele Boden *(Lawrence Boden 5, Anna Gurba 4, Semen 3, Stefan 2, Daniel 1)* was born in 1926.

> Adele married **Frank Borawski**.
>
> Children from this marriage were:
>
> 309 M i. **? Borawski**.
>
> 310 F ii. **? Borawski**.

132. Mary Anne Britt *(Frances A. Budynski 5, Anna Gurba 4, Semen 3, Stefan 2, Daniel 1)* was born on 11 Apr 1929.

> Mary married **John Forsyth**. John was born on 23 Mar 1927 and died on 2 Mar 1994 in Lockport, Niagara, New York aged 66.
>
> Children from this marriage were:
>
> + 311 M i. **Thomas Forsyth** was born on 21 Jun 1953 in Lockport, Niagara, New York and died on 3 Jun 2008 in Lockport, Niagara, New York aged 54.
>
> 312 F ii. **Linda Forsyth**.
>
> > Linda married someone **Gargalino**.

313 M iii. **John S. Forsyth**.

John married **Judy**.

314 F iv. **Mary (Becky) Forsyth**.

315 M v. **David Forsyth**.

316 F vi. **Ellen Forsyth**.

Ellen married **Marc Watkins**.

317 F vii. **Amy Forsyth**.

Amy married **Louis Juliano**.

134. Elizabeth Loretta Britt *(Frances A. Budynski 5, Anna Gurba 4, Semen 3, Stefan 2, Daniel 1)* was born on 21 Sep 1935.

Elizabeth married **Robert Anderson**. Robert was born on 26 Sep 1923 and died on 20 Mar 2005 in Lockport, Niagara, New York aged 81.

The child from this marriage was:

318 M i. **Jim Anderson**.

139. John Boychuk *(Rosalia (Rosa) Stecyk 5, Kate Gurba 4, Semen 3, Stefan 2, Daniel 1)* was born on 16 Jun 1925 in Hardyville.
John married **Rose Kowal** in 1948. Rose was born on 27 Mar 1925 in Radway, Alberta. Another name for Rose is Rose Boychuk.

The child from this marriage was:

+ 319 F i. **Darlene Boychuk** was born on 18 Jan 1950 in Radway, Alberta.

140. Antonia Boychuk *(Rosalia (Rosa) Stecyk 5, Kate Gurba 4, Semen 3, Stefan 2, Daniel 1)* was born in 1927 in Radway, Alberta, died in 2007 aged 80, and was buried in Evergreen Cemetery, Edmonton, Alberta. Another name for Antonia was Antonia Gubersky.

Antonia married **Mike Gubersky**.

Children from this marriage were:

320 M i. **Richard Gubersky**.

321 F ii. **Shirley Gubersky**.

322 M iii. **David Gubersky.**

323 F iv. **Jackie Gubersky.**

141. Steve Boychuk *(Rosalia (Rosa) Stecyk 5, Kate Gurba 4, Semen 3, Stefan 2, Daniel 1)* was born in 1928, died on 23 Jan 2004 in Edmonton, Alberta aged 76, and was cremated on 28 Jan 2004 in with inurnment at St. Michael's Cemetary, Edmonton, Alberta.

Steve married **Mary Small**. Another name for Mary is Mary Boychuk.

Children from this marriage were:

+ 324 F i. **Jane Boychuk.**

325 M ii. **Douglas Boychuk.**

+ 326 F iii. **Cindy Boychuk.**

327 M iv. **Randy Boychuk.**

328 M v. **Joseph Boychuk** died date unknown.

329 M vi. **Gary Boychuk** died date unknown.

142. Mary Boychuk *(Rosalia (Rosa) Stecyk 5, Kate Gurba 4, Semen 3, Stefan 2, Daniel 1)* was born in 1930. Another name for Mary is Mary Popil.

Mary married **Edward Popil**. Edward died in Apr 2002.

Children from this marriage were:

330 F i. **Karen Popil.**

+ 331 F ii. **Leslie Popil.**

+ 332 M iii. **Chris Popil.**

333 M iv. **James Popil.**

143. Winnie Boychuk *(Rosalia (Rosa) Stecyk 5, Kate Gurba 4, Semen 3, Stefan 2, Daniel 1)* was born in 1932. Another name for Winnie is Winnie Prokuda.

Winnie married **Walter Prokuda**.

Children from this marriage were:

+ 334 F i. **Linda Prokuda.**

335 M ii. **Ronald Prokuda.**

+ 336 F iii. **Debbie Prokuda.**

144. Paul Boychuk *(Rosalia (Rosa) Stecyk 5, Kate Gurba 4, Semen 3, Stefan 2, Daniel 1)* was born in 1935.

> Paul married **Marlene Huntley.** Another name for Marlene is Marlene Boychuk.
>
> The child from this marriage was:
>
> 337 F i. **Tracy Boychuk.** Another name for Tracy is Tracy Francis.
>
> Tracy married **Malcolm Francis.**

145. George Boychuk *(Rosalia (Rosa) Stecyk 5, Kate Gurba 4, Semen 3, Stefan 2, Daniel 1)* was born in 1938.

> George married **Florence Riggs.** Another name for Florence is Florence Boychuk.
>
> Children from this marriage were:
>
> 338 M i. **Louis Boychuk.**
>
> 339 F ii. **Laurel Boychuk.**
>
> 340 F iii. **Lydia Boychuk.**

146. Sandy Boychuk *(Rosalia (Rosa) Stecyk 5, Kate Gurba 4, Semen 3, Stefan 2, Daniel 1)* was born in 1940.

> Sandy married **Edel Genille.** Another name for Edel is Edel Boychuk.
>
> Children from this marriage were:
>
> 341 M i. **Darren Boychuk.**
>
> 342 M ii. **Bobby Boychuk.**

147. Alexandra Boychuk *(Rosalia (Rosa) Stecyk 5, Kate Gurba 4, Semen 3, Stefan 2, Daniel 1)* was born in 1942. Other names for Alexandra are Alexandra Verbitsky, and Alexandra Olexin.

> Alexandra married **Robert Olexin.**

Children from this marriage were:

+ 343 F i. **Patricia Joanne Olexin**.

+ 344 M ii. **Robert Mitchell Olexin**.

Alexandra next married **Jack Verbitsky**.

148. Gloria Boychuk *(Rosalia (Rosa) Stecyk 5, Kate Gurba 4, Semen 3, Stefan 2, Daniel 1)* was born in 1946. Other names for Gloria are Gloria Dombrosky, and Gloria Wallace.

Gloria married **Richard Dombrosky**. Richard died in 1985.

Children from this marriage were:

345 M i. **Glen Dombrosky**.

Glen married **Caroline Taylor**. Another name for Caroline is Caroline Dombrosky.

+ 346 M ii. **Rick Dombrosky**.

Gloria next married **Douglas Wallace**.

The child from this marriage was:

347 F i. **Tanya Wallace**. Another name for Tanya is Tanya Foley.

Tanya married **Clint Foley**.

150. Elizabeth Boychuk *(Rosalia (Rosa) Stecyk 5, Kate Gurba 4, Semen 3, Stefan 2, Daniel 1)* was born in 1951. Another name for Elizabeth is Elizabeth Polanski.

Elizabeth married **Richard Polanski**. Richard was born on 30 Jan 1950, died on 19 Jun 1997 aged 47, and was buried in St. Joseph's Roman Catholic Cemetery, Radway, Alberta.

Children from this marriage were:

+ 348 M i. **Kevin Charles Polanski**.

349 F ii. **Christina Rose Polanski**.

350 F iii. **Angela Rae Polanski**.

151. Julia Piontkowski *(Annie Czternastek 5, Rozalia (Rose) Gurba 4, Semen 3, Stefan 2, Daniel 1)* was born on 11 Jun 1907 and died on 15 May 1990 aged 82. Another name for Julia was Julia Palvakavich (Palmer).

Julia married **Peter Pawlukiewicz (Palmer)**. Peter was born in 1893 and died in 1976 aged 83.

Children from this marriage were:

+ 351　F　i.　**Lucy Pawlukiewicz (Palmer)** was born on 19 Jul 1925.

+ 352　F　ii.　**Josephine Pawlukiewicz (Palmer)** was born on 8 Sep 1926 and died on 20 Nov 1995 aged　69.

+ 353　F　iii.　**Irene Pawlukiewicz (Palmer)** was born on 31 Jan 1927 and died on 26 Dec 1996 aged 69.

+ 354　M　iv.　**Mitch Pawlukiewicz (Palmer)** was born on 8 Oct 1929.

+ 355　M　v.　**Larry Pawlukiewicz (Palmer)** was born on 8 Jan 1938.

+ 356　M　vi.　**Darrel Pawlukiewicz (Palmer)** was born on 3 Jun 1943.

153. John Piontkowski (Point) *(Annie Czternastek 5, Rozalia (Rose) Gurba 4, Semen 3, Stefan 2, Daniel 1)* was born on 12 Dec 1909.

John married **Josie Pinkoski**. Josie was born on 20 Jul 1912 and died on 8 Feb 1997 aged 84. Another name for Josie was Josie Piontkowski (Point).

Children from this marriage were:

+ 357　F　i.　**Patricia Piontkowski (Point)** was born on 11 Jan 1940.

+ 358　M　ii.　**Reg Piontkowski (Point)** was born on 5 Dec 1941.

155. Edward Piontkowski *(Annie Czternastek 5, Rozalia (Rose) Gurba 4, Semen 3, Stefan 2, Daniel 1)* was born on 27 May 1914 in Round Hill, Alberta, died on 24 Jul 2005 in Camrose, Alberta aged 91, and was buried on 29 Jul 2005 in St. Stanislaus Roman Catholic Cemetery, Round Hill, Alberta.

Edward married **Mary Ann Maruszeczka** in 1944. Mary was born on 12 Jan 1919 in Kopernik, Camrose, Alberta, died on 14 Oct 2006 in Camrose, Alberta aged 87, and was buried on 28 Oct 2006 in St. Stanislaus Roman Catholic Cemetery, Round Hill, Alberta. Another name for Mary was Mary Ann Piontkowski.

Children from this marriage were:

359　M　i.　**David Albert Piontkowski** was born on 15 Mar 1945, died on 23 Apr 2006 in Camrose, Alberta aged 61, and was buried on 29 Apr 2006.

360　F　ii.　**Lorraine Piontkowski** was born in 1946, died in 1946, and was buried in St. Stanislaus Roman Catholic Cemetery, Round Hill, Alberta.

+ 361　F　iii.　**Joyce Piontkowski** was born on 13 Apr 1947.

362　M　iv.　**Donald Piontkowski** was born in 1948, died in 1948, and was buried in St. Stanislaus Roman Catholic Cemetery, Round Hill, Alberta.

+ 363　M　v.　**Arnold Piontkowski** was born on 26 Feb 1951.

364　M　vi.　**Raymond Piontkowski** was born on 25 Jan 1955 and died on 16 Feb 1987 in St. Stanislaus Roman Catholic Cemetery, Round Hill, Alberta aged 32.

157. Frederick Paul Pointkoski *(Annie Czternastek 5, Rozalia (Rose) Gurba 4, Semen 3, Stefan 2, Daniel 1)* was born on 17 Mar 1918, died on 24 Nov 2004 in Edmonton, Alberta aged 86, and was buried on 26 Nov 2004 in Camrose Cemetary, Camrose, Alberta.

Frederick married **Mabel Gogol**. Mabel was born on 17 Aug 1920, died on 5 Dec 2006 in Edmonton, Alberta aged 86, and was buried on 8 Dec 2006 in Camrose Cemetery, Camrose, Alberta. Another name for Mabel was Mabel Piontkowski.

Children from this marriage were:

+ 365　F　i.　**Dianna Pointkoski** was born on 10 Sep 1949.

+ 366　M　ii.　**Duane Pointkoski** was born on 26 Oct 1950.

+ 367　F　iii.　**Arlene Pointkoski** was born on 26 Aug 1958.

368　M　iv.　**Randy Pointkoski** was born on 20 Oct 1961.

Randy married **Myrna Macneil**. Myrna was born on 14 Apr 1957. Another name for Myrna is Myrna Piontkowski.

158. Walter Piontkowski *(Annie Czternastek 5, Rozalia (Rose) Gurba 4, Semen 3, Stefan 2, Daniel 1)* was born on 5 Aug 1919 and died on 3 Mar 2000 aged 80.

Walter married **Emma Kushnerick**. Emma was born on 11 Jan 1926. Another name for Emma is Emma Piontkowski.

Children from this marriage were:

+ 369　M　i.　**Gary Piontkowski** was born on 17 Jul 1947.

+ 370 M ii. **Kenneth Piontkowski** was born on 15 Apr 1950.

371 F iii. **Marilyn Piontkowski** was born on 23 Mar 1957. Another name for Marilyn is Marilyn Olson.

Marilyn married **Gary Olson**. Gary was born in 1948.

372 F iv. **Joan Piontkowski** was born on 2 Jun 1960. Another name for Joan is Joan Burnett.

Joan married **Craig Darren Burnett** on 18 Sep 1999. Craig was born on 5 May 1970.

159. Margaret Piontkowski *(Annie Czternastek 5, Rozalia (Rose) Gurba 4, Semen 3, Stefan 2, Daniel 1)* was born on 24 Nov 1920. Another name for Margaret is Margaret Nahirniak.

Margaret married **Joe Nahirniak**. Joe was born on 26 Aug 1913, died on 24 Jun 2000 in Round Hill, Alberta aged 86, and was buried on 28 Jun 2000 in Transfiguration of Our Lord Ukrainian Catholic Church, Round Hill, Alberta.

Children from this marriage were:

+ 373 F i. **Teresa Nahirniak** was born on 6 Jun 1949.

+ 374 M ii. **Darryl Nahirniak** was born on 3 Jan 1952.

375 F iii. **Debbie Nahirniak** was born on 3 Jan 1952. Another name for Debbie is Debbie Murdoch.

Debbie married **Jim Murdoch**. Jim was born on 14 Nov 1935.

161. Bernice Piontkowski *(Annie Czternastek 5, Rozalia (Rose) Gurba 4, Semen 3, Stefan 2, Daniel 1)* was born on 20 Dec 1928. Another name for Bernice is Bernice Nedohin. Bernice married **Bill Nedohin**. Bill was born on 6 May 1926 and died on 9 Sep 2000 aged 74.

Children from this marriage were:

376 F i. **Linda Nedohin** was born on 9 Nov 1959.

377 F ii. **Tracey Nedohin** was born on 28 Jul 1969.

162. Carl (Adamoski) Adams *(Mary Czternastek 5, Rozalia (Rose) Gurba 4, Semen 3, Stefan 2, Daniel 1)* was born on 7 Apr 1913, died in Jan 1984 in Batavia, Genesee, New York aged 70, and was buried in St. Joseph's Cemetery, Albion, Orleans, New York.

Carl married **Leona ?**. Leona was born on 7 Jul 1917 and died in Aug 1995 in Rochester, Monroe, New York aged 78. Another name for Leona was Leona (Adamoski) Adams.

Children from this marriage were:

> 378 F i. **Mary Ann (Adamoski) Adams** died in Rochester New York. Another name for Mary was Mary Ann Conley.
>
> > Mary married **Conley**.
>
> 379 F ii. **Judy (Adamoski) Adams** died in Alabama, USA. Another name for Judy was Judy Lomabardo.
>
> > Judy married **Lomabardo**.

164. Steve E. (Adamoski) Adams *(Mary Czternastek 5, Rozalia (Rose) Gurba 4, Semen 3, Stefan 2, Daniel 1)* was born on 2 Sep 1916 and died on 11 Aug 2002 in Spencerport, Monroe, New York aged 85.

Steve married **Margaret Shevlin**. Margaret was born on 1 Dec 1917. Another name for Margaret is Margaret (Adamoski) Adams.

Children from this marriage were:

> 380 M i. **Richard (Adamoski) Adams** was born on 23 Nov 1943.
>
> > Richard married **Gloria**. Another name for Gloria is Gloria (Adamoski) Adams.
>
> + 381 M ii. **Robert (Adamoski) Adams** was born on 2 Sep 1945.
>
> + 382 F iii. **Kathy (Adamoski) Adams** was born on 25 Jan 1947.
>
> + 383 F iv. **Patti (Adamoski) Adams** was born on 11 Dec 1949.
>
> + 384 M v. **Paul (Adamoski) Adams** was born on 26 Oct 1958.

165. John Maxwell *(Kathleen P. Czternastek 5, Rozalia (Rose) Gurba 4, Semen 3, Stefan 2, Daniel 1)* was born in 1928.

John married **Gloria ?**.

Children from this marriage were:

> 385 M i. **John T. Maxwell**.
>
> 386 F ii. **Barbara Maxwell**.

166. Marlene Johnson *(Francis Czternastek 5, Rozalia (Rose) Gurba 4, Semen 3, Stefan 2, Daniel 1)*. Another name for Marlene is Marlene Bowers.

Marlene married **Bob Bowers**.

Children from this marriage were:

387 F i. **Lisa Bowers**.

388 F ii. **Lori Bowers**.

389 F iii. **Bonnie Bowers**.

168. James Phillip Romball *(Anthony Joseph Romball 5, Rozalia (Rose) Gurba 4, Semen 3, Stefan 2, Daniel 1)* was born on 6 May 1945.

James married **Diane Janice Mickow**. Diane was born on 11 Jun 1947 in Wabash, Minnesota. Another name for Diane is Diane Janice Romball.

Children from this marriage were:

390 F i. **Lori Ann Romball** was born on 14 Sep 1969. Another name for Lori is Lori Ann Norbeck.

Lori married **Christoph Norbeck** on 11 Oct 1997. Christoph was born on 14 Jan 1971.

391 F ii. **Lisa Jo Romball** was born on 8 Aug 1970.

169. Tony Jr. Romball *(Anthony Joseph Romball 5, Rozalia (Rose) Gurba 4, Semen 3, Stefan 2, Daniel 1)* was born on 20 Sep 1947, died on 7 Apr 1976 in South Minneapolis, Minnesota aged 28, and was buriedon 12 Apr 1976.

Tony married **Kuang Mits Wei**.

The child from this marriage was:

392 F i. **Lily Wei Romball** was born on 24 Jul 1972.

176. Walter Tychkowsky *(Ksenia (Cassie) Dombrosky 5, Sofia Gurba 4, Semen 3, Stefan 2, Daniel 1)* was born in 1922 and died in Warspite, Alberta.

Walter married **Angline Olynik**.

The child from this marriage was:

393 M i. **David Tychkowsky**.

177. Lena Tychkowsky *(Ksenia (Cassie) Dombrosky 5, Sofia Gurba 4, Semen 3, Stefan 2, Daniel 1)* was born in 1924.

> Lena married **Nick Sloboda**. Nick was born in 1919.
>
> Children from this marriage were:
>
> 394 M i. **Mark Sloboda**.
>
> 395 M ii. **Neil Sloboda**.
>
> 396 M iii. **Myron Sloboda**.

178. George Tychkowsky *(Ksenia (Cassie) Dombrosky 5, Sofia Gurba 4, Semen 3, Stefan 2, Daniel 1)* was born in 1926.

> George married **Nadia Margaret Korpak**.
>
> Children from this marriage were:
>
> 397 M i. **Gregory Mark Tychkowsky**.
>
> 398 M ii. **James Tychkowsky**.
>
> 399 F iii. **Janet Tychkowsky** was born in 1955. Another name for Janet is Janet Brzezicki.
>
> Janet married **Tony Brzezicki**.
>
> 400 F iv. **Betty Nadia Tychkowsky** was born in 1960. Another name for Betty is Betty Nadia Schrider.
>
> Betty married **Dan Schrider**.
>
> 401 M v. **Richard George Tychkowsky** was born in 1962 and died in 1988 aged 26.
>
> 402 F vi. **Barbara Joan Tychkowsky** was born in 1972.

179. Adam Tychkowsky *(Ksenia (Cassie) Dombrosky 5, Sofia Gurba 4, Semen 3, Stefan 2, Daniel 1)* was born in 1928.

> Adam married **Arda Fae Fletcher**.
>
> Children from this marriage were:
>
> + 403 F i. **Dianna Michelle Tychkowsky**.

404   F   ii.   **Jennifer Elaine Tychkowsky**. Another name for Jennifer is Jennifer Elaine Seguin.

Jennifer married **John Gillies Seguin**.

405   M   iii.   **Michael Eric Tychkowsky**.

Michael married **Lea Marie Topuzoglu**. Another name for Lea is Lea Marie Tychkowski.

406   F   iv.   **Darlene Fae Tychkowsky** was born in 1963 and died in 1987 aged 24.

182. Francis Tychkowsky *(Ksenia (Cassie) Dombrosky 5, Sofia Gurba 4, Semen 3, Stefan 2, Daniel 1)* was born in 1933.

Francis married **Earl W. L. Deamude**.

Children from this marriage were:

+ 407   M   i.   **David Thomas Deamude**.

408   M   ii.   **Daniel Deamude**.

+ 409   M   iii.   **John Richard Deamude**.

+ 410   M   iv.   **Paul Douglas Deamude**.

+ 411   M   v.   **Donald Michael Deamude**.

+ 412   F   vi.   **Karen Loy Deamude**.

+ 413   M   vii.   **Robert Christopher Deamude**.

+ 414   M   viii.   **Edward Wayne Deamude**.

415   F   ix.   **Sharon Francis Deamude**.

+ 416   F   x.   **Barbara Lynn Deamude**.

183. Nestor Tychkowsky *(Ksenia (Cassie) Dombrosky 5, Sofia Gurba 4, Semen 3, Stefan 2, Daniel 1)* was born in 1937 and died in 1984 aged 47.

Nestor married **Margaret Arsenault**.

Children from this marriage were:

+ 417   F   i.   **Pauline Naomi Tychkowsky**.

418 F ii. **Naomi Cassie Tychkowsky**. Another name for Naomi is Naomi Cassie Reed.

Naomi married **Robert Reed**.

419 M iii. **Nestor Michael Tychkowsky**.

184. Eddie Dziwenka *(Tillie Dombrosky 5, Sofia Gurba 4, Semen 3, Stefan 2, Daniel 1)* died in Sep 1999 in Edmonton, Alberta and was buried on 1 Oct 1999 in Evergreen Cemetery, Edmonton.

Eddie married **Jean Pullishy**.

Children from this marriage were:

+ 420 F i. **Dianna Dziwenka**.

+ 421 F ii. **Judy Dziwenka**.

+ 422 F iii. **Elizabeth Dziwenka**.

423 F iv. **Cindy Dziwenka**.

185. Emma Dziwenka *(Tillie Dombrosky 5, Sofia Gurba 4, Semen 3, Stefan 2, Daniel 1)* was born in 1930. Another name for Emma is Emma Elliot.

Emma married **Bill Wilson**.

Children from this marriage were:

+ 424 M i. **Robert Wilson** was born in 1957.

+ 425 M ii. **Murray Wilson** was born in 1958.

Emma next married **Keith Elliot**.

186. Pat McNee *(Bessie Dombrosky 5, Sofia Gurba 4, Semen 3, Stefan 2, Daniel 1)*.

Pat married **Bob Chapman**.

The child from this marriage was:

426 M i. **Michael Chapman**.

Seventh Generation (4th Great-Grandchildren)

191. Joy Keymel *(Jean Budynski 6, Tylda Gurba 5, Antoni 4, Semen 3, Stefan 2, Dan iel 1)* was born in Jun 1941.

> Joy married **Anthony Ciarfella**.
>
> Children from this marriage were:
>
> > 427 M i. **Tony Ciarfella**.
> >
> > 428 F ii. **Jeanie Ciarfella** was born in 1966.
> >
> > 429 F iii. **Julie Ciarfella** was born in 1975.

198. Evelyn Marie Gordash *(Pauline Gurba 6, Lucas 5, Antoni 4, Semen 3, Stefan 2, Daniel 1)* was born on 3 Jul 1938 in Radway, Alberta. Another name for Evelyn is Evelyn Marie Chwok.

> Evelyn married **Mike Paul Chwok** on 7 Sep 1957 in Darling, Alberta, son of **Pete Chwok** and **Mary Chwok**. Mike was born on 10 Jul 1934, died on 26 Sep 2003 in Edmonton, Alberta aged 69, and was buried on 29 Sep 2003 in St. Michael's Cemetary, Edmonton, Albereta.
>
> Children from this marriage were:
>
> > + 430 M i. **Michael Wayne Chwok** was born on 18 Jan 1958 in Edmonton.
> >
> > + 431 M ii. **Steven Terry Chwok** was born on 1 Sep 1964 in Edmonton.

200. Joseph John Gordash *(Pauline Gurba 6, Lucas 5, Antoni 4, Semen 3, Stefan 2, Daniel 1)* was born on 14 Sep 1942 in Darling, Alberta.

> Joseph married **Evelyn Jean Kotylak** on 27 Feb 1965 in Edmonton, Alberta. Evelyn was born on 20 Jul 1943 in Radway, Alberta, died on 21 Feb 2003 aged 59, and was buried on 24 Feb 2003. Another name for Evelyn was Evelyn Jean Gordash.
>
> Children from this marriage were:
>
> > + 432 F i. **Maureen Ann Gordash** was born on 5 Jul 1965 in Edmonton, Alberta.
> >
> > 433 M ii. **Paul Gordash** was born on 5 Apr 1970 in Edmonton, Alberta.

201. Betty Lorraine Gordash *(Pauline Gurba 6, Lucas 5, Antoni 4, Semen 3, Stefan 2, Daniel 1)* was born on 28 Jan 1946 in Radway, Alberta. Another name for Betty is Betty Lorraine Screpnek.

> Betty married **George Screpnek** on 5 Jun 1971. George was born on 3 May 1939 in Peace River, Alberta.
>
> The child from this marriage was:
>
> > 434 M i. **Wade Matthew Screpnek** was born on 5 Feb 1973 in Edmonton, Alberta.

202. Phyllis Helen Horyn *(Lily Gurba 6, Lucas 5, Antoni 4, Semen 3, Stefan 2, Daniel 1)* was born on 18 Nov 1938 in Darling, Alberta. Another name for Phyllis is Phyllis Osadchuk.

> Phyllis married **Ernie Osadchuk** on 11 Jun 1960 in Waskatenau, Alberta, son of **Nick Osadchuk** and **Sophie Osadchuk**. Ernie was born on 16 Apr 1933 in Edmonton, Alberta and died on 6 Feb 1992 aged 58.
>
> Children from this marriage were:
>
> > 435 F i. **Loretta Kim Osadchuk** was born on 4 Dec 1961 in Smoky Lake, Alberta.
> >
> > + 436 M ii. **Gerald Nicholas Osadchuk** was born on 6 Feb 1963 in Smoky Lake, Alberta.
> >
> > + 437 M iii. **Walter (Wally) Ernest Osadchuk** was born on 20 Jun 1964 in Smoky Lake, Alberta.

205. Edward Victor Horyn *(Lily Gurba 6, Lucas 5, Antoni 4, Semen 3, Stefan 2, Daniel 1)* was born on 14 May 1943 in Radway, Alberta.

> Edward married **Diana Marie Orichowski** on 11 Jun 1965. Diana was born on 29 Jul 1946 in Radway, Alberta. Another name for Diana is Diana Marie Horyn.
>
> Children from this marriage were:
>
> > + 438 M i. **Dean Vincent Horyn** was born on 26 Nov 1965 in Edmonton, Alberta.
> >
> > 439 M ii. **Brent Elliott Horyn** was born on 25 Oct 1968 in Edmonton, Alberta.
> >
> > 440 F iii. **Trina Nadine Horyn** was born on 27 Mar 1977 in Edmonton, Alberta.

206. David Horyn *(Lily Gurba 6, Lucas 5, Antoni 4, Semen 3, Stefan 2, Daniel 1)* was born on 30 May 1949, died on 23 Sep 1984 aged 35, and was buried in Nativity BV Mary Ruthenian Greek Catholic Cemetery, Newbrook (nearby Darling, Alberta).

> David married **Doris Zukiwski**. Another name for Doris is Doris Horyn.
>
> Children from this marriage were:
>
> > 441　M　i.　**Stephan Horyn** was born in Apr 1973.
> >
> > + 442　F　ii.　**Christie Horyn** was born in 1975.

207. Donald Frederick Horyn *(Lily Gurba 6, Lucas 5, Antoni 4, Semen 3, Stefan 2, Daniel 1)* was born on 5 Oct 1951.

> Donald married **Linda Ryley**. Another name for Linda is Linda Horyn.
>
> The child from this marriage was:
>
> > 443　F　i.　**Crystal Dawn Horyn** was born on 10 Nov 1982 in Edmonton, Alberta.
> >
> > > Crystal married **Dale Matyjanka**. Dale was born in 1975 in Edmonton, Alberta.

208. Cynthia Lillian Horyn *(Lily Gurba 6, Lucas 5, Antoni 4, Semen 3, Stefan 2, Daniel 1)* was born on 13 Dec 1956 in Radway, Alberta. Another name for Cynthia is Cynthia Lillian Humm.

> Cynthia married **Doug Humm** on 1 Jun 1985 in Newbrook, Alberta. Doug was born on 27 Jul 1949.
>
> Children from this marriage were:
>
> > 444　M　i.　**David Humm**.
> >
> > 445　F　ii.　**Jaqueline Humm**.
> >
> > 446　M　iii.　**Jeffrey Humm**.
> >
> > 447　F　iv.　**Wendy Humm**.
> >
> > 448　M　v.　**Jason Humm**.

209. Gerald Gurba *(Joseph 6, Lucas 5, Antoni 4, Semen 3, Stefan 2, Daniel 1)* was born on 8 Jul 1952 inMyrnam, Alberta.

Gerald married **Elaine Hardy** on 7 Dec 1974. Elaine was born on 1 Jul 1953. Another name for Elaine is Elaine Gurba.

Children from this marriage were:

449 F i. **Leslie Kathryn Gurba** was born on 25 Oct 1984 in Calgary, Alberta.

450 F ii. **Leah Christine Gurba** was born on 24 Nov 1986.

211. Monica Gurba *(Joseph 6, Lucas 5, Antoni 4, Semen 3, Stefan 2, Daniel 1)* was born on 9 Apr 1955. Another name for Monica is Monica Stack.

Monica married **Peter Stack** on 20 Sep 1986. Peter was born on 12 Feb 1956.

Children from this marriage were:

451 M i. **Andrew Stack** was born on 20 Mar 1989 in Calgary, Alberta.

452 M ii. **Evan Stack** was born on 29 May 1991.

214. Rose Marie Gurba *(Joseph 6, Lucas 5, Antoni 4, Semen 3, Stefan 2, Daniel 1)* was born on 7 Feb 1962 in Edmonton, Alberta. Another name for Rose is Rose Marie McGee.

Rose married **Brian McGee**. Brian was born in 1962.

Children from this marriage were:

453 M i. **Michael McGee** was born on 29 Dec 1995.

454 M ii. **Patrick McGee** was born on 7 Jun 1997.

455 F iii. **Rebecca McGee** was born on 23 Mar 1999.

456 F iv. **Sarah McGee** was born on 25 Jan 2001.

215. Robert William Gurba *(Bill 6, Lucas 5, Antoni 4, Semen 3, Stefan 2, Daniel 1)* was born on 8 Sep 1949 in Radway, Alberta.

Robert married **Gail May Pasay** on 2 Jun 1973 in Darling, Alberta, daughter of **Frank Pasay** and **Olga Latka**. Gail was born on 26 Sep 1955 in Edmonton, Alberta. Another name for Gail is Gail Gurba.

Children from this marriage were:

457 F i. **Pamela Brandy Gurba** was born on 4 Jun 1980 in Edmonton, Alberta. Another name for Pamela is Pamela Brandy Northam.

Pamela married **Craig Northam** on 9 Oct 2003 in Bremerton, Washington. Craig was born on 25 Jul 1980 in Columbia, South Carolina.

 458 M ii. **Terence Robert Gurba** was born on 4 Jul 1983 in Inuvik, N.W.T..

Robert next married **Teri Dyanne Green** on 14 May 2000 in Plano, Texas. Teri was born on 21 Oct 1965 in Dardanelle, Arkansas. Another name for Teri is Teri Dyanne Gurba.

Children from this marriage were:

 459 F i. **Ashley Kay Sims** was born on 7 Aug 1985.

 460 F ii. **Tara Diane Sims** was born on 25 Feb 1987.

 461 F iii. **Rebecca Jo Becker** was born on 21 May 1991.

Robert next married **Janet Wilgus** on 23 Sep 2007.

216. Judith Ann Gurba *(Bill 6, Lucas 5, Antoni 4, Semen 3, Stefan 2, Daniel 1)* was born on 24 Jul 1951 in Radway, Alberta. Another name for Judith is Judith Ann Paranich.

Judith married **Stanley Vincent Paranich** on 19 Aug 1972 in Darling, Alberta. Stanley was born on 6 Aug 1951 in Edmonton, Alberta.

The child from this marriage was:

 462 F i. **Holly Ann-Marie Paranich** was born on 10 Jan 1982 in Edmonton, Alberta.

217. Theodore Wayne Gurba *(Bill 6, Lucas 5, Antoni 4, Semen 3, Stefan 2, Daniel 1)* was born on 13 Jun 1953 in Radway, Alberta.

Theodore married **Doreen Norell** on 1 Sep 1976. Doreen was born on 19 Apr 1960. Another name for Doreen is Doreen Gurba.

The child from this marriage was:

 463 M i. **Donald Michael Corey Gurba** was born on 13 Aug 1977 in Edmonton, Alberta.

Theodore next married **Lorie Calihoo** on 13 Aug 1988 in Fort Saskatchewan, Alberta. Another name for Lorie is Lorie Gurba.

218. Carol Lynn Gurba *(Bill 6, Lucas 5, Antoni 4, Semen 3, Stefan 2, Daniel 1)* was born on 8 Dec 1956 in Radway, Alberta. Another name for Carol is Carol Lynn Sauchuk.

Carol married **Gerald Wayne Sauchuk** on 19 Jun 1976 in Darling, Alberta. Gerald was born on 26 May 1953 in Smoky Lake, Alberta.

Children from this marriage were:

> 464   M   i.   **Jason William Sauchuk** was born on 31 Jul 1982 in Smoky Lake, Alberta.
>
> > Jason married **Erin Lindsay Penner** on 13 Oct 2007 in Darling, Alberta. Erin was born on 9 Dec.
>
> 465   M   ii.   **Jeffrey Stefan Sauchuk** was born on 30 Jan 1986 in Smoky Lake, Alberta.

219. Bernard James Gurba *(Bill 6, Lucas 5, Antoni 4, Semen 3, Stefan 2, Daniel 1)* was born on 1 Feb 1959 in Radway, Alberta.

> Bernard married **Karen Onyschuk** on 18 Jul 1981 in Darling, Alberta, daughter of **Jack Onyschuk** and **Lena Wonsik**. Karen was born on 26 Mar 1959 in Thorhild, Alberta. Another name for Karen is Karen Gurba.

Children from this marriage were:

> 466   M   i.   **Bernard Jacob (BJ) Gurba** was born on 28 Oct 1986 in Edmonton, Alberta.
>
> 467   M   ii.   **Joshua James Gurba** was born on 24 Jan 1990 in Edmonton, Alberta.

221. Zenon Lester Gurba *(Bill 6, Lucas 5, Antoni 4, Semen 3, Stefan 2, Daniel 1)* was born on 1 Apr 1963 in Radway, Alberta.

> Zenon married **Sharlene Gail Toronchuk** on 5 Jul 1986 in Darling, Alberta, daughter of **Lorne Toronchuk** and **June Pelechaty**. Sharlene was born on 28 Aug 1965 in Edmonton, Alberta. Another name for Sharlene is Sharlene Gurba.

Children from this marriage were:

> 468   F   i.   **Lisa Marie Gurba** was born on 6 Mar 1990 in Fort Saskatchewan, Alberta.
>
> 469   M   ii.   **Stefan Zenon Gurba** was born on 10 Feb 1992 in Fort Saskatchewan, Alberta.

222. Randy Joseph Wosnack *(Nettie Gurba 6, Lucas 5, Antoni 4, Semen 3, Stefan 2, Daniel 1)* was born on 5 Jan 1952 in Edmonton, Alberta.

Randy married **Terry Smith** on 17 Aug 1974 in Redwater, Alberta. Terry was born on 16 Feb 1954 in Edmonton, Alberta. Another name for Terry is Terry Wosnack.

Children from this marriage were:

470 F i. **Tianna Roberta Wosnack** was born on 26 Sep 1980 in Edmonton, Alberta.

471 M ii. **Scott Randall Wosnack** was born on 24 Oct 1984 in Edmonton, Alberta.

Randy next married **Debra Murray Ogrodiuk** on 3 Jan 2000 in Ashmont, Alberta. Debra was born on 4 Sep 1953. Another name for Debra is Debbie Wosnack.

223. Sidney Wosnack *(Nettie Gurba 6, Lucas 5, Antoni 4, Semen 3, Stefan 2, Daniel 1)* was born on 29 Jul 1953 in Edmonton, Alberta.

Sidney married **Rose Landman** on 19 Jun 1975 in Coeur d'Alene, Idaho. Rose was born on 30 May 1956 in Creston, B.C.. Another name for Rose is Rose Wosnack.

Children from this marriage were:

472 M i. **Cory Dean Wosnack** was born on 1 May 1974 in Pincher Creek, Alberta.

Cory married **Antara Spitzig** on 5 May 2001 in Edmonton, Alberta. Antara was born on 27 Dec 1976. Another name for Antara is Antara Wosnack.

473 M ii. **Kelly James Wosnack** was born on 8 Jan 1981 in Redwater, Alberta.

224. Linda Mae Wosnack *(Nettie Gurba 6, Lucas 5, Antoni 4, Semen 3, Stefan 2, Daniel 1)* was born on 24 Nov 1962 in Edmonton, Alberta. Another name for Linda is Linda Mae Simpson.

Linda married **John Charest**. John was born on 28 Sep 1958 and died on 26 Nov 1992 aged 34.

The child from this marriage was:

474 M i. **Mathew Joseph Charest** was born on 20 Aug 1986 in Edmonton, Alberta.

Linda next married **Dean Simpson** on 7 Jun 1997 in Sherwood Park, Alberta. Dean was born on 8 Nov 1960 in Edmonton, Alberta.

225. Jerome Russell Toronchuk *(Olga Tillie Gurba 6, Lucas 5, Antoni 4, Semen 3, Stefan 2, Daniel 1)* was born on 26 Jan 1958 in Edmonton, Alberta.

Jerome married **Coralie Alison Cawston** on 16 Feb 1985 in Vancouver, British Columbia, daughter of **Leslie Cawston** and **Alison Hibbs**. Coralie was born on 24 May 1965. Another name for Coralie is Coralie Alison Toronchuk.

Children from this marriage were:

> 475 F i. **Rachel Elizabeth Toronchuk** was born on 20 Aug 1986 in Edmonton, Alberta.

> 476 M ii. **Jonathan Lucas Toronchuk** was born on 22 Apr 1988 in Edmonton, Alberta.

228. James Bradley Gurba *(Paul Bohdan 6, Lucas 5, Antoni 4, Semen 3, Stefan 2, Daniel 1)* was born on 29 Oct 1968 in Edmonton, Alberta.

James married **Cindy Keith** on 20 Aug 2005 in Edmonton, Alberta.

The child from this marriage was:

> 477 M i. **Cody Keith**.

231. Richard Joseph Gurba *(Peter Roman 6, Lucas 5, Antoni 4, Semen 3, Stefan 2, Daniel 1)* was born on 23 Nov 1969 in Norman Wells, NWT.

Richard married **Cheryl Ann Gray** in Jul 2000 in Edmonton, Alberta. Cheryl was born on 5 Nov 1975. Another name for Cheryl is Cheryl Gurba.

Children from this marriage were:

> 478 M i. **Jordan William Gurba** was born on 20 May 2001 in Edmonton, Alberta.

> 479 M ii. **Jonathan Michael Gurba** was born on 28 Oct 2004 in St. Albert, Alberta.

> 480 M iii. **Jayden John Dale Krembil** was born on 9 Feb 1996.

233. Jason Maurice Luke Gurba *(Maurice 6, Lucas 5, Antoni 4, Semen 3, Stefan 2, Daniel 1)* was born on 5 Jun 1976 in Athabasca, Alberta.

Jason married **Marie Lee Patrick** on 18 Jun 2005 in Edmonton, Alberta. Marie was born on 24 Jan 1977 in Westlock, Alberta. Another name for Marie is Marie Lee Gurba.

The child from this marriage was:

481　F　i.　**Avery Madison Gurba** was born on 16 Dec 2007.

234. Sheryl Lynn Marie Wenger *(Nester F. Wenger 6, Rose Gurba 5, Antoni 4, Semen 3, Stefan 2, Daniel 1)* was born on 11 Jun 1963 in Smoky Lake, Alberta. Another name for Sheryl is Sheryl Lynn Marie Karba.

Sheryl married **Fred Karba** on 8 Jun 1985. Fred was born on 9 Jun 1960 in Edmonton, Alberta.

The child from this marriage was:

482　M　i.　**Shane Michael George Karba** was born on 9 Jun 1989 in Edmonton, Alberta

237. Randolph Sawchuk *(Rose Wenger 6, Rose Gurba 5, Antoni 4, Semen 3, Stefan 2, Daniel 1)* was born on 10 Oct 1961 in Smoky Lake, Alberta.

Randolph married **Lorelei Michalow** on 28 Jun 1986. Lorelei was born on 28 May 1963 in Fort Smith, N.W.T.. Another name for Lorelei is Lorelei Sawchuk.

The child from this marriage was:

483　M　i.　**Alek John Sawchuk** was born in Aug 1992.

238. Katherine Anne Mykytiuk *(Helen Bezborodka 6, Francesca Gurba 5, Antoni 4, Semen 3, Stefan 2, Daniel 1)* was born on 8 Feb 1955 in Edmonton, Alberta. Another name for Katherine is Katherine Anne Rosadiuk.

Katherine married **John Rosadiuk** on 17 Aug 1974 in Wildwood, Alberta. John was born on 12 Jun 1954 in Evansburg, Alberta.

Children from this marriage were:

484　M　i.　**Adam Rosadiuk** was born on 21 Nov 1978 in Edmonton, Alberta.

485　M　ii.　**Kristopher Rosadiuk** was born on 30 Apr 1981 in Edmonton, Alberta.

486　F　iii.　**Stacy Rosadiuk** was born on 17 Feb 1984 in Edmonton, Alberta.

487　F　iv.　**Elyssa Rosadiuk** was born on 14 Dec 1995 in Edmonton, Alberta.

243. Ryan Nicholas McMurdo *(Mae Mary-Pearl Bezborodka 6, Francesca Gurba 5, Antoni 4, Semen 3, Stefan 2, Daniel 1)* was born on 6 Jun 1961 in Red Deer, Alberta.

Ryan married **Shonna Lajeunesse** on 22 Sep 1990 in Red Deer, Alberta. Shonna was born in 1961. Another name for Shonna is Shonna McMurdo.

Children from this marriage were:

488　F　i.　**Natalie Mae McMurdo** was born in 1992 in Calgary, Alberta.

489　M　ii.　**Lyndan Nicholas McMurdo** was born in 1996 in Calgary, Alberta.

244. Gwen Gurba *(Walter 6, Steve 5, Antoni 4, Semen 3, Stefan 2, Daniel 1)* was born on 11 Dec 1961 in Edmonton, Alberta.

Gwen married **Ted Linkewich**. Ted was born on 26 Aug 1960 in Edmonton, Alberta.

The child from this marriage was:

490　F　i.　**Brandi Mary Linkewich** was born on 1 Aug 1997 in Edmonton, Alberta.

245. George Walter Gurba *(Walter 6, Steve 5, Antoni 4, Semen 3, Stefan 2, Daniel 1)* was born on 18 Apr 1964 in Edmonton, Alberta.

George married **Cindy Sawchyn** on 19 May 1990 in Edmonton, Alberta. Cindy was born on 19 Apr 1965 in Edmonton, Alberta. Another name for Cindy is Cindy Gurba.

Children from this marriage were:

491　M　i.　**Tyler Steven Gurba** was born on 27 Jun 1994 in Edmonton, Alberta.

492　M　ii.　**Ryan Michael Gurba** was born on 15 Apr 1997 in Edmonton, Alberta.

493　F　iii.　**Kyleigh Sarah Gurba** was born on 11 Mar 2003.

246. Gordon Gurba *(Walter 6, Steve 5, Antoni 4, Semen 3, Stefan 2, Daniel 1)* was born on 7 Apr 1966 in Edmonton, Alberta.

Gordon married **Michelle Mix** on 14 Jun 1997. Another name for Michelle is Michelle Gurba.

Children from this marriage were:

494 M i. **Gregory Norman Gurba** was born on 6 Apr 2001 in Edmonton, Alberta.

495 M ii. **Geoffrey Gurba**.

247. Gary Gurba *(Walter 6, Steve 5, Antoni 4, Semen 3, Stefan 2, Daniel 1)* was born on 7 Jan 1972 in Edmonton, Alberta.

Gary married **Lisa Billey** on 20 Jul 2002. Lisa was born on 20 Jan 1968 in Edmonton, Alberta. Another name for Lisa is Lisa Gurba.

Children from this marriage were:

496 F i. **Layne Gurba** was born in Feb 1996.

497 M ii. **Luka Gurba**.

250. Brigitte Marie Gurba *(Eugene Adolf 6, Steve 5, Antoni 4, Semen 3, Stefan 2, Daniel 1)* was born on 8 Nov 1968 in Lamont, Alberta. Another name for Brigitte is Brigitte Large.

Brigitte married **Dirk Arthur Large** on 19 Sep 1992 in Edmonton, Alberta. Dirk was born on 28 Dec 1960 in Winnipeg, Manitoba.

Children from this marriage were:

498 F i. **Shawna Marie Large** was born on 17 Oct 1996 in Edmonton, Alberta.

499 M ii. **Joshua Large** was born on 29 May 2000 in Edmonton, Alberta.

253. William Pietz *(Sylvia Gurba 6, Steve 5, Antoni 4, Semen 3, Stefan 2, Daniel 1)* was born on 13 Sep 1963 in Edmonton, Alberta.

William married **Karen Atkinson** on 22 Jun 2002. Another name for Karen is Karen Pietz.

Children from this marriage were:

500 F i. **Teegan Pietz** was born in 1994.

501 M ii. **Blake Pietz** was born in 1996.

258. Brenda Gurba *(Sylvester 6, Steve 5, Antoni 4, Semen 3, Stefan 2, Daniel 1)* was born on 5 Mar 1969 in Edmonton, Alberta. Another name for Brenda is Brenda Mazzuca.

Brenda married **Gino Mazzuca** in Edmonton, Alberta. Gino was born in 1966 in Edmonton, Alberta.

Children from this marriage were:

    502 M i. **Alissandro Mazzuca** was born on 10 Jul 1998 in Edmonton, Alberta.

    503 F ii. **Isabella Justine Mazzuca** was born on 9 Mar 2002 in Edmonton, Alberta.

261. Wayne Budynski *(Louie Budynski 6, Wladek (William) Budynski 5, Anna Gurba 4, Semen 3, Stefan 2, Daniel 1)* was born in Jul 1945 and died on 5 Jul 1994 aged 49.

Wayne married **Julie Zukiwsky**. Julie was born in 1945. Another name for Julie is Julie Budynski.

The child from this marriage was:

+ 504 M i. **Wayne Budynski** was born on 2 Oct 1962.

262. Ken Budynski *(Louie Budynski 6, Wladek (William) Budynski 5, Anna Gurba 4, Semen 3, Stefan 2, Daniel 1)* was born on 10 Jan 1947.

Ken married **Sharon Tough**. Sharon was born on 13 Aug 1948. Another name for Sharon is Sharon Budynski.

Children from this marriage were:

    505 M i. **Dean Wesley Budynski** was born on 17 Apr 1972.

    506 M ii. **Darcy Stuart Budynski** was born on 7 Feb 1975.

263. Anna Mae Budynski *(Kaizer (Clarence) Budynski 6, Wladek (William) Budynski 5, Anna Gurba 4, Semen 3, Stefan 2, Daniel 1)* was born on 16 May 1937. Another name for Anna is Anna Mae Dyson.

Anna married **John Dyson**.

Children from this marriage were:

+ 507 M i. **John Jr. Dyson** was born on 28 Jun 1960.

    508 M ii. **Duane Dyson** was born on 29 Nov 1963.

266. Chester Doulis *(Marie Budynski 6, Wladek (William) Budynski 5, Anna Gurba 4, Semen 3, Stefan 2, Daniel 1)* was born on 23 Apr 1948.

Chester married **Diane.**

Children from this marriage were:

509 F i. **Alexis Doulis.**

510 F ii. **Casandra Doulis.**

271. Orville Budynski *(Joseph Lawrence Budynski 6, Wladek (William) Budynski 5, Anna Gurba 4, Semen 3, Stefan 2, Daniel 1)* was born on 25 Mar 1937 in Dinant, Alberta.

Orville married **Janet Mould.**

Children from this marriage were:

511 M i. **Dale Budynski.**

512 F ii. **Debra Budynski.**

Orville next married **Roselyn Lanzorotta** on 25 Mar 1965. Roselyn was born on 12 Jan 1940 in Toronto, Ontario.

Children from this marriage were:

513 F i. **Linda May Budynski** was born on 27 Apr 1960.

+ 514 M ii. **Darryl Wayne Budynski** was born on 27 Dec 1962.

515 M iii. **Brian Joseph Budynski** was born on 8 Jan 1964.

516 F iv. **Sherry (Sheryl) Doreen Budynski** was born on 22 Jul 1965.

517 F v. **Charlene Budynski** was born on 2 Nov 1970.

276. Daniel Budynski *(Joseph Lawrence Budynski 6, Wladek (William) Budynski 5, Anna Gurba 4, Semen 3, Stefan 2, Daniel 1)* died in 1988 in Kitchner, Ontario and was buried in Royal Oak Burial Park, Victoria, British Columbia.

Daniel married **Christine.**

Children from this marriage were:

518 M i. **Shaun Budynski.**

519 F ii. **Jessica Budynski.**

277. Norma Rossell *(Virginia (Ginnie) Budynski 6, Wladek (William) Budynski 5, Anna Gurba 4, Semen 3, Stefan 2, Daniel 1)*.

Norma married **? Perkins**.

Children from this marriage were:

    520 M i. **? Perkins**.

    521 M ii. **? Perkins**

278. Judy Rossell *(Virginia (Ginnie) Budynski 6, Wladek (William) Budynski 5, Anna Gurba 4, Semen 3, Stefan 2, Daniel 1)*.

Judy married **? Rigby**.

Children from this marriage were:

    522 M i. **Chris Rigby** was born in 1971.

    523 M ii. **Banji Rigby** was born in 1973.

279. Carl David Mack *(Carl Anthony Mack 6, Rose Budynski 5, Anna Gurba 4, Semen 3, Stefan 2, Daniel 1)* was born on 24 Sep 1941.

Carl married **Mary Jacobs**. Mary was born on 21 Sep 1939. Another name for Mary is Mary Mack.

Children from this marriage were:

  + 524 M i. **Keith Mack** was born on 13 Mar 1962.

  + 525 M ii. **Roger Mack** was born on 1 May 1967.

  + 526 M iii. **Steve Mack** was born on 25 Feb 1970.

280. Barbara Sis Mack *(Carl Anthony Mack 6, Rose Budynski 5, Anna Gurba 4, Semen 3, Stefan 2, Daniel 1)* was born on 30 May 1943. Another name for Barbara is Barbara Sis Gaver.

Barbara married **Tom Gaver Jr.** on 8 Apr 1967. Tom was born on 30 Oct 1941.

Children from this marriage were:

    527 M i. **Jason Gaver** was born on 25 May 1970.

    528 F ii. **Melissa Gaver** was born on 15 Jan 1972.

    529 M iii. **Jonathan Gaver** was born on 5 Oct 1987.

281. Sandra Mack *(Carl Anthony Mack 6, Rose Budynski 5, Anna Gurba 4, Semen 3, Stefan 2, Daniel 1)* was born on 21 Aug 1944. Another name for Sandra is Sandra Kimball.

> Sandra married **Joe B. Kimball**. Joe was born on 19 Nov 1942.
>
> Children from this marriage were:
>
> + 530 M i. **Joey Kimball**.
>
> + 531 F ii. **Brenda Kimball**.

283. Nestor Robert Mack *(Nestor Mack 6, Rose Budynski 5, Anna Gurba 4, Semen 3, Stefan 2, Daniel 1)* was born on 24 Nov 1942.

> Nestor married **Ellen Totsie Roberts** on 14 Jan 1977 in Houston, Texas. Ellen was born on 21 Jun 1955. Another name for Ellen is Ellen Totsie Mack.
>
> Children from this marriage were:
>
> 532 F i. **Christina Shawn Mack** was born on 18 Oct 1968 in San Benito, Texas. Another name for Christina is Christina Shawn Snaples.
>
>> Christina married **Noble Lee Snaples Jr.** on 25 May 1991 in San Benito, Texas. Noble was born on 18 Aug 1968 in San Benito, Texas.
>
> + 533 M ii. **Kenneth Robert Mack** was born on 28 Jan 1972 in Houston, Texas.
>
> Nestor next married **Suzanne Carol Rockwell**. Another name for Suzanne is Suzanne Carol Mack

284. Constance Rose Russell *(Verna Mack 6, Rose Budynski 5, Anna Gurba 4, Semen 3, Stefan 2, Daniel 1)* was born on 22 Sep 1942 in Rochester New York. Another name for Constance is Constance Tilley.

> Constance married **David Haskell Tilley** on 18 Jul 1964 in San Benito, Texas. David was born on 13 Jun 1939 in Ada, Oklahoma.
>
> Children from this marriage were:
>
> 534 M i. **Mathew David Tilley** was born on 6 May 1968 in Olongapo, Zambales, Phillipines.
>
> + 535 F ii. **Karen Glynn Tilley** was born on 18 May 1967 in Olongapo, Zambales, Phillipines.

+ 536   M   iii.   **Russell Backus Tilley** was born on 15 Oct 1978 in Kingsville, Texas.

285. Kenneth Joseph Russell *(Verna Mack 6, Rose Budynski 5, Anna Gurba 4, Semen 3, Stefan 2, Daniel 1)* was born on 3 Oct 1940 in Rochester, New York.

Kenneth married **Charlotte (Cherry) Voorhies** on 20 Feb 1965. Charlotte was born on 30 Mar 1941 in Lake Charles, Louisana and died on 31 Mar 2003 in Houston, Texas aged 62. Another name for Charlotte was Charlotte (Cherry) Russell.

Children from this marriage were:

+ 537   F   i.   **Robin Russell** was born on 6 May 1970 in Houston, Texas.

538   F   ii.   **Laurie Russell** was born on 28 Sep 1972 in Houston, Texas. Another name for Laurie is Laurie Abreo.

Laurie married **Damian Abreo** on 22 Jun 2002. Damian was born on 6 Dec 1972 in Houston, Texas.

286. Richard Dick Matwyshen *(Helen Mack 6, Rose Budynski 5, Anna Gurba 4, Semen 3, Stefan 2, Daniel 1)* was born on 3 Sep 1948.

Richard married **Bonnie Maginnis**. The marriage ended in divorce. Another name for Bonnie is Bonnie Matwyshen.

The child from this marriage was:

539   F   i.   **Suzanne Matwyshen**. Another name for Suzanne is Suzanne Gillen.

Suzanne married **Paul Gillen**.

287. Gary Mack *(Wilfred (Will) Barney Mack 6, Rose Budynski 5, Anna Gurba 4, Semen 3, Stefan 2, Daniel 1)* was born on 21 Oct 1952.

Gary married **Pam Thompson**. The marriage ended in divorce. Another name for Pam is Pam Mack.

Children from this marriage were:

540   M   i.   **David Mack** was born on 28 Nov 1972.

541   M   ii.   **Daniel Lee Mack** was born on 21 Jun 1974 and died on 3 Jan 1976 aged 1.

542   F   iii.   **Leigh Ann Mack** was born on 30 Jan 1980.

Gary next married **Nita C. Barker**. Nita was born on 6 Jan 1952. Another name for Nita is Nita C. Mack.

288. Paula Mack *(Wilfred (Will) Barney Mack 6, Rose Budynski 5, Anna Gurba 4, Semen 3, Stefan 2, Daniel 1)* was born on 27 Jun 1954. Another name for Paula is Paula Sargent.

Paula married **Greg Sargent**.

Children from this marriage were:

    543 M i. **Mack Sargent**.

    544 F ii. **Samantha Sargent**.

289. Michael Demmert *(Stella Bernice Mack 6, Rose Budynski 5, Anna Gurba 4, Semen 3, Stefan 2, Daniel 1)* was born on 16 Aug 1948 and died on 17 Nov 2004 in Lady Lake, Florida aged 56.

Michael married **Andrea Pasino**. The marriage ended in divorce. Another name for Andrea is Andrea Demmeret.

The child from this marriage was:

    545 F i. **Andrea Demmert**.

290. Judi Demmert *(Stella Bernice Mack 6, Rose Budynski 5, Anna Gurba 4, Semen 3, Stefan 2, Daniel 1)* was born on 10 Jun 1952 in Rochester New York. Another name for Judi is Judi Tancrede.

Judi married **Robert Tancrede** on 15 Apr 1995. Robert was born on 12 May 1948 in LeRoy, New York.

Children from this marriage were:

+ 546 F i. **Kristin Tancrede** was born on 17 Jul 1981 in Rochester New York.

    547 F ii. **Michelle Tancrede** was born on 23 Aug 1986 in Rochester New York.

291. Robert (Bobby) Demmert *(Stella Bernice Mack 6, Rose Budynski 5, Anna Gurba 4, Semen 3, Stefan 2, Daniel 1)* was born on 27 Feb 1954.

Robert married **Carol Fortin**. Another name for Carol is Carol Demmeret.

Children from this marriage were:

548   M   i.   **Scott Clausen**.

549   M   ii.   **Eric Clausen**.

292. Eddy Mack *(Edward A. Mack 6, Rose Budynski 5, Anna Gurba 4, Semen 3, Stefan 2, Daniel 1)* was born on 31 Mar 1956.

Eddy married **Denice Kolasinski** on 21 Oct 1980. Denice was born on 5 May 1955. Another name for Denice is Denice Mack.

Children from this marriage were:

550   F   i.   **Kristen Mack** was born on 9 Jul 1982.

551   M   ii.   **Eric Mack** was born on 7 May 1985.

293. Wilfred D. Mack *(Edward A. Mack 6, Rose Budynski 5, Anna Gurba 4, Semen 3, Stefan 2, Daniel 1)* was born on 4 Apr 1957.

Wilfred married **Rene Taylor** on 10 Apr 1980. Rene was born on 3 Oct 1957. Another name for Rene is Rene Mack.

Children from this marriage were:

+ 552   M   i.   **Ryan Mack** was born on 18 Jan 1981.

553   M   ii.   **Shane Mack** was born on 13 Oct 1989.

294. Joseph M. Mack *(Edward A. Mack 6, Rose Budynski 5, Anna Gurba 4, Semen 3, Stefan 2, Daniel 1)* was born on 18 Apr 1960.

Joseph married **Norina Cranmer** on 14 Feb 1996. Norina was born on 23 Jun 1968. Another name for Norina is Norina Mack.

The child from this marriage was:

554   M   i.   **Tyler Mack** was born on 29 Apr 1989.

Joseph next married **Maria Walentik** in 1981. The marriage ended in divorce. Another name for Maria is Maria Mack.

295. Linda Mack *(Edward A. Mack 6, Rose Budynski 5, Anna Gurba 4, Semen 3, Stefan 2, Daniel 1)* was born on 10 Sep 1961. Another name for Linda is Linda Arnott.

Linda married **James Arnott** on 27 Mar 1982. James was born on 7 May 1959.

Children from this marriage were:

555 M i. **Stephen Arnott** was born on 20 Apr 1983.

556 M ii. **Christopher Arnott** was born on 19 Jan 1985.

557 F iii. **Tiffanie Arnott** was born on 16 Nov 1990.

297. Betty Mack *(Edward A. Mack 6, Rose Budynski 5, Anna Gurba 4, Semen 3, Stefan 2, Daniel 1)* was born on **8 Sep 1968**. Another name for Betty is Betty Burke.

Betty married **Bob Burke** on 10 Aug 1996. Bob was born on 6 Mar 1969.

Children from this marriage were:

558 F i. **Courtney Burke** was born on 8 Apr 1998.

559 F ii. **Cassidy Burke** was born on 10 Jun 2002.

298. Jerry Mack *(Edward A. Mack 6, Rose Budynski 5, Anna Gurba 4, Semen 3, Stefan 2, Daniel 1)* was born on **25 Aug 1970**.

Jerry married **Faye Martin**. Another name for Faye is Faye Mack.

Children from this marriage were:

560 F i. **Amber Mack**.

561 M ii. **Jacob Mack** was born on 16 Nov 1994 and died on 10 Feb 1996 aged 1.

562 M iii. **Trystan Mack** was born on 16 Sep 1996.

299. Rosie Mack *(Edward A. Mack 6, Rose Budynski 5, Anna Gurba 4, Semen 3, Stefan 2, Daniel 1)* was born on **31 Jul 1971**. Another name for Rosie is Rosie Perrin.

Rosie married **Jim Perrin**. The marriage ended in divorce.

The child from this marriage was:

563 F i. **Katie Perrin** was born on 3 Jul 1996.

300. Marilyn K. Mack *(Florian Sy Mack 6, Rose Budynski 5, Anna Gurba 4, Semen 3, Stefan 2, Daniel 1)* was born on **3 Feb 1952** in San Benito, Texas. Other names for Marilyn are Marilyn K. Collins, and Marilyn K. Pineda.

Marilyn married **Thomas Collins** on 24 Jun 1973 in Tucson, Arizona. The marriage ended in divorce.

The child from this marriage was:

564 M i. **Jason Thomas Collins** was born on 30 Mar 1974 in Tucson, Arizona and died on 29 Jun 1994 in Tucson, Arizona aged 20.

Marilyn next married **Roberto Joseph Pineda** on 21 Mar 1979 in Okanogan, Washington. Roberto was born on 9 Mar 1942 in Guatamala.

Children from this marriage were:

565 F i. **Emelina Maria Pineda** was born on 21 Mar 1980 in Omak, Washington.

+ 566 F ii. **Lana Michelle Pineda** was born on 4 Sep 1983 in Omak, Washington.

Marilyn next married **Paul Sheldon**.

302. Michelle Marie Mack *(Florian Sy Mack 6, Rose Budynski 5, Anna Gurba 4, Semen 3, Stefan 2, Daniel 1)* was born on 29 Nov 1962 in Tucson, Arizona. Another name for Michelle is Michelle Marie Landess.

Michelle married **Thomas Wade Landess** on 1 Jun 1980 in Tucson, Arizona. Thomas was born on 30 Nov 1958 in Roswell, New Mexico.

Children from this marriage were:

567 F i. **Ellen Rene Landess** was born on 13 Aug 1985 in Soldotna, Alaska.

568 F ii. **Leslie Elaine Landess** was born on 13 Jul 1988 in Soldotna, Alaska.

569 F iii. **Melissa Michelle Landess** was born on 12 Jun 1991 in Soldotna, Alaska.

303. James Jimmy Jordan *(Gloria Mack 6, Rose Budynski 5, Anna Gurba 4, Semen 3, Stefan 2, Daniel 1)* was born on 6 Aug 1950 and died on 2 Mar 1993 in Harlingen, Texas aged 42.

James married someone

His children were:

570 M i. **Christopher Jordan** was born on 19 Sep 1980.

571 F ii. **Katalean Jordan** was born on 28 Feb 1985.

306. Stephen Jordan *(Gloria Mack 6, Rose Budynski 5, Anna Gurba 4, Semen 3, Stefan 2, Daniel 1)* was born on 31 Mar 1955.

Stephen married **Beverly Clark** on 7 Jan 1979. Beverly was born on 17 Sep 1958. Another name for Beverly is Beverly Jordan.

Children from this marriage were:

572 F i. **Kimberly Jordan** was born on 17 Apr 1986.

573 F ii. **Michelle Jordan** was born on 12 Jun 1990.

307. Margaret Jordan *(Gloria Mack 6, Rose Budynski 5, Anna Gurba 4, Semen 3, Stefan 2, Daniel 1)* was born on 12 Aug 1957. Another name for Margaret is Margaret Ferris.

Margaret married **Jerry Ferris**.

Children from this marriage were:

574 M i. **Kelly Ferris**.

575 M ii. **Matthew Ferris**.

311. Thomas Forsyth *(Mary Anne Britt 6, Frances A. Budynski 5, Anna Gurba 4, Semen 3, Stefan 2, Daniel 1)* was born on 21 Jun 1953 in Lockport, Niagara, New York and died on 3 Jun 2008 in Lockport, Niagara, New York aged 54.

Thomas married someone

His child was:

+ 576 M i. **Thomas Forsyth Jr.**

319. Darlene Boychuk *(John Boychuk 6, Rosalia (Rosa) Stecyk 5, Kate Gurba 4, Semen 3, Stefan 2, Daniel 1)* was born on 18 Jan 1950 in Radway, Alberta. Another name for Darlene is Darlene Tchir.

Darlene married **Dennis Tchir**. Dennis was born on 8 Sep 1946 in Lamont, Alberta.

Children from this marriage were:

577 F i. **C rystal Tchir** was born on 20 Oct 1978 in Edmonton, Alberta.

578 M ii. **Jason Tchir** was born on 8 Apr 1980 in Edmonton, Alberta.

324. Jane Boychuk *(Steve Boychuk 6, Rosalia (Rosa) Stecyk 5, Kate Gurba 4, Semen 3, Stefan 2, Daniel 1)* . Another name for Jane is Jane Fletcher.

Jane married **? Fletcher**.

The child from this marriage was:

+ 579   F   i. **Lacey Fletcher**.

326. Cindy Boychuk *(Steve Boychuk 6, Rosalia (Rosa) Stecyk 5, Kate Gurba 4, Semen 3, Stefan 2, Daniel 1)*. Another name for Cindy is Cindy Starkevich.

Cindy married **Brian Starkevich**.

Children from this marriage were:

580   F   i. **Diane Starkevich**.

581   M   ii. **Colin Starkevich**.

582   F   iii. **Lisa Starkevich**.

331. Leslie Popil *(Mary Boychuk 6, Rosalia (Rosa) Stecyk 5, Kate Gurba 4, Semen 3, Stefan 2, Daniel 1)*. Another name for Leslie is Leslie Gardener.

Leslie married **Ron Gardener**.

Children from this marriage were:

583   M   i. **Colten Gardener**.

584   M   ii. **Mackenzie Gardener**.

332. Chris Popil *(Mary Boychuk 6, Rosalia (Rosa) Stecyk 5, Kate Gurba 4, Semen 3, Stefan 2, Daniel 1)*.

Chris married **Jackie Fox**. Another name for Jackie is Jackie Popil.

Children from this marriage were:

585   M   i. **Dean Popil**.

586   M   ii. **Mitchell Popil**.

587   F   iii. **Tawnee Popil**.

334. Linda Prokuda *(Winnie Boychuk 6, Rosalia (Rosa) Stecyk 5, Kate Gurba 4, Semen 3, Stefan 2, Daniel 1).*

Linda married **? Lagaden.**

Children from this marriage were:

588 F i. **Melinda Lagaden.**

589 M ii. **Robert Lagaden.**

590 M iii. **Dustin Lagaden.**

591 F iv. **Clancy Lagaden.**

336. Debbie Prokuda *(Winnie Boychuk 6, Rosalia (Rosa) Stecyk 5, Kate Gurba 4, Semen 3, Stefan 2, Daniel 1).* Another name for Debbie is Debbie Gillis.

Debbie married **? Gillis.**

The child from this marriage was:

592 F i. **Amanda Rose Gillis.**

343. Patricia Joanne Olexin *(Alexandra Boychuk 6, Rosalia (Rosa) Stecyk 5, Kate Gurba 4, Semen 3, Stefan 2, Daniel 1).* Another name for Patricia is Patricia Joanne Lang.

Patricia married **Michael Lang.**

The child from this marriage was:

593 M i. **Harley Gray Lang**

\
344. Robert Mitchell Olexin *(Alexandra Boychuk 6, Rosalia (Rosa) Stecyk 5, Kate Gurba 4, Semen 3, Stefan 2, Daniel 1).*

Robert married **Joy Dragon.** Another name for Joy is Joy Olexin.

The child from this marriage was:

594 M i. **Talston Robert Olexin.**

346. Rick Dombrosky *(Gloria Boychuk 6, Rosalia (Rosa) Stecyk 5, Kate Gurba 4, Semen 3, Stefan 2, Daniel 1).*

Rick married **Lorraine Lastiwka**. Another name for Lorraine is Lorraine Dombrosky.

Children from this marriage were:

595 F i. **Bobbi-Delisa Dombrosky**.

596 F ii. **Cassidy Dombrosky**.

348. Kevin Charles Polanski *(Elizabeth Boychuk 6, Rosalia (Rosa) Stecyk 5, Kate Gurba 4, Semen 3, Stefan 2, Daniel 1)*.

Kevin married someone

His child was:

597 M i. **Deven Polanski**.

351. Lucy Pawlukiewicz (Palmer) *(Julia Piontkowski 6, Annie Czternastek 5, Rozalia (Rose) Gurba 4, Semen 3, Stefan 2, Daniel 1)* was born on 19 Jul 1925. Another name for Lucy is Lucy Auger.

Lucy married **Fran Auger**.

Children from this marriage were:

598 M i. **David Auger**.

599 F ii. **Mary Ellen Auger**.

600 M iii. **Steven Auger**.

601 F iv. **Kathy Auger** was born in 1947.

602 F v. **Susan Auger** was born in 1961 and died in 1986 aged 25.

352. Josephine Pawlukiewicz (Palmer) *(Julia Piontkowski 6, Annie Czternastek 5, Rozalia (Rose) Gurba 4, Semen 3, Stefan 2, Daniel 1)* was born on 8 Sep 1926 and died on 20 Nov 1995 aged 69. Another name for Josephine was Josephine Hazlett.

Josephine married **David George Hazlett**. David was born on 27 Oct 1921.

Children from this marriage were:

+ 603 F i. **Gail Hazlett** was born on 30 Jun 1950 and died on 31 Jul 1993 aged 43.

+ 604 F ii. **Karen Hazlett** was born on 24 Jan 1955.

+ 605   M   iii.   **Thomas Hazlett** was born on 24 Aug 1961.

+ 606   F   iv.   **Donna Hazlett** was born on 17 Jul 1964.

+ 607   M   v.   **David James Hazlett** was born on 14 Jan 1967.

353. Irene Pawlukiewicz (Palmer) *(Julia Piontkowski 6, Annie Czternastek 5, Rozalia (Rose) Gurba 4, Semen 3, Stefan 2, Daniel 1)* was born on 31 Jan 1927 and died on 26 Dec 1996 aged 69. Another name for Irene was Irene Tetrault.

Irene married **Charles Tetrault**. Charles was born on 11 Dec 1928.

Children from this marriage were:

+ 608   F   i.   **Charmaine Tetrault** was born on 14 Jun 1952.

+ 609   M   ii.   **Alvah Tetrault** was born on 10 Mar 1954.

+ 610   M   iii.   **Charlie Tetrault** was born on 20 Jun 1956.

611   M   iv.   **Francis Tetrault** was born on 31 Oct 1962.

354. Mitch Pawlukiewicz (Palmer) *(Julia Piontkowski 6, Annie Czternastek 5, Rozalia (Rose) Gurba 4, Semen 3, Stefan 2, Daniel 1)* was born on 8 Oct 1929.

Mitch married **Jean Davidson**. Jean was born in 1929 and died in 1975 aged 46. Another name for Jean was Jean Palvakavich (Palmer).

Children from this marriage were:

612   F   i.   **Holly Palvakavich (Palmer)** was born on 24 Dec 1955.

+ 613   M   ii.   **Kelly Palvakavich (Palmer)** was born on 12 Feb 1959.

+ 614   M   iii.   **Scott Palvakavich (Palmer)** was born on 26 Jun 1962.

Mitch next married **Dorothy McKechnie**. Dorothy was born in 1932. Another name for Dorothy is Dorothy Palvakavich (Palmer).

355. Larry Pawlukiewicz (Palmer) *(Julia Piontkowski 6, Annie Czternastek 5, Rozalia (Rose) Gurba 4, Semen 3, Stefan 2, Daniel 1)* was born on 8 Jan 1938.

Larry married **Jan ?**. Another name for Jan is Jan Palvakavich (Palmer).

Children from this marriage were:

615   F   i.   **Jane Palvakavich (Palmer)**.

616 M ii. **Rick Palvakavich (Palmer)** was born in 1954.

617 F iii. **Kim Palvakavich (Palmer)** was born in 1960.

356. Darrel Pawlukiewicz (Palmer) *(Julia Piontkowski 6, Annie Czternastek 5, Rozalia (Rose) Gurba 4, Semen 3, Stefan 2, Daniel 1)* was born on 3 Jun 1943.

>Darrel married **Sandra Vicki Mills**. Sandra was born on 13 Oct 1944. Another name for Sandra is Sandra Vicki Palvakavich (Palmer).

>Children from this marriage were:

>>618 F i. **Corinne Pawlukiewicz (Palmer)** was born on 15 Jan 1964. Another name for Corinne is Corinne Petrukovich.

>>Corinne married **Martin Petrukovich**.

>+ 619 F ii. **Darlene Pawlukiewicz (Palmer)** was born on 29 Jun 1965.

357. Patricia Piontkowski (Point) *(John Piontkowski (Point) 6, Annie Czternastek 5, Rozalia (Rose) Gurba 4, Semen 3, Stefan 2, Daniel 1)* was born on 11 Jan 1940. Another name for Patricia is Patricia Poulin.

>Patricia married **Roger Poulin**. Roger was born on 10 May 1940.

>Children from this marriage were:

>+ 620 F i. **Kim Poulin** was born on 30 Jun 1966.

>+ 621 F ii. **Lesa Poulin** was born on 28 May 1968.

>+ 622 F iii. **Nathalie Jo Poulin** was born on 4 Sep 1971.

358. Reg Piontkowski (Point) *(John Piontkowski (Point) 6, Annie Czternastek 5, Rozalia (Rose) Gurba 4, Semen 3, Stefan 2, Daniel 1)* was born on 5 Dec 1941.

>Reg married **Joanne Boucher**. Joanne was born on 1 Jan 1941. Another name for Joanne is Joanne Piontkowski (Point).

>Children from this marriage were:

>+ 623 F i. **Susan Piontkowski (Point)** was born on 8 Dec 1966.

>624 M ii. **Greg Piontkowski (Point)** was born on 3 Mar 1968.

Greg married **Audrey Toal** on 5 Sep 1998. Audrey was born on 16 Apr 1969. Another name for Audrey is Audrey Piontkowski (Point).

361. Joyce Piontkowski *(Edward Piontkowski 6, Annie Czternastek 5, Rozalia (Rose) Gurba 4, Semen 3, Stefan 2, Daniel 1)* was born on 13 Apr 1947. Other names for Joyce are Joyce Kotke, and Joyce Welch.

Joyce married **Don Welch**. Don was born on 1 May 1954.

The child from this marriage was:

625　M　i.　**Keith Welch** was born on 22 Aug 1990.

Joyce next married **Harvey Kotke**. Harvey was born in 1943 and died in 1977 aged 34.

363. Arnold Piontkowski *(Edward Piontkowski 6, Annie Czternastek 5, Rozalia (Rose) Gurba 4, Semen 3, Stefan 2, Daniel 1)* was born on 26 Feb 1951.

Arnold married **Janice Meakin**. Janice was born on 21 Jun 1955. Another name for Janice is Janice Piontkowski.

Children from this marriage were:

626　M　i.　**Richard Ian Piontkowski** was born on 9 Jul 1979.

627　F　ii.　**Angela Mae Piontkowski** was born on 10 Oct 1981.

365. Dianna Pointkoski *(Frederick Paul Pointkoski 6, Annie Czternastek 5, Rozalia (Rose) Gurba 4, Semen 3, Stefan 2, Daniel 1)* was born on 10 Sep 1949. Another name for Dianna is Dianna Spychka.

Dianna married **Orest Spychka**. Orest was born on 10 Oct 1947.

Children from this marriage were:

628　F　i.　**Jolene Spychka** was born on 18 Nov 1979. Another name for Jolene is Jolene Nissen.

Jolene married **Aaron Nissen**.

629　F　ii.　**Tasha Spychka** was born on 13 Jul 1981.

366. Duane Pointkoski *(Frederick Paul Pointkoski 6, Annie Czternastek 5, Rozalia (Rose) Gurba 4, Semen 3, Stefan 2, Daniel 1)* was born on 26 Oct 1950.

Duane married **Paulette Gibbons**. Paulette was born on 26 Jan 1946. Another name for Paulette is Paullette Piontkowski.

Children from this marriage were:

630   F   i.   **Nicole Pointkoski** was born on 10 Feb 1977.

631   M   ii.   **Chad Pointkoski** was born on 18 Mar 1979.

632   F   iii.   **Joceyln Piontkowski** was born on 6 Oct 1981.

367. Arlene Piontkoski *(Frederick Paul Pointkoski 6, Annie Czternastek 5, Rozalia (Rose) Gurba 4, Semen 3, Stefan 2, Daniel 1)* was born on 26 Aug 1958. Another name for Arlene is Arlene Kakoulakis.

Arlene married **Nick Kakoulakis**.

Children from this marriage were:

633   M   i.   **Alex Kakoulakis**.

634   M   ii.   **Fotis Kakoulakis**.

635   M   iii.   **George Kakoulakis** was born in Oct 1982.

369. Gary Piontkowski *(Walter Piontkowski 6, Annie Czternastek 5, Rozalia (Rose) Gurba 4, Semen 3, Stefan 2, Daniel 1)* was born on 17 Jul 1947.

Gary married **Yvonne Szott**. Yvonne was born on 8 Jul 1954. Another name for Yvonne is Yvonne Piontkowski.

The child from this marriage was:

636   M   i.   **Jason Piontkowski** was born on 10 Oct 1972.

370. Kenneth Piontkowski *(Walter Piontkowski 6, Annie Czternastek 5, Rozalia (Rose) Gurba 4, Semen 3, Stefan 2, Daniel 1)* was born on 15 Apr 1950.

Kenneth married **Debbie Lynn Roth**. Debbie was born in 1959. Another name for Debbie is Debbie Lynn Piontkowski.

The child from this marriage was:

637   F   i.   **Tara Leanne Piontkowski** was born on 6 Sep 1981.

373. Teresa Nahirniak *(Margaret Piontkowski 6, Annie Czternastek 5, Rozalia (Rose) Gurba 4, Semen 3, Stefan 2, Daniel 1)* was born on 6 Jun 1949. Another name for Teresa is Teresa Routledge.

Teresa married **Jim Routledge**. Jim was born on 8 Mar 1948.

Children from this marriage were:

638　M　i.　**Joel Routledge** was born on 25 Jun 1970.

> Joel married **Pritchard Shawna**. Pritchard was born on 13 Jan 1973. Another name for Pritchard is Pritchard Routledge.

639　M　ii.　**Morgan Routledge** was born on 8 Jan 1980.

640　F　iii.　**Brandy Routledge** was born on 3 Feb 1983.

374. Darryl Nahirniak *(Margaret Piontkowski 6, Annie Czternastek 5, Rozalia (Rose) Gurba 4, Semen 3, Stefan 2, Daniel 1)* was born on 3 Jan 1952.

Darryl married **Kathy Bochenek**. Kathy was born on 21 Jan 1953. Another name for Kathy is Kathy Nahirniak.

Children from this marriage were:

641　F　i.　**Kimberley Nahirniak** was born on 18 Aug 1973.

642　M　ii.　**Scott Nahirniak** was born on 12 Jan 1978.

381. Robert (Adamoski) Adams *(Steve E. (Adamoski) Adams 6, Mary Czternastek 5, Rozalia (Rose) Gurba 4, Semen 3, Stefan 2, Daniel 1)* was born on 2 Sep 1945.

Robert married **??**.

Children from this marriage were:

643　M　i.　**Mark (Adamoski) Adams**.

644　M　ii.　**John (Adamoski) Adams**.

382. Kathy (Adamoski) Adams *(Steve E. (Adamoski) Adams 6, Mary Czternastek 5, Rozalia (Rose) Gurba 4, Semen 3, Stefan 2, Daniel 1)* was born on 25 Jan 1947. Another name for Kathy is Kathy Paul.

Kathy married **? Paul**.

Children from this marriage were:

645 F i. **Christine Paul.**

646 F ii. **Tracy Paul.**

647 F iii. **Amy Paul.**

383. Patti (Adamoski) Adams *(Steve E. (Adamoski) Adams 6, Mary Czternastek 5, Rozalia (Rose) Gurba 4, Semen3, Stefan 2, Daniel 1)* was born on 11 Dec 1949. Another name for Patti is Patti Nadiak.

Patti married **Jerry Nadiak.**

Children from this marriage were:

648 F i. **Melinda Nadiak.**

649 F ii. **Tricia Nadiak.**

650 F iii. **Kadia Nadiak.**

384. Paul (Adamoski) Adams *(Steve E. (Adamoski) Adams 6, Mary Czternastek 5, Rozalia (Rose) Gurba 4, Semen 3, Stefan 2, Daniel 1)* was born on 26 Oct 1958.

Paul married **Sandy Gerici.** Another name for Sandy is Sandy (Adamoski) Adams.

Children from this marriage were:

651 F i. **Amanda (Adamoski) Adams**

652 M ii. **Jake (Adamoski) Adams.**

403. Dianna Michelle Tychkowsky *(Adam Tychkowsky 6, Ksenia (Cassie) Dombrosky 5, Sofia Gurba 4, Semen 3, Stefan 2, Daniel 1).*

Dianna married **Martino Dell Fine.**

Children from this marriage were:

653 F i. **Carolina Fine.**

654 F ii. **Arda Fae Fine.**

407. David Thomas Deamude *(Francis Tychkowsky 6, Ksenia (Cassie) Dombrosky 5, Sofia Gurba 4, Semen 3, Stefan 2, Daniel 1).*

David married **Susan Fraser.**

Children from this marriage were:

655 M i. **Corey Dusing Deamude.**

656 M ii. **Christi Lynne Deamude.**

Christi married **Greta Kaleniak**. Another name for Greta is Greta Deamude.

657 F iii. **Jennifer Lynne Deamude.**

658 M iv. **David Christopher Earl Deamude.**

659 F v. **Greta Elizabeth Anne Deamude.**

409. John Richard Deamude *(Francis Tychkowsky 6, Ksenia (Cassie) Dombrosky 5, Sofia Gurba 4, Semen 3, Stefan 2, Daniel 1).*

John married **Dawna Elanor Matthews.**

Children from this marriage were:

660 F i. **Amber Dawn Deamude.**

661 F ii. **Tarah Eden Deamude.**

410. Paul Douglas Deamude *(Francis Tychkowsky 6, Ksenia (Cassie) Dombrosky 5, Sofia Gurba 4, Semen 3,Stefan 2, Daniel 1).*

Paul married **Lorraine Elizabeth Wood.**

Children from this marriage were:

662 M i. **Andrew Douglas Deamude.**

663 F ii. **April Kristin Deamude.**

411. Donald Michael Deamude *(Francis Tychkowsky 6, Ksenia (Cassie) Dombrosky 5, Sofia Gurba 4, Semen 3, Stefan 2, Daniel 1).*

Donald married **Debbie Lorraine Degram.**

Children from this marriage were:

664 F i. **Amanda Marie Deamude.**

665 M ii. **Brandon Donald Deamude.**

666 M iii. **Matthew Curtis Deamude**.

412. Karen Loy Deamude *(Francis Tychkowsky 6, Ksenia (Cassie) Dombrosky 5, Sofia Gurba 4, Semen 3, Stefan 2, Daniel 1)*.

Karen married **John James Humphries**.

The child from this marriage was:

667 F i. **Rebekah Margaret Frances Humphries**.

413. Robert Christopher Deamude *(Francis Tychkowsky 6, Ksenia (Cassie) Dombrosky 5, Sofia Gurba 4, Semen 3, Stefan 2, Daniel 1)*.

Robert married **Cindy Lee Beauchemin**.

The child from this marriage was:

668 F i. **Cassondra Marie Deamude**.

414. Edward Wayne Deamude *(Francis Tychkowsky 6, Ksenia (Cassie) Dombrosky 5, Sofia Gurba 4, Semen 3, Stefan 2, Daniel 1)*.

Edward married **Kathy Lorraine Milton**.

Children from this marriage were:

669 F i. **Caitlin Deamude**.

670 F ii. **Courtney Meghan Deamude**.

416. Barbara Lynn Deamude *(Francis Tychkowsky 6, Ksenia (Cassie) Dombrosky 5, Sofia Gurba 4, Semen 3, Stefan 2, Daniel 1)*.

Barbara married **Mark Spencer Thompson**.

The child from this marriage was:

671 F i. **Alyssa Lynne Thompson**.

417. Pauline Naomi Tychkowsky *(Nestor Tychkowsky 6, Ksenia (Cassie) Dombrosky 5, Sofia Gurba 4, Semen 3, Stefan 2, Daniel 1)*.

Pauline married **Daniel Dmytryshyn**.

Children from this marriage were:

672 F i. **Cassandra Melessia Dmytryshyn.**

673 F ii. **Madeline Rose Dmytryshyn.**

420. Dianna Dziwenka *(Eddie Dziwenka 6, Tillie Dombrosky 5, Sofia Gurba 4, Semen 3, Stefan 2, Daniel 1)*

Dianna married **Lee Brosius.**

Children from this marriage were:

674 F i. **Heather Brosius.**

675 F ii. **Lenora Brosius.**

676 M iii. **Matthew Brosius.**

677 M iv. **Harry Brosius.**

421. Judy Dziwenka *(Eddie Dziwenka 6, Tillie Dombrosky 5, Sofia Gurba 4, Semen 3, Stefan 2, Daniel 1)*

Judy married **Donald Brosius.**

Children from this marriage were:

678 M i. **Dion Brosius.**

679 F ii. **April Brosius.**

422. Elizabeth Dziwenka *(Eddie Dziwenka 6, Tillie Dombrosky 5, Sofia Gurba 4, Semen 3, Stefan 2, Daniel 1).*

Elizabeth married **Jose Ferrara.**

Children from this marriage were:

680 F i. **Cindy Ferrara.**

681 M ii. **John Ferrara.**

424. Robert Wilson *(Emma Dziwenka 6, Tillie Dombrosky 5, Sofia Gurba 4, Semen 3, Stefan 2, Daniel 1)* was born in 1957.

Robert married **Bonnie Sundquist.**

The child from this marriage was:

682   M   i.   **Nicolas William Wilson.**

425. Murray Wilson *(Emma Dziwenka 6, Tillie Dombrosky 5, Sofia Gurba 4, Semen 3, Stefan 2, Daniel 1)* was born in 1958.

Murray married **May Barr.**

Children from this marriage were:

683   M   i.   **Marlo Robert Wilson.**

684   F   ii.   **Marlis Marie Wilson.**

Eighth Generation (5th Great-Grandchildren)

430. Michael Wayne Chwok *(Evelyn Marie Gordash 7, Pauline Gurba 6, Lucas 5, Antoni 4, Semen 3, Stefan 2, Daniel 1)* was born on 18 Jan 1958 in Edmonton.

Michael married **Holly Algajer** on 16 Sep 1995 in Edmonton, Alberta. Holly was born on 15 Nov 1964. Another name for Holly is Holly Chwok.

Children from this marriage were:

685   M   i.   **Zachary Chwok** was born on 5 Jul 1996 in Edmonton, Alberta.

686   F   ii.   **Mikaela Kristina Chwok** was born on 17 Apr 1998 in Edmonton, Alberta.

431. Steven Terry Chwok *(Evelyn Marie Gordash 7, Pauline Gurba 6, Lucas 5, Antoni 4, Semen 3, Stefan 2, Daniel 1)* was born on 1 Sep 1964 in Edmonton.
Steven married **Deonne Flasha** on 5 Sep 1992 in Edmonton. Deonne was born on 4 Dec 1969. Another name for Deonne is Deonne Chwok.

The child from this marriage was:

687   F   i.   **Annalise Marie Chwok** was born on 26 Nov 1998.

432. Maureen Ann Gordash *(Joseph John Gordash 7, Pauline Gurba 6, Lucas 5, Antoni 4, Semen 3, Stefan 2, Daniel 1)* was born on 5 Jul 1965 in Edmonton, Alberta. Another name for Maureen is Maureen Ann Halldorson.

Maureen married **Brad Halldorson** on 6 Oct 1990 in Edmonton, Alberta. Brad was born on 3 Mar 1962 in Edmonton, Alberta.

Children from this marriage were:

688   M   i.   **Erik Halldorson** was born on 18 Apr 1994 in Edmonton, Alberta.

689   F   ii.   **Lauren Halldorson** was born on 14 Apr 1998 in Edmonton, Alberta.

436. Gerald Nicholas Osadchuk *(Phyllis Helen Horyn 7, Lily Gurba 6, Lucas 5, Antoni 4, Semen 3, Stefan 2, Daniel 1)* was born on 6 Feb 1963 in Smoky Lake, Alberta.

Gerald married **Laural Berg** on 25 Jun 1994. Laural was born on 21 May 1963 in St. Catherines, Ontario. Another name for Laural is Laura Osadchuk.

Children from this marriage were:

690 M i. **Cameron Osadchuk**.

691 M ii. **Duncan Osadchuk**.

437. Walter (Wally) Ernest Osadchuk *(Phyllis Helen Horyn 7, Lily Gurba 6, Lucas 5, Antoni 4, Semen 3, Stefan 2, Daniel 1)* was born on 20 Jun 1964 in Smoky Lake, Alberta.

Walter married **Karen Ewasiuk** in Jul 1993. Karen was born on 18 Mar 1970 in Edmonton, Alberta. Another name for Karen is Karen Osadchuk.

The child from this marriage was:

692 F i. **Ryley Dawn Osadchuk** was born on 5 Oct 1995 in Edmonton, Alberta

438. Dean Vincent Horyn *(Edward Victor Horyn 7, Lily Gurba 6, Lucas 5, Antoni 4, Semen 3, Stefan 2, Daniel 1)* was born on 26 Nov 1965 in Edmonton, Alberta.

Dean married **Janet Elaine Zimmerman**. Janet was born in 1968. Another name for Janet is Janet Elaine Horyn.

Children from this marriage were:

693 M i. **Graham Edward Horyn** was born on 18 Aug 2001 in Edmonton, Alberta.

694 M ii. **Cameron George Horyn** was born on 5 Jul 2004 in Edmonton, Alberta.

442. Christie Horyn *(David Horyn 7, Lily Gurba 6, Lucas 5, Antoni 4, Semen 3, Stefan 2, Daniel 1)* was born in 1975.

Christie married someone

Her child was:

695 F i. **Chance Horyn**.

504. Wayne Budynski *(Wayne Budynski 7, Louie Budynski 6, Wladek (William) Budynski 5, Anna Gurba 4, Semen 3, Stefan 2, Daniel 1)* was born on 2 Oct 1962.

Wayne married **Judy Topma**. Judy was born on 29 Apr 1967.

Children from this marriage were:

696 F i. **Stephanie Budynski** was born on 27 May 1994.

697   F   ii.   **Kelsey Anne Budynski** was born on 27 May 1994.

507. John Jr. Dyson *(Anna Mae Budynski 7, Kaizer (Clarence) Budynski 6, Wladek (William) Budynski 5, Anna Gurba 4, Semen 3, Stefan 2, Daniel 1)* was born on 28 Jun 1960.

John married **Arlene**.

The child from this marriage was:

698   F   i.   **Crystal Danielle Dyson** was born in May 1995.

514. Darryl Wayne Budynski *(Orville Budynski 7, Joseph Lawrence Budynski 6, Wladek (William) Budynski 5,Anna Gurba 4, Semen 3, Stefan 2, Daniel 1)* was born on 27 Dec 1962.

Darryl married **Michaela** on 7 Sep 1991. Michaela was born in Bristol, England.

Children from this marriage were:

699   F   i.   **Malyna Louise Budynski** was born on 31 May 1992.

700   M   ii.   **Joshua Daniel Budynski** was born on 18 May 1985.

524. Keith Mack *(Carl David Mack 7, Carl Anthony Mack 6, Rose Budynski 5, Anna Gurba 4, Semen 3, Stefan 2, Daniel 1)* was born on 13 Mar 1962.

Keith married **Carol** on 17 May 1987. Carol was born on 29 Oct 1961. Another name for Carol is Carol Mack.

Children from this marriage were:

701   F   i.   **K.C. Mack** was born on 28 Mar 1990.

702   M   ii.   **Cory Mack** was born on 17 Sep 1991.

525. Roger Mack *(Carl David Mack 7, Carl Anthony Mack 6, Rose Budynski 5, Anna Gurba 4, Semen 3, Stefan 2, Daniel 1)* was born on 1 May 1967.

Roger married **Robin** on 29 Aug 2000. Robin was born on 20 Nov 1957. Another name for Robin is Robin Mack.

Children from this marriage were:

703   M   i.   **Nathaniel Mack** was born on 21 Jul 1991.

704 M ii. **Travis Mack** was born on 9 Jul 1992.

526. Steve Mack *(Carl David Mack 7, Carl Anthony Mack 6, Rose Budynski 5, Anna Gurba 4, Semen 3, Stefan 2, Daniel 1)* was born on 25 Feb 1970.

Steve married **Deanna Lawson**. The marriage ended in divorce. Another name for Deanna is Deanna Mack.

The child from this marriage was:

705 F i. **Jessica Mack** was born on 23 Oct 1991.

Steve next married **Shannon** on 15 Apr 1995. Shannon was born on 11 Oct 1970. Another name for Shannon is Shannon Mack.

Children from this marriage were:

706 M i. **Reese Mack** was born on 21 Jun 1998.

707 M ii. **Colden Mack** was born on 17 Dec 2000.

530. Joey Kimball *(Sandra Mack 7, Carl Anthony Mack 6, Rose Budynski 5, Anna Gurba 4, Semen 3, Stefan 2, Daniel 1)*.

Joey married **Shellie**. Another name for Shellie is Shellie Kimball.

The child from this marriage was:

708 M i. **Joey Kimball Jr.**

531. Brenda Kimball *(Sandra Mack 7, Carl Anthony Mack 6, Rose Budynski 5, Anna Gurba 4, Semen 3, Stefan 2, Daniel 1)*.
Brenda married someone
Her children were:
709 F i. **Crystal Kimball**.
710 F ii. **Rachael Taie**.
711 M iii. **Troy Jacob**.
712 M iv. **Trevor Jacob**.

533. Kenneth Robert Mack *(Nestor Robert Mack 7, Nestor Mack 6, Rose Budynski 5, Anna Gurba 4, Semen 3, Stefan 2, Daniel 1)* was born on 28 Jan 1972 in Houston, Texas.

Kenneth married **Kerri Ann Kertesz** on 5 Aug 1995 in San Antonio, Texas. Kerri was born on 2 Nov 1970 in Bethesda, Maryland. Another name for Kerri is Kerri Ann Mack.

The child from this marriage was:

713 M i. **Lynden Mack** was born on 30 Jul 1998 in San Antonio, Texas

535. Karen Glynn Tilley *(Constance Rose Russell 7, Verna Mack 6, Rose Budynski 5, Anna Gurba 4, Semen 3, Stefan 2, Daniel 1)* was born on 18 May 1967 in Olongapo, Zambales, Phillipines. Another name for Karen is Karen Wheeler.

Karen married **Darby Wheeler** on 14 Nov 1987.

Children from this marriage were:

714 M i. **Christian Brons Wheeler** was born on 24 Sep 1992 in Reno, Nevada.

715 M ii. **Ty Backus Wheeler** was born on 23 Sep 1996 in San Benito, Texas.

536. Russell Backus Tilley *(Constance Rose Russell 7, Verna Mack 6, Rose Budynski 5, Anna Gurba 4, Semen 3, Stefan 2, Daniel 1)* was born on 15 Oct 1978 in Kingsville, Texas.
Russell married **Mary Grayson Clesi** on 14 Jun 2002. Another name for Mary is Mary Tilley.

Children from this marriage were:

716 F i. **Veronica Krey Tilley** was born on 2 Sep 2004 in Houston, Texas.

717 F ii. **Clesi Rose Tilley** was born on 23 Apr 2007.

537. Robin Russell *(Kenneth Joseph Russell 7, Verna Mack 6, Rose Budynski 5, Anna Gurba 4, Semen 3, Stefan 2, Daniel 1)* was born on 6 May 1970 in Houston, Texas. Another name for Robin is Robin Lindle.

Robin married **Jonathan Lindle** on 24 Jun 1995. Jonathan was born on 18 Apr 1969 in Huntsville, Alabama.

Children from this marriage were:

718 F i. **Allison Charlotte Lindle** was born on 12 Dec 2003 in Houston, Texas.

719 M ii. **Andrew Joseph Lindle** was born on 8 May 2007 in Houston, Texas.

546. Kristin Tancrede *(Judi Demmert 7, Stella Bernice Mack 6, Rose Budynski 5, Anna Gurba 4, Semen 3, Stefan 2, Daniel 1)* was born on 17 Jul 1981 in Rochester New York.

Kristin married **Jeremy Spacek** on 6 Jul 2000.

The child from this marriage was:

720 M i. **Bradley Robert Spacek** was born on 23 Nov 2007 in Pottstown, Pennsylvania.

552. Ryan Mack *(Wilfred D. Mack 7, Edward A. Mack 6, Rose Budynski 5, Anna Gurba 4, Semen 3, Stefan 2, Daniel 1)* was born on 18 Jan 1981.

Ryan married someone

His child was:

721 M i. **Maccartney Mack**.

566. Lana Michelle Pineda *(Marilyn K. Mack 7, Florian Sy Mack 6, Rose Budynski 5, Anna Gurba 4, Semen 3, Stefan 2, Daniel 1)* was born on 4 Sep 1983 in Omak, Washington.

Lana married someone

Her child was:

722 M i. **Jason R. Blochowitz** was born on 6 Feb 2008 in Tucson, Arizona.

576. Thomas Forsyth Jr. *(Thomas Forsyth 7, Mary Anne Britt 6, Frances A. Budynski 5, Anna Gurba 4, Semen 3, Stefan 2, Daniel 1)*.

Thomas married **Nancy**.

The child from this marriage was:

723 M i. **Patrick Forsyth**.

579. Lacey Fletcher *(Jane Boychuk 7, Steve Boychuk 6, Rosalia (Rosa) Stecyk 5, Kate Gurba 4, Semen 3, Stefan 2, Daniel 1)*. Another name for Lacey is Lacey Janke.

Lacey married **Ben Janke**.

Children from this marriage were:

724 M i. **Levi John Janke**.

725 F ii. **Victoria Janke**.

603. Gail Hazlett *(Josephine Pawlukiewicz (Palmer)* 7, *Julia Piontkowski* 6, *Annie Czternastek* 5, *Rozalia (Rose) Gurba* 4, *Semen* 3, *Stefan* 2, *Daniel* 1*)* was born on 30 Jun 1950 and died on 31 Jul 1993 aged 43. Another name for Gail was Gail Williams.

Gail married **Wes Williams.**

Children from this marriage were:

726　F　i.　**Fionia Williams** was born on 21 Jun 1981.

727　M　ii.　**Matthew Williams** was born in 1983.

728　F　iii.　**Naomia Williams** was born on 11 Feb 1985.

604. Karen Hazlett *(Josephine Pawlukiewicz (Palmer)* 7, *Julia Piontkowski* 6, *Annie Czternastek* 5, *Rozalia (Rose) Gurba* 4, *Semen* 3, *Stefan* 2, *Daniel* 1*)* was born on 24 Jan 1955. Other names for Karen are Karen Symington, and Karen Thomson.

Karen married **Jim Symington.**

Children from this marriage were:

729　M　i..　**Wheaton Symington.**

730　F　ii.　**Erin Symington** was born in 1986.

731　M　iii.　**Benjamin Symington** was born in 1988.

Karen next married **Bruce Thomson.**

The child from this marriage was:

732　M　i.　**William Thomson** was born in 1995.

605. Thomas Hazlett *(Josephine Pawlukiewicz (Palmer)* 7, *Julia Piontkowski* 6, *Annie Czternastek* 5, *Rozalia(Rose) Gurba* 4, *Semen* 3, *Stefan* 2, *Daniel* 1*)* was born on 24 Aug 1961.

Thomas married **Janice Hiniuk.** Another name for Janice is Janice Hazlett.

Children from this marriage were:

733　M　i.　**Mark Hazlett** was born on 6 Feb 1990.

734　M　ii.　**Ryan Hazlett** was born on 9 Mar 1992.

606. Donna Hazlett *(Josephine Pawlukiewicz (Palmer) 7, Julia Piontkowski 6, Annie Czternastek 5, Rozalia (Rose) Gurba 4, Semen 3, Stefan 2, Daniel 1)* was born on 17 Jul 1964. Another name for Donna is Donna Matovinovic.

Donna married **Frank Matovinovic**.

The child from this marriage was:

735   F   i.   **Kaja Matovinovic** was born on 20 Sep 1996.

607. David James Hazlett *(Josephine Pawlukiewicz (Palmer) 7, Julia Piontkowski 6, Annie Czternastek 5, Rozalia (Rose) Gurba 4, Semen 3, Stefan 2, Daniel 1)* was born on 14 Jan 1967.

David married **Lisa Rurak**. Another name for Lisa is Lisa Hazlett.

The child from this marriage was:

736   M   i.   **Jake Hazlett** was born on 10 Jul 1997.

608. Charmaine Tetrault *(Irene Pawlukiewicz (Palmer) 7, Julia Piontkowski 6, Annie Czternastek 5, Rozalia(Rose) Gurba 4, Semen 3, Stefan 2, Daniel 1)* was born on 14 Jun 1952. Another name for Charmaine is Charmaine Baker.

Charmaine married **Robert Baker**. Robert was born on 16 Apr 1946.

Children from this marriage were:

737   M   i.   **Nicholas Baker** was born on 16 Jun 1981.

738   F   ii.   **Natalie Baker** was born on 26 Jan 1983.

609. Alvah Tetrault *(Irene Pawlukiewicz (Palmer) 7, Julia Piontkowski 6, Annie Czternastek 5, Rozalia (Rose) Gurba 4, Semen 3, Stefan 2, Daniel 1)* was born on 10 Mar 1954.

Alvah married **Shirley Buchkowsky**. Shirley was born on 16 Feb 1954. Another name for Shirley is Shirley Tetrault.

The child from this marriage was:

739   M   i.   **Adam Tetrault** was born on 26 Nov 1984.

610. Charlie Tetrault *(Irene Pawlukiewicz (Palmer) 7, Julia Piontkowski 6, Annie Czternastek 5, Rozalia (Rose) Gurba 4, Semen 3, Stefan 2, Daniel 1)* was born on 20 Jun 1956.

Charlie married **Marlene Poloway**. Marlene was born on 25 Oct 1956. Another name for Marlene is Marlene Tetrault.

Children from this marriage were:

740　F　i.　**Sarah Tetrault** was born on 4 May 1986.

741　F　ii.　**Lauren Tetrault** was born on 24 Jun 1988.

613. Kelly Palvakavich (Palmer) *(Mitch Pawlukiewicz (Palmer) 7, Julia Piontkowski 6, Annie Czternastek 5, Rozalia (Rose) Gurba 4, Semen 3, Stefan 2, Daniel 1)* was born on 12 Feb 1959.

Kelly married **Gwen Stewart**. Gwen was born on 24 Aug 1963. Another name for Gwen is Gwen Palvakavich (Palmer).

Children from this marriage were:

742　F　i.　**Olivia Palvakavich (Palmer)** was born on 7 Jun 1996.

743　F　ii.　**Julia Lauren Palvakavich (Palmer)** was born on 22 May 1998.

614. Scott Palvakavich (Palmer) *(Mitch Pawlukiewicz (Palmer) 7, Julia Piontkowski 6, Annie Czternastek 5, Rozalia (Rose) Gurba 4, Semen 3, Stefan 2, Daniel 1)* was born on 26 Jun 1962.

Scott married **Nancy Carter**. Another name for Nancy is Nancy Palvakavich (Palmer).

Children from this marriage were:

744　F　i.　**Kelsey Palvakavich (Palmer)** was born on 21 Apr 1988.

745　F　ii.　**Sarah Palvakavich (Palmer)** was born on 3 Jan 1992.

619. Darlene Pawlukiewicz (Palmer) *(Darrel Pawlukiewicz (Palmer) 7, Julia Piontkowski 6, Annie Czternastek 5, Rozalia (Rose) Gurba 4, Semen 3, Stefan 2, Daniel 1)* was born on 29 Jun 1965. Another name for Darlene is Darlene Lemay.

Darlene married **Keith Lemay**.

Children from this marriage were:

746　M　i.　**Russel Lemay** was born on 27 Sep 1991.

747　F　ii.　**Hillary Lemay** was born on 30 Jul 1993.

748 M   iii. **Mitchell Lemay** was born on 18 Jun 1995.

749 F   iv. **Neil Austin Lemay** was born on 21 Aug 1997.

620. Kim Poulin *(Patricia Piontkowski (Point)* 7, *John Piontkowski (Point)* 6, *Annie Czternastek* 5, *Rozalia (Rose) Gurba* 4, *Semen* 3, *Stefan* 2, *Daniel* 1*)* was born on 30 Jun 1966. Another name for Kim is Kim Lakeman.

Kim married **Brent Lakeman**. Brent was born on 25 Nov 1966.

Children from this marriage were:

750 M   i. **Emmet Lakeman** was born on 11 Dec 1995.

751 F   ii. **Avery Lakeman** was born on 16 Mar 1998.

621. Lesa Poulin *(Patricia Piontkowski (Point)* 7, *John Piontkowski (Point)* 6, *Annie Czternastek* 5, *Rozalia (Rose) Gurba* 4, *Semen* 3, *Stefan* 2, *Daniel* 1*)* was born on 28 May 1968. Another name for Lesa is Lesa Gennaro.

Lesa married **Nazz Gennaro**. Nazz was born on 8 May 1968.

Children from this marriage were:

752 M   i. **Mateo Gennaro** was born on 31 Mar 1997.

753 F   ii. **Kiara Gennaro** was born on 16 Apr 2000.

622. Nathalie Jo Poulin *(Patricia Piontkowski (Point)* 7, *John Piontkowski (Point)* 6, *Annie Czternastek* 5, *Rozalia (Rose) Gurba* 4, *Semen* 3, *Stefan* 2, *Daniel* 1*)* was born on 4 Sep 1971. Another name for Nathalie is Nathalie Jo Langstaedtler.

Nathalie married **Bernd Langstaedtler**. Bernd was born on 2 Feb 1968.

The child from this marriage was:

754 M   i. **Eli Sebastian Langstaedtler** was born on 23 Feb 2001.

623. Susan Piontkowski (Point) *(Reg Piontkowski (Point)* 7, *John Piontkowski (Point)* 6, *Annie Czternastek* 5, *Rozalia (Rose) Gurba* 4, *Semen* 3, *Stefan* 2, *Daniel* 1*)* was born on 8 Dec 1966. Another name for Susan is Susan Graci.

Susan married **Adrien Graci**. Adrien was born on 24 Dec 1966.

The child from this marriage was:
755 M i. **Benjamin Pointe-Graci** was born on 18 May 2001.